WOMEN WRITERS AND
NATIONAL IDENTITY
Bachmann, Duden, Özdamar

In *Women Writers and National Identity*, Stephanie Bird offers a detailed analysis of the twin themes of female identity and national identity in the works of three major twentieth-century German-language women writers. Bird argues for the importance of an understanding of ambiguity, tension and contradiction in the fictional narratives of Ingeborg Bachmann, Anne Duden and Emine Özdamar. She aims to demonstrate how ambiguity is itself central to the development of an understanding of identity and that literary texts are uniquely able to point to the ethical importance of ambiguity through their stylistic complexity. Bird gives close readings of the three writers and draws on feminist theory and psychoanalysis to elucidate the complex nature of individual identity. This book will be of interest to literary and women's studies scholars as well as Germanists.

STEPHANIE BIRD is Lecturer in German at University College London. She is the author of *Recasting Historical Women* (1998) and of articles in journals, including *MLR, Austrian Studies* and *FMLS*.

CAMBRIDGE STUDIES IN GERMAN

General editors
H. B. Nisbet, University of Cambridge
Martin Swales, University of London

Advisory editor
Theodore J. Ziolkowski, Princeton University

Also in the series

WOMEN WRITERS AND NATIONAL IDENTITY

Bachmann, Duden, Özdamar

STEPHANIE BIRD

University College London

CAMBRIDGE
UNIVERSITY PRESS

PUBLISHED BY THE PRESS SYNDICATE OF THE UNIVERSITY OF CAMBRIDGE
The Pitt Building, Trumpington Street, Cambridge, United Kingdom

CAMBRIDGE UNIVERSITY PRESS
The Edinburgh Building, Cambridge, CB2 2RU, UK
40 West 20th Street, New York, NY 10011–4211, USA
477 Williamstown Road, Port Melbourne, VIC 3207, Australia
Ruiz de Alarcón 13, 28014 Madrid, Spain
Dock House, The Waterfront, Cape Town 8001, South Africa

http://www.cambridge.org

© Stephanie Bird 2003

First published 2003

Printed in the United Kingdom at the University Press, Cambridge

Typeface Adobe Garamond 11/12.5 pt.   *System* LaTeX 2ε   [TB]

A catalogue record for this book is available from the British Library

Library of Congress Cataloguing in Publication data
Bird, Stephanie.
Women writers and national identity: Bachmann, Duden, Özdamar / by Stephanie Bird.
p.   cm. – (Cambridge studies in German)
Includes bibliographical references and index.
ISBN 0 521 82406 0
1. German literature – Women authors   History and criticism.   2. Identity (Psychology) in
literature.   3. Bachmann, Ingeborg, 1926–1973 – Criticism and interpretation.   4. Duden,
Anne, 1942 – Criticism and interpretation.   5. èzdamar, Emine Sevgi, 1946 – Criticism and
interpretation.   I. Title.   II. Series.
PT167.B57   2003   833'.91409353 – dc21   2003043581

ISBN 0 521 82406 0 hardback

For my mother

Contents

Acknowledgements

I am grateful to many people who in various ways and at different stages helped me with this project, especially Timothy McFarland, Judith Beniston, Mark Hewitson, Mererid Puw Davies, Anthony Bird, Sabine Bird-Santer and Adil Shamky. I would like to thank the manuscript readers, in particular my British reader, for their critical engagement with the text. I owe Matthew Fox special thanks for his advice and support.

Introduction

Even if it is likely that Euripides was the first dramatist to make Medea murder her children, there are plenty of other murders to her name.[1] She slaughtered her brother and scattered his remains into the Black Sea, she was involved in the murder of Jason's uncle, Pelias, and finally killed Creon and his daughter, Jason's new wife. Yet in Christa Wolf's *Medea* she is absolved of all these crimes.[2] The narrator, in a brief introductory section, assumes a tone of insistent moral authority, justifying her desire to reopen the secrets of the past by reference to the afflictions of the present: 'Das Eingeständnis unserer Not, damit müßten wir anfangen' (9). (We should start with the admission of our distress.) The narrator makes the astonishing assertion that the Ancient Greeks are 'fremde Gäste, uns gleich' (9) (strange guests who are like ourselves) and that Medea's age is one which speaks more clearly to us than others. Thus the 'erwünschte Begegnung' (desired encounter) with Medea will not only expose how sorely she has been misjudged, a misrepresentation perpetuated by the myths, but will also confront us with our own processes of misjudgement and self-deceit.

There follow eleven dramatic monologues by six characters, which convey how the woman Medea has been made the scapegoat for crimes of the state. Medea discovers that Creon's assertion of power and wealth rests upon the sacrifice of his daughter. Against the wishes of a faction in which his wife Merope has a strong voice, Creon rejects a plan to marry Iphinoe to a neighbouring king, who would in future be his heir, thereby forging an alliance which would bring Corinth increased security. Instead he murders Iphinoe to consolidate his position, and encourages the incapacitating neurotic illness of his second daughter, Glauke, who has repressed all knowledge of what has occurred. In order to sustain the public lie that Iphinoe's disappearance is due to her marriage to a foreign prince, Medea's knowledge is invalidated by defaming her and casting her in the role of criminal. Thus the rumour begins that she murdered her brother, Absyrtos. But we then learn from her monologue that he was in fact killed for similar reasons;

her father Aietes 'sacrificed' him in order to retain power in the face of opposition to his incompetence and greed, which included the opposition of his wise wife and daughters. Thus Medea's conflict is not only portrayed as the individual against the state, but as a gendered struggle in which men's humanity is diminished by their lust for power and wealth, and women fall victim to male arrogance and pride. This conflict is further inflected by the Colchians' immigrant status, and the way in which the threat that Medea poses as a woman not willing to conform to oppressive Corinthian values can be countered by official encouragement of xenophobia.

As is clear from the narrator's 'Eingeständnis unserer Not' (9) (admission of our distress) and the themes of state power, murder, gender and immigration, Wolf's text, first published in 1996, can be viewed as a contemporary feminist critique of German, and more broadly, of western values. As Helen King comments, for Wolf, the Greeks

are 'our strange guests who are like ourselves', but their philosophical dualism is also to blame for getting us into the fine mess which is 20th-century Europe . . . Her aim is to confront 'the corpse in the cellar', as Germany comes to terms with its Nazi past, with its division after 1945 and its recent reunification, and with the presence in the country of immigrant communities. More generally, she is concerned with the way our reconstructions of the past act to suppress our knowledge of what has made us who we are. The 'blind spot' she detects in Western civilisation, the catalyst of moral breakdown, is the conflict between 'Thou shalt not kill' and the consent given by societies to judicial execution and war.[3]

King praises this 'cogent and impressive novel';[4] it undeniably touches upon important issues. Wolf's project involves examining the way in which questions of gender, national and cross-cultural identity are interlinked, and how the discourses affect and even sustain each other. Fictional representation remains potentially the most radical medium for exploring and confronting the relationship of individual and corporate identity and for revealing the way in which identity is often perceived and expressed as incoherent or contradictory. 'Free *from* . . . artists must still render themselves free *for* . . .'[5] By creatively incorporating the freedom for ambiguity, irresolution and irony, fiction can revolt against normative or totalizing explanation, be that in the form of feminist theory, historical analysis or literary criticism. Indeed, in dialogue with the fictional interrogation of historical and personal experience, such explanatory disciplines are themselves challenged by the need to account for textual ambiguity or unresolved conflict.

It is the themes approached by Wolf, those of female identity and how it interlinks with the field of national identity at the level of the individual woman, which form the basis of my analysis. The conceptual linking of the

two is crucial. Feminist theories have long been concerned with the roots of female identity, wherein its difference to male identity lies, how it can be expressed in a language that is male, or whether there is such a thing at all. In varying degrees (and with the obvious exception of essentialist theorists) feminists have emphasized the historical roots of identity, arguing that identity is historically specific and therefore variable, and that gender is linked with questions of national identity, ethnicity and class. Similarly, the term 'national identity' remains much discussed. There are those who hold the view that national identity is based on essential characteristics or qualities that remain stable through time, a view that usually corresponds to an essentializing notion of ethnicity. More suggestive definitions of national identity are those which hold it to be constructed, a myth or creation that frequently has ascribed to it foundational value. As Mary Fulbrook makes clear, however, the 'constructionist' approach is far from uniform:

Broadly, one may say that [Ernest] Gellner, [Benedict] Anderson and [Eric] Hobsbawm each focus on different aspects of changing conditions in 'modernity': the social processes concomitant on industrialization (Gellner); the emergence of 'print capitalism' which allowed a broadening of the 'imagined community' (Anderson); and the state system of modern capitalism (Hobsbawm). Their contribution has been to focus attention on the substantive conditions under which, historically, conceptions of the nation could emerge and develop in the last two centuries.[6]

The emphasis on the concept of nation as constructed has led to interesting debates about the relationship between nation and literature. Far from being an innocent medium of representation, literature, and particularly the novel, has played a decisive role in creating and consolidating the sense of a national community. As Timothy Brennan argues:

Nations, then, are imaginary constructs that depend for their existence on an apparatus of cultural fictions in which imaginative literature plays a decisive role. And the rise of European nationalism coincides especially with one form of literature – the novel . . . It was the novel that historically accompanied the rise of nations by objectifying the 'one, yet many' of national life, and by mimicking the structures of the nation, a clearly bordered jumble of languages and styles.[7]

Clearly, both female and national identity have been the subject of considerable interdisciplinary study: my interest in this book is to examine the way in which national identity manifests itself at the individual level and how it relates to female identity; the way in which the two identities are shown to interact and inflect each other; and the critical response invited by the text.[8] It is not my purpose here, however, to draw on the explosion of non-literary work on identity, but to focus on the contribution that

fictional works can make to how we understand and interrogate identity. Thus my project is unashamedly literary in its emphasis, rather than being emphatically 'interdisciplinary' in approach. There is a reason for this. When the study of literature is incorporated into a broader, cultural-studies approach to a theme, it can too easily become part of a body of evidence within a general study of an issue; the literary text's function becomes illustrative and it is presented as a mirror of specific kinds of sociopolitical and historical context. Such studies are valuable, for of course literature is written at a particular time under particular conditions. However, by concentrating closely on narrative texts I hope to demonstrate that prose fiction can offer an understanding of identity that is qualitatively different from definitions of identity reached through theoretical and historical analysis. The fictional exploration of the relationship between female and national identity is potentially so fruitful because such a portrayal need not function in the service of an argument. It can, through the creative interchange of plot, narrative voice, perspective and language, both construct and challenge preconceptions, and can variously and actively depict contradiction in a way that analytical discourses (historical and theoretical) too often cannot or do not. The devices of narrative fiction facilitate the depiction of the complex nature of identity; the way in which it can shift in relation to context is often constructed on the basis of opposition and how it manifests itself through contradictory desires and emotions. Narrative fiction can itself be contradictory or ambiguous in its representation, while yet making contradiction and ambiguity a subject of exploration. Representations that allow for such complexity then serve both to extend and to complicate the way in which identity, whether individual female or national, must be understood.

However, in Wolf's *Medea* there is unfortunately no such challenge posed to our understanding of identity. By eschewing ambiguity in favour of idealization, Wolf has transformed the woman implicated in at least six murders to a vehicle for all she values. Whereas the interest and challenge of Euripides' *Medea* resides precisely in the portrayal of a woman who elicits sympathy because she is wronged, but whose anger is then horrific even to herself, Wolf rejects a figure who could both encompass and provoke such ambivalent emotions. Instead her protagonist is very much as Leukon describes her: 'das unschuldige Opfer, frei . . . von innerem Zwiespalt' (206) (the innocent victim, free . . . of inner conflict). The characters are largely structured around polarities of good or bad, innocent or manipulative, thus reproducing a crass dualism that is absent in Euripides: 'der Riß [ging] nicht durch sie, sondern [klaffte] zwischen ihr und jenen, die sie

verleumdet, verurteilt hatten' (206). (The rift did not run through her, but gaped between her and those who had slandered and condemned her.)

So Medea becomes the perfect woman; wild (10), proud (19), beautiful (42), witty (47), assured and knowing. In Colchis she was known as 'die guten Rat Wissende' (55) (the woman of good council); she comprehends and sees through people's relationships and power structures to which others are blind. Thus Jason admits, 'Zu hoch für mich, all diese schwierigen verborgenen Zusammenhänge' (45) (all of these difficult, hidden connections are too elevated for me), and even Akamas appears dimwitted in comparison: 'Warum, konnte sie fragen, warum gibt es diese zwei Kreons. Der eine steif im Thronsaal, der andere locker bei Tisch, wenn wir unter uns sind. Mir war nie der Gedanke gekommen, daß es anders sein könnte' (111). (Why, she could ask, why are there these two Creons. The one sits stiff in his throne room, the other relaxed at the table when we are together by ourselves. It had never occurred to me that it could be different.) In relation to Glauke, Medea becomes the skilled therapist who encourages the princess to confront what she has repressed, and more generally she advocates the free-play of emotions, presumably with the assumption that emotions are always positive: 'Ach Leukon, sagt sie, du nimmst deine Gefühle mit deinen Gedanken gefangen. Laß sie doch einfach frei' (155). (Oh Leukon, she said, you allow your ideas to imprison your feelings. Just let them free.) Certainly in her case, there are no destructive emotions in the first place and no desire for revenge on Jason since 'Es hat so kommen müssen' (48). (It had to be this way.)

This dazzling Medea dominates the characterization of the other main figures. Jason is a weak misogynist who has forgotton the wisdom and healing arts taught to him by Cheiron to become a despicable, abuse-hurling ruffian: 'Wir sollen die Weiber nehmen. Wir sollen ihren Widerstand brechen' (202). (We should take the women. We should break their resistance.) Agameda hates Medea because Medea never showed her enough love; Akamas is the arch-manipulator who admires Medea but recognizes the threat she poses to the prevailing system; Glauke is the neurotic victim whose final act of dissent, hurling herself down the palace well, is a refusal to conform to the role expected of her as Jason's new wife, and whose sudden strength of resolve is due to the affection and help Medea gave her. Only Leukon arouses more interest as a character, aware of and appalled by the actions of Creon and Akamas, but keeping silent, accepting his marginalization as astronomer without political influence and increasingly withdrawing from court in order to survive.

This schematization does not only apply to the main characters. Thus those individuals who are loyal friends of Medea are as exceptional as she is. Lyssa, Medea's companion from Colchis, exemplifies female loyalty and uncloying motherliness. She leaves Colchis with Medea, leaving behind the man she loved, cares for Medea and her sons, shows admirable common sense in times of crisis and goes into exile with Medea. In Leukon's words, 'Sie gehört zu den Frauen, die die Erde wieder anstoßen würden, falls sie einmal stehenbleiben sollte, sie hält das Leben der Menschen, die ihr anvertraut sind, fest in den Händen, man kann jeden beneiden, der in ihrer Obhut aufwachsen darf' (163). (She is one of those women who would start the world turning again, should it ever stand still; she holds the life of the people who are entrusted to her firmly in her hands. One can envy those who are allowed to grow up in her care.) Oistros, the man who rescued Medea from the pursuing crowds and who becomes her lover, is the perfect man with all the right fairytale credentials. An orphan of humble origin, he was adopted by a childless family, was trained as a stonemason by his adopted father, whom he soon overtook in skill, and is now a sought-after artist who is influenced by neither money nor power: 'Geld scheint so wenig an ihm zu haften wie Neid, dafür ist er ein Menschenfänger, immer ist er umgeben von jungen Leuten' (151). (Money seems to make as little impression on him as envy, but instead he attracts people and is always surrounded by the young.) His presence has a healing effect, and 'Sein Gleichmut und seine Unabhängigkeit strahlen auf jeden aus, der zu ihm kommt, ob hoch oder niedrig' (151). (His equanimity and independence shine on all who come to him, whether grand or lowly.)

Extremes of idealization and of defamation also inform the aspects of the text that are concerned with state power and the comparison of cultures. Thus Corinth 'ist besessen von der Gier nach Gold . . . Man mißt den Wert eines Bürgers von Korinth nach der Menge des Goldes, die er besitzt, und berechnet nach ihr die Abgaben, die er dem Palast zu leisten hat' (35) (is obsessed with the greed for gold . . . The worth of a citizen of Corinth is measured according to how much gold he possesses, and calculated by the taxes he must pay to the palace). The Corinthian government is corrupt and nepotistic (122), what is good is defined through its usefulness (112), duty takes preference over personal inclination (121) and the subtle and manipulative workings of power means that citizens have developed 'eine feine Witterung für die kleinsten Veränderungen der Atmosphäre um die Mächtigen, von der wir . . . auf Leben und Tod abhängig sind' (154) (a fine sense for the smallest changes in the atmosphere surrounding the powerful, on whom we . . . depend for life and death). Furthermore, the Corinthians

consider themselves superior to all around and are therefore blind to what they themselves are really like (164). The Corinthian men never show their emotions (29) and the women are nothing but 'sorgfältig gezähmte Haustiere' (18) (carefully tamed pets), who resent the self-confidence of the Colchian women in their midst. In contrast, Colchis was a state in which the ideals of a just regent, harmonious community and equality of ownership still governed people's political consciousnesses. The king still only lived in a wooden palace (49), the women's voices were heard and taken seriously (53) and the men showed their emotions freely. Even in Corinth the women from Colchis hold their heads high despite doing the dirty work (155), and their celebratory approach to childbirth is catching on in Corinth (110).

It matters little whether in the juxtaposition of Corinth and Colchis parallels are drawn between present-day consumer-based Germany and the early and still idealistic East Germany, or more generally between the developed West and its underdeveloped but corruptible Other. The level of idealization and simplification that sustains the polarity is such that Wolf does little more than assert the evils of greed, state power and xenophobia against the virtues of individual respect, inner strength and emotional integrity. The clichés of the noble savage and the natural woman are superimposed upon the utopia of equality to produce a vapid heroine whose greatest insight is in her admission that someone like her cannot really exist: 'Es ist dahin gekommen, das es für meine Art, auf der Welt zu sein, kein Muster mehr gibt, oder daß noch keines entstanden ist, wer weiß' (161). (It has reached the point where there is no longer any scope for living in the world as I do, or maybe there never was, who knows.) The challenge to the reader of the uncompromising and cruel Medea of myth has been sacrificed for a contemporary didacticism that simplifies in order to enhance its moral impact. Thus Wolf's Medea does not even know why she must act as she does and remain in Corinth as a knowing victim instead of escaping to the rebel women with Arinna: 'Es geht nicht, Arinna, sagte ich, und sie: Warum nicht. Ich konnte es ihr nicht erklären' (183). (It won't work Arinna, I said, and she replied: why not. I could not explain it to her.)

Despite her evident interest in the question of how female identity interacts with perceptions of national identity, Wolf's impossible utopian vision interferes with the creative exploration of the complex, shifting and often contradictory elements that constitute any identity. In her text the good are very, very good and the bad are horrid, but, unlike the girl with the curl, they are never both. Her Medea so totally inhabits the role of persecuted heroine that suffering, with the hatred, destruction and self-obsession it can engender, is replaced by the unselfish quest for enlightenment and willing

self-sacrifice. There is little here that either acknowledges or contributes to contemporary debates surrounding female identity. The escape into a new myth produces, but does not acknowledge, new blind spots.

My purpose in this book, as outlined above, is to focus closely on representations of female and national identity in fictional narrative and to demonstrate the importance of ambiguity, tension and contradiction for challenging and developing an understanding of what constitutes female and national identity. I hope to achieve this in two main ways. First, by focusing on the complexity of the texts themselves. The authors whose work forms the subject of the study – Ingeborg Bachmann, Anne Duden and Emine Sevgi Özdamar – in different ways establish a conceptual link between individual female identity and national identity, making a connection between individual and national psychosis or exposing the idealization, prejudice or deceit upon which identity is often justified. They explore this link without seeking to reconcile any ambiguity or tension which may arise. Although the emphasis of the study is literary, it is not narrowly so in scope, and this, then, relates to my second aim. I do not apply one methodology to all the texts, nor bring to them one particular understanding of what constitutes identity, but instead seek to incorporate a hermeneutic awareness into the analysis. It is not my desire to argue for one theory of identity, but to show the ways in which quite different theories may elucidate a text. Furthermore, and this is crucial, these theories are themselves, when seen in interaction with specifically literary features, elucidated and challenged by the stylistic and cognitive complexity of the literary text. It is for this reason that I do not ascribe to theoretical discourse the authority with which to validate the argument that ambiguity and contradiction are central to understanding identity.[9] Theoretical discussions of identity, of course, also recognize ambiguity as central, but they do so in the service of an argument. In the texts studied here, ambiguity and irresolution are constructed and explored through very different textual means that do not have simple parallels with historical or cultural studies. The creative dimension of fiction offers a qualitatively different understanding of identity from other disciplines, and far from being seen to be in thrall to their 'authority', of illustrating theoretical insights, narrative fiction in its own terms extends our intellectual and emotional comprehension of what constitutes identity. Furthermore, to use theoretical discourse as an 'authority' in relation to fictional texts, rather than in a relationship of mutual elucidation, not only confers upon it a truth claim greater than that which fiction offers, but also assumes a level of consensus over the question of identity formation that belies the reality. Thus, rather than casting non-fictional discourse as

authoritative, I hope to incorporate into my analysis a critical awareness of theoretical debates and disagreements, so that those debates too remain open to scrutiny.

There is a degree of imbalance in this book which relates largely to the nature of the project. Most obviously, all three authors are of different nationality, and so the issues they confront vary. Whereas Bachmann and Duden both consider Austrian and German identity respectively in relation to the Holocaust, with very different emphases, Özdamar's discussion of national identity is inseparable from questions of ethnicity. Similarly, female identity is variously represented: in the work of Bachmann and Duden, suffering and victimhood are important constituents of identity, yet Özdamar focuses more explicitly on the central role of language and performance. Nor do the texts treat the themes equally. Thus, for example, in Duden's short stories there is almost no interest in national identity, whereas in *Das Judasschaf* it is vital. However, the issues raised by the short stories provide the theoretical basis for the subsequent analysis of Duden's novel and furthermore are crucial to the discussion of feminist theory and methodology which forms an integral part of this project. And in contrast to the explicit consideration of theory in the later chapters, I start with two chapters in which my argument is based on close textual analysis of Bachmann's narrative technique, crucial as it is in revealing the complex relationship between identities, deceit and desire.

Ingeborg Bachmann: the Todesarten *prose*

CHAPTER I

Franza and the Righteous Servant

In her recently published introduction to Ingeborg Bachmann, Stefanie Golisch quotes Christa Wolf's comment on Bachmann's relationship to her protagonists in the fourth Frankfurt lecture: 'Die Bachmann aber ist jene namenlose Frau aus *Malina*, sie ist jene Franza aus dem Romanfragment, die ihre Geschichte einfach nicht in den Griff, nicht in die Form kriegt.'[1] (Yet Bachmann is that nameless woman in *Malina*, she is the Franza of the unfinished novel who simply does not get her story in hand, cannot give it form.) Although Golisch admits that the ability of an artist to attain a reflexive distance from his or her experience when incorporated into their work is not dependent on the sex of the author but is 'eine Frage der psychischen Disposition einer kreativen Natur'[2] (a question of the psychological disposition of a creative personality), she nevertheless argues that Wolf is pointing in the right direction:

Es ist für Schriftstellerinnen offenbar bis in die Gegenwart hinein schwieriger als für ihre männlichen Kollegen, jenen überlegenen Blickwinkel einzunehmen, der ihre Werke erst aus der Befangenheit der eigenen Betroffenheit entließe und somit unanfechtbar machte.[3]

(Until now it is clearly harder for female authors than their male colleagues to adopt an elevated perspective, such as would allow the works to escape the intense personal investment of their authors, thereby becoming unassailable.)

This is a frustrating critical response, for Golisch perpetuates the naive identification of Bachmann with her protagonist, equating the suffering of the fictional figures with Bachmann's inability to maintain a sovereign distance from her own emotions. It is a response which fails to explore the significance of narrative technique for interpretation and which overlooks previous scholarship addressing precisely that question.

Thus in her much earlier article tracing the structural development of the *Todesarten* fragments, of *Das Buch Franza*, *Requiem für Fanny Goldmann* and the posthumously named *Goldmann/Rottwitz-Roman* fragment,

Monika Albrecht emphasizes the increasing sophistication of Bachmann's narrative stance. As she points out, *Das Buch Franza* and *Requiem für Fanny Goldmann* were both published after the death of the author, so without her express consent, and furthermore, they were abandoned by her in order to write *Malina*, and to work on the *Goldmann/Rottwitz* novel:

Die diesen Texten [*Das Buch Franza* and *Requiem für Fanny Goldmann*] eingeschriebene Gegenüberstellung von Mann und Frau als Täter und Opfer ist mit dem Konzeptionswandel um 1966 und dem Beginn der Arbeit an *Malina* zugunsten einer differenzierteren Position aufgegeben. Zwar liegt mit den Binnengeschichten von Fanny Goldmann und Aga Rottwitz auch weiterhin tendenziell eine Mörder/Opfer- Konstellation vor, allerdings nur tendenziell, denn die Multiperspektivität der Fragmente aus der dritten Phase des *Todesarten-Romans* arbeitet dieser Konstellation entgegen.[4]

(The opposition of man and woman as culprit and victim that is found in these texts was given up in favour of a more differentiated position in around 1966, when there was a shift in Bachmann's conception and she started work on *Malina*. Although in the stories of Fanny Goldmann and Aga Rottwitz there is still a tendency towards a murder/victim constellation, this remains only a tendency, since the multiple perspectives of the *Todesarten* novel fragments written in the third phase opposes this constellation.)

The fact that Bachmann did not consider *Das Buch Franza* publishable in its existing form, but showed herself happy with the narrative structure of *Malina*, with its rigorous questioning of perspective and identification, makes the assumption that Bachmann's experience is represented in the figure of Franza all the more frustrating. Nor did she even consider *Das Buch Franza* a text that she would necessarily return to, writing to Klaus Piper in November 1970, '(DAS BUCH FRANZA ist zudem in einer Schublade verschwunden und wird von mir, aus verschiedenen Gründen, noch lange nicht oder überhaupt nicht veröffentlicht werden, ich weiß es selber noch nicht)'.[5] (Moreover, *Das Buch Franza* has disappeared into a drawer, and for various reasons won't be published by me for a long time, if at all. I don't know myself yet.)

   Albrecht's analysis is fascinating and she convincingly argues that there is greater narrative sophistication in the later *Goldmann/Rottwitz* fragments and in *Malina* than there is in the earlier fragment. This is a view she elaborates in a later study, in which she argues that occasional moments of narrative irony do not serve to relativize the questionable perspective of the protagonist, Franza.[6] Albrecht's analyses are excellent, yet I would suggest that she underestimates the potential of the narrative structure of *Das Buch Franza*. Although the male/female, oppressor/victim juxtaposition is

obvious, as it is in *Malina*, this is not in itself (as Albrecht makes clear) a reflection of a simplistic position; there are important textual indications that these dualities are not to be taken at face value, and that the woman Franza represents one facet of a destructive polarity. Weigel has already pointed to this polarity, arguing that Franza represents the type of thinking that leads to death, without which the thinking of the 'Whites', exemplified in the figure of Jordan, could not function.[7] However, Weigel still sees in Franza's confrontation with her illness in the Egyptian desert the possibility of utopia; according to her, Franza has done what the female narrator of *Malina* has failed to do and has overcome her victim self, even though this entails death. In her fluctuation between states she has moved ever closer to the language of Egyptian hieroglyphs, in which Weigel sees the indication for a mythical utopia. This is based on her assessment of hieroglyphs as possibly the earliest form of autobiography: 'In der ägyptischen Grabinschriften ist vermutlich auch der Beginn der Ich-Perspektive in der Literatur zu sehen, denn die Biographien wurden (noch zu Lebzeiten) von den sogenannten Grabherren verfaßt und in der Ich-Form formuliert.'[8] (It may also be possible to see in the Egyptian grave inscriptions the beginning of the I-perspective in literature, for the biographies were composed by the so-called grave masters (during their lifetime) and formulated in the first person.)

Weigel's desire to situate Franza in relation to a utopia despite her victimhood and death is in keeping with Franza's seductive idealistic vision. In contrast, Sara Lennox's recent study, in which she seeks to demonstrate that the identity of Bachmann's female protagonists is based on racist and imperialistic discourses, refuses any such idealization. Lennox argues that while Bachmann emphasizes 'die Verstrickung aller EuropäerInnen in die imperiale/neokoloniale und rassistische Ordnung des Westens' (the entanglement of all Europeans in the imperial/neo-colonial and racist order of the West), she nevertheless, as author, perpetuates racist stereotypes.[9] On the one hand Lennox points to the complex narrative technique of the *Todesarten* texts as evidence for Bachmann's critical questioning of the subjectivity of the 'White Lady' that depends upon the abjection of the black or oriental Other; on the other hand she considers that Bachmann is caught up in the same discourses as her white protagonists. Thus she concludes 'daß Bachmann selbst nicht ganz von der Kritik auszunehmen ist, der sie ihre Figuren unterwirft'[10] (that Bachmann is herself not innocent of the criticism that she makes of her figures). Lennox argues her thesis convincingly. The final emphasis of her study is such, however, that the imaginative potential of her argument is constrained by a limiting understanding

of literature's ability to write about its time. She rightly asserts that Bachmann, while responding critically to her epoch, is also a product of it, and that therefore neither the texts nor the protagonists escape the tension between critical momentum and conformity. Yet to conclude here, without returning to the question of how the literary text itself allows or enables us to understand that tension is to assign to literature the function of mere seismograph. So while recognizing the importance of narrative technique for the *Todesarten* texts' critical dimension, Lennox does not pursue the significance of the narrative *insistence* upon irresolution, seeing it merely as symptomatic of Bachmann's historical situation, rather than understanding it as an important response to that historical situation.

That individuals are trapped within the discourses language makes available to them, but that in reacting against those discourses they become the vehicle of their perpetuation is a dominating theme of *Das Dreißigste Jahr* collection. Bachmann was all too aware of her own entrapment in the 'schlechte Sprache' (bad language), but held out the theoretical hope that 'im Widerspiel des Unmöglichen mit dem Möglichen erweitern wir unsere Möglichkeiten'[11] (in the interplay of the impossible with the possible, we broaden our possibilities). The extent to which her creative writing achieves this opening up of new possibilities is of central importance for understanding 'wie Literatur angemessen "über die Zeit schreiben" könne'[12] (how literature can adequately write 'about its time'). Karen McAuley, in her outstanding study of *Kindlichkeit* in Bachmann's prose, remains unconvinced that Bachmann's subversive qualities offer emancipatory potential, pointing to the fact that the 'hyperbolic conformity' of so many of the female protagonists might lead to further self-injury.[13] Although, unlike Lennox, McAuley does not include the author Bachmann in her assessment of the texts' profound ambivalence, she too concludes her study without further considering whether this ambivalence might be understood as an integral part of the texts' response to their epoch.

In the following analyses of Bachmann's *Todesarten* prose I hope to show that the texts, however much they fail to resolve the tension between critique and conformity, also, through their complex narrative structures, insist on irresolution as a timely and ethical response to their time. I shall begin by discussing the way in which the narrative complexity of *Das Buch Franza* serves to expose and criticize Franza's idealism and her hankering for an absolute as profoundly limiting and destructive, not as a utopian release. In chapter 2 I shall also trace the theme of idealization and self-deception in the *Requiem für Fanny Goldmann* and the *Goldmann/Rottwitz-Roman* fragments, showing how closely the exploration of naive and narcissistic

female identity is linked to a questioning of Austrian identity. For my analysis of *Das Buch Franza* I refer to the edited final draft in Volume 11 of the *'Todesarten'-Projekt*, and for the analysis of *Requiem für Fanny Goldmann* and the *Goldmann/Rottwitz-Roman* I refer to the edited drafts in Volume 1.[14]

DAS BUCH FRANZA: NARRATIVE PERSPECTIVE

Das Buch Franza depicts the devastating results of Franza's marriage with Leo Jordan, a psychiatrist whose research is on the long-term effects of experiments on Holocaust victims. The story begins with her 'escape' to her childhood home in Galicia after discovering that Jordan had been using her as the object of his experiment. Her brother, Martin Ranner, who is shortly to leave on a trip to Egypt, comes to help her and then takes her with him. They travel through the desert and return to Cairo, where Franza meets a doctor, an old Nazi who had been involved in giving lethal injections to Jews. She asks him to give her a lethal injection, convinced that she is ill beyond saving, but he refuses, horrified. Finally, she is assaulted at the pyramids and dies, apparently as the result of a fall.

There are three perspectives represented in *Das Buch Franza* – that of the narrator, of Martin and of Franza – but they are not equally present, varying in each of the three sections. The omniscient third-person narrator is in evidence throughout, although her voice is frequently submerged in the perspective of either Martin or Franza. Thus in the first section, 'Heimkehr nach Galicien' (Homecoming to Galicia), the perspective is predominantly Martin's, although the narrator is keen to point to the constructed nature of her story in the passage 'Exkurs, während ein Zug durch den Semmering-Tunnel fährt' (Digression while a train drives through the Semmering tunnel). She insists that drawing the reader's attention to the fictionality of her figures does not detract from their significance, 'denn die Tatsachen, die die Welt ausmachen – sie brauchen das Nichttatsächliche, um von ihm aus erkannt zu werden' (134) (for the facts that determine the world need the non-factual as a basis from which to be recognized). Thus she begins the narrative by distinguishing between a reality and its fictional representation, and, more importantly, by emphasizing the distance between herself and her characters. She reinforces this distance shortly afterwards by informing the reader that the biblical reference to Matthew 12. 20,[15] and the statement 'Die Liebe aber ist unwiderstehlich' (But love is irresistible), are not part of Martin's thought processes, but her own comment on his search for his sister: 'ihm ging nichts dergleichen durch den Kopf, er kannte solche

Sätze nicht' (149–50).[16] (Nothing of the sort went through his mind, he did not know such phrases.)

In the second section, 'Jordanische Zeit' (The time with Jordan), the perspective is Franza's, either in the form of her first-person recollection in response to Martin's brief questions, or through the narrator, who recounts some episodes from her marriage, and most obviously tells us of Franza's 'schönsten Frühling' (loveliest spring), but always from her point of view. In 'Die ägyptische Finsternis' (The Egyptian darkness), the final section, there is undoubtedly a greater coalescence of the narrator's perspective with that of Franza, and although Martin's perspective is also present, the narrator's interest is with Franza. As Sabine Grimkowski points out, 'Der Erzähler ist keine neutrale Instanz, sondern weist eine besondere Affinität zu Franza auf.'[17] (The narrator is not a neutral voice, but shows a special affinity for Franza.) She points to the increasing similarity of the narrator's and Franza's language, and argues that at times they even become one voice, as for example when the narrator seems to have become Franza's partner in dialogue; 'Wo ist der Golf von Akaba! Gehetzt immer noch . . . in der Nacht am Nil, im Segelschatten, der allein dunkel ist. Was willst du in dieser Wüste' (277). (Where is the Gulf of Aqaba! Still harassed, . . . at night by the Nile, in the sail's shadow, which alone is dark. What are you seeking in this desert.) It is the proximity of the narrator and Franza in the last section which has made it the particular focus of much feminist interest, often at the expense of engaging with the narrative strategies of the preceding two sections. The skewed focus that results has also been exacerbated by the exclusion of certain final draft sections of the 'Jordanische Zeit' from the collected works.[18] These sections focus on Franza in the time before her relationship with Jordan and on her first meeting with him, and are crucial for understanding her and the nature of her victimhood. As Albrecht remarks, 'Die Episoden über den "schönsten Frühling" und die "Vor-Jordanische Zeit" mit einem Pianistenprinzen [haben] die Funktion, Franzas Grunddisposition und damit ihre Prädestination für die "Ermordung" durch Jordan darzustellen.'[19] (The episodes depicting the 'loveliest spring' and the 'time before Jordan' spent with a piano-prince, serve to portray Franza's basic disposition and her predestination to be 'murdered' by Jordan.) Nevertheless, despite this assertion, Albrecht remains sceptical as to whether the narrator adds a critical dimension to the text, remarking that 'Insgesamt gewinnt die Relativierung von Franzas fragwürdiger Perspektive in dem Roman . . . wenig kontur.'[20] (Overall the relativizing of Franza's questionable perspective in the novel . . . has little definition.)

My purpose now is not to deny the reality of Franza's suffering, but to show that the narrator, deeply sympathetic to her protagonist though she is, does invite the reader to adopt a critical position in relation to her anguish. Indeed, not only does the narrator recognize Franza's contributory role in her plight, but by making us aware of the destructive potential of Franza's position, she questions the validity of Franza's judgements and values.

FRANZA'S SUBSERVIENCE TO THE ABSOLUTE

Franza's suffering is not disputed in the texts, but her innocence is. This co-existence of suffering and complicity is initially indicated by Martin, who, even if he never fully understands his sister, does not deny or reject the severity of her despair. While there is no question in his mind that Jordan is to blame for Franza's collapse, he is not blind to her participation in the destructive process. Martin has long been disturbed by Jordan and was discomforted by aspects of Franza's behaviour when she and Leo were still together. Martin has always been tempted to tell Jordan 'wie ihm alles immer auf die Nerven gegangen war, die paar belehrenden Sätze, mit denen er abgefertigt worden war, was Franza nie gestört hatte, den überlegenen Ton, der . . . nicht nötig gewesen wäre' (147–8) (how everything had always got on his nerves; the couple of didactic sentences with which he had been fobbed-off but which had never bothered Franza; the superior tone, which . . . had been unnecessary). But 'Am meisten erschreckt hatten ihn in Wien diese Altarblicke von ihr' (192). (What had shocked him most in Vienna was her devotional expression.) Martin observed that Franza 'immer mit einem Gebet auf den Lippen herumging' (193) (always went around with a prayer on her lips), and when the siblings met in cafés he had to hear about her beloved Leo, her 'großartiges Fossil' (193) (marvellous fossil), whether he liked it or not.

Martin's observations of his sister's marital life point to Franza's willing subsumation into her husband's values and aspirations. However, Martin has, if anything, underestimated the extent to which her passivity has made her an occasional accomplice to Jordan's murderous methods in relation to his previous wives. Martin's assessment of the relationship is not only confirmed but also extended by Franza's own devastating realization of her passive complicity. So whereas Martin attempts to exculpate her from what she now sees as the ignominy of her life with Jordan by claiming 'Das ist doch keine Schande, mit einem Schwein gelebt zu haben' (207) (But it's no shame to have lived with a pig), Franza realizes that she is deeply

implicated in his cruelty through her condescending and scornful attitude
to his ex-wives:

Erst jetzt habe ich mich nach den anderen Frauen gefragt . . . warum die eine nicht
mehr aus dem Haus geht, warum die andere den Gashahn aufgedreht hat . . . und
wie bereitwillig habe ich geglaubt, sie seien dumm, verständnislos, defekt gewesen, nichtswürdige Kreaturen, die sich mit einem Abgang ins Schweigen selbst
bestraften für ihr Scheitern . . . Ich fühlte mich noch erhoben, geschmeichelt, daß
ich vielleicht den Ritterschlag mir verdienen könnte . . .

(Only now have I asked myself . . . about the other wives, why one no longer
leaves the house, why the other turned the gas tap on . . . How willingly I believed
that they were stupid, lacking in understanding, flawed, unworthy creatures who
punished themselves for their failure by retreating into silence . . . I felt edified,
flattered, that I could perhaps earn the knighthood . . .)

She participates in his lifestyle without reflection, admitting 'Nie fragte ich
mich, wie wir denn leben und ob wir richtig leben' (218). (I never asked
myself how we lived and whether we were living the right way.) Now she
wonders 'Warum ist mir das nie aufgefallen, daß er alle Menschen zerlegte,
bis nichts mehr da war' (219). (Why did I never notice that he dissected
people until nothing was left.) When in one fragment Martin asks her when
it all began, she describes a process of self-deceit that was present from the
beginning, and which then feeds on itself: 'der Betrug zeugt neuen Betrug'
(227) (deceit breeds new deceit). She now acknowledges this process of
deceit and willing self-deceit in which she participated as more than an
innocent victim as 'eine Schande, eine Schandgeschichte' (228) (a disgrace,
a shameful story).

   However, it is not only the fact of her subservience and self-deceit that
is of interest here, but the nature of that submission to her husband.
When Martin comments on Jordan's condescending tone, he also refers to
'etwas Hochmoralisches, das noch diesen Ton überlagerte und dem seine
Schwester aufgesessen war' (148) (something highly moralistic that over-
lapped with this tone and that his sister was taken in by). Again Martin's observation is confirmed by Franza's own admission that she thought Jordan's
two previous wives 'sich . . . selbst bestraften für ihr Scheitern an einer
höheren Moral, an einer Instanz, einem Maßstab, den ich zu dem meinen
machen wollte' (207) (punished themselves for their failure to attain a
higher morality, an authority, a yardstick that I wanted to make my own).
Her struggle to admit her mistake is related to the consequent need to
relinquish this idealized moral absolute that Jordan represented in her eyes:
'Wenn ich zugebe, daß ich mich getäuscht habe. Altarblicke, sagst du. Wenn

ich das zugebe . . . dann sterb ich zweimal, einmal noch mit für ihn, für mein Idol' (216). (If I admit that I was mistaken. A devotional expression, you say. If I admit that . . . then I die twice, the second time for him, for my idol.) Jordan has not been her only idol. Her yearning for the absolute and her desire to see in certain men the embodiment of an ideal to which she can then willingly submit as representative of a higher moral authority, is a pattern that is established before meeting Jordan. Herein lies the crucial role of both the section on Franza's relationship with the English army captain in the spring of 1945, and that on her time with the two Csobadi brothers when she is a medical student, leading to her first meetings with Jordan.

In her depiction of the young Franza's meeting with 'Sire', the narrator clearly shows the process by which a man assumes symbolic value for her. He is the personification of freedom even before he is an individual: 'Und sie sagte zu dem Frieden und diesem Mann Sire' (181). (And to Peace and to this man she said Sire.) He is at once 'Sire und der Frieden, dieser König und der erste Mann in ihrem Leben' (181) (Sire and Peace, this King and the first man in her life), and it is not the person who speaks to her, but the 'ein Meter neunzig lange dürre Frieden' (181) (one-metre-ninety-tall, scrawny Peace). Her desire transcends the individual and has the man as its object only as the personification of the ideal. This difference is again emphasized when she meets the Captain, now Percival Glyde, years later in England. She does not admit to him who she is, but wonders to herself afterwards whether she should ring him and consummate the love she had, now that she is no longer a skinny girl. Her considerations bear the trace of the self-sacrificial language that later culminates in the adoring devotional expression to her husband, although at this stage Franza is still able to laugh at the split between ideal and man: 'Sie . . . überlegte, ob sie anrufen solle und zu ihm gehen, denn jetzt hatte sie einen Körper, und den war sie ihm noch schuldig, ihm ja nicht, aber Sire, und dann lachte sie, weil kein Percival Glyde und kein ehemaliger Captain in einer Armee sie verstehen würde' (189). (She . . . wondered whether she should ring up and go to him, for now she had a body, and she still owed it to him, well, not to him, but to Sire, and then she laughed because no Percival Glyde and no former captain in the army would understand her.)

Franza's relationship with the pianist Ödön Csobadi during her time as a medical student in Vienna again confirms the pattern of subsumation which later reaches its extreme with Jordan. Very different in character from her time with either Glyde or Jordan, her time with Ödön is a 'halbverstandenes musikalisches Abenteuer' (236) (half-understood musical adventure) in

which she gets caught up. He is dependent on her for his emotional equanimity, for practical arrangements and for stability when plagued by depressive moods; in response to his dependence and the excitement of the new lifestyle, she suspends her studies. In the context of this relationship she is not at ease with the decision to delay her studies, although their total cessation is not identified as a problem when she is married. She retains an underlying dissatisfaction with a relationship that does not offer her a greater moral meaning, despite the joy it gives her:

Das schönste an Ödön war, daß er, selbst wenn ihn die Traurigkeit um die Ecke schwemmte, Franza nie traurig, sondern immer stark machte und fröhlich. Sie hatte nie soviel gelacht, sie ging in lauter Lachen und Glanz auf, ohne es zu merken, und es [gab] nichts, was [sie] ihm je hätte übel nehmen können. (237)

(The nicest thing about Ödön was that he never made Franza sad, but always made her strong and happy, even if sadness was just around the corner for him. She had never laughed so much, she was subsumed by all the laughter and radiance without noticing, and there was nothing she could ever have resented him for.)

But despite this joy she cannot escape the feeling of 'Schwerfälligkeit' (236) (ponderousness), cannot refrain from murmuring ' "unnütz" ' (236) (pointless) to herself, and instead wants stability and a meaning that exceeds the moment. Ödön is a man who represents the moment, the pleasure of instant gratification of desire. As he says, 'Ich weiß nur, was ich jetzt will, ich will dich. Und jetzt möcht ich Eis dazu' (238). (I only know what I want now, I want you. And now I want ice-cream too.) Franza's role is to satisfy the demand for 'jetzt' (now) with a 'sofort' (straight away): 'Warum möcht man dir eigentlich immer alles sofort geben und holen?'(238). (Why do people always want to give and fetch everything for you straight away?) However, it is not the giving and fetching in themselves which are a problem for Franza, but that they are not done in the service of a greater good, so when the relationship ends, 'Franza akzeptiert Ödöns Selbstbeschuldigung, weil er das Ordinäre ad absurdum führt' (243). (Franza accepted Ödön's self-castigation because he took the ordinary to its absurd extreme.) In contrast, Jordan, a man whose research is concerned with the experiments done on Holocaust victims, provides a ready cause, one for which she can give and fetch by working as an assistant on his book. Once she has met Jordan there is no further mention of resuming her studies.

The desert is, of course, the final object of Franza's need to sacrifice herself to an absolute. It becomes the last of the moral authorities that will save her from oppression, the 'große Heilanstalt' (248) (large sanatorium),

the uncompromising extreme in which she need no longer be afraid of the 'Whites': 'Ich werde nie mehr auf die Knie fallen, vor keinem Menschen, vor keinem Weißen' (255). (I will never go down on my knees again, not before any human, not before any white man.) When she arrives she links the desert with the attainment of her first desire: 'Sire, ich werde ankommen' (249). (Sire, I will arrive.) She knows that this final desire can be consummated because the desert is an object which has no voice, a perfect surface for projection and hallucination. The desert offers no answers to the fundamental question it poses: 'Was suchst du in dieser Wüste, sagte die Stimme in der Wüste, in der nichts zu hören ist . . . Und die Stimme antwortet nicht, da es in der Wüste still ist' (260). (What are you seeking in this desert, said the voice in the desert, in which there is nothing to be heard . . . And the voice did not answer, because it is still in the desert.) It remains permanently and irreducibly absolute, and is the logical conclusion of what has gone before. Indeed, it is the fulfilment of Franza's own youthful fantasies, for in her student days she dreamed about the grand ethical gestures she could make when she was qualified as a doctor. She felt that only such grand gestures would be 'real', and would avoid becoming ordinary, a prospect that is intolerable for her: 'Es mußte etwas Wirkliches sein, später Afrika oder Asien, unter den härtesten Bedingungen, mit Opferbringen, mit Heroismus, Opferbringen mußte unbedingt dazugehören, und großartig sollte es sein, voller Anstrengung, aber glorreich für sie selber, mit frühem Tod' (233–4). (It had to be something real, later Africa or Asia, under the hardest conditions, with sacrifice and heroism; sacrifice absolutely had to be part of it, and it would be marvellous, full of effort, but glorious for her, with an early death.) How well she succeeds in her ambition! She dies her early death in the desert of North Africa, the female sacrifice to the dominance of 'die Weißen' (the Whites). And, at the risk of being too caustic, the glorious postscript is provided not by the surreptitious removal of her body from the Cairo hotel, but by some critical attempts to see her story as a model for utopia.

While in the last section, 'Die ägyptische Finsternis', the narrator remains consistently sympathetic to her protagonist, she nevertheless continues to point to Franza's pathological compulsion to make absolute the ordinary as a necessary element in the story of her death. The episode of her seaside vision of God is a grotesque microcosm of the repeated process that is fundamental to her destruction, whereby idealization is followed by the terrible confrontation with the real object. In a walk along a beach she sees an object which she initially believes is Jordan, then her father, but who she then realizes is God: 'Gott kommt auf mich zu, und ich komme auf Gott

zu . . . Ich habe Gott gesehen' (286–7). (God is coming towards me and I am approaching God . . . I have seen God.) Weeping, she runs to the object, falls, and kneels before it, 'Und da lag Er vor ihr, ein schwarzer Strunk, aus dem Wasser geschwemmt, eine Seewalze, ein zusammengeschrumpftes Ungeheuer . . . Darauf war sie zugerannt' (287). (And there He lay in front of her, a black stalk washed up out of the water, a sea cucumber, a wrinkled-up monster . . . That is what she had run towards.) The disparity between God and sea cucumber throws her into convulsions, an existential crisis in which she feels herself trampled down, and from which Martin then carries her away. The narrator's crucial comment comes last: 'Die arabische Wüste ist von zerbrochenen Gottesvorstellungen umsäumt' (288). (The Arabian desert is lined with shattered images of God.) The narrator's voice is quite distinct from Franza's preceding perspective, and although her comment does of course link Franza to the prophets, it concurrently ironizes that association, coming as it does immediately after a vision based on a sea cucumber. It recalls another remark made by the narrator, this time on the occasion of the young Franza's first meeting with 'Sire', and exposes the degree of irony present in that early judgement: 'Da bewies Franza zum erstenmal in ihrem Leben den Instinkt, der sie später außerhalb Galiciens sich zurechtfinden ließ, ihre Unterscheidungsfähigkeit' (180). (There Franza demonstrated for the first time in her life the instinct that later enabled her to cope outside Galicia: her power of discernment.)

NATIONAL IDENTITY

Franza's suffering victimhood is inseparable from her need to idealize; she seeks a moral absolute and attempts to assimilate with it, thereby winning for herself the moral worth she aspires to. She fluctuates between self-deceit and denial, seeing only the absolute, and the inability to live in a state of moral compromise or ambiguity. At a wider level, her dependence on an idealized object, and the licence to ignore present reality which it offers, are fundamental to her perception of national identity. Franza idealizes the past of the Habsburg Empire and the oriental present. In her, the two are related, both imagined realms where she will be uncompromised, realms that signify the return to an origin, to authenticity, away from the deceit, manipulation and denial of contemporary society. The Empire offers an image of an 'innocent' Austria, untainted by complicity with German National Socialism, and the Orient offers escape from the morally tainted post-war Austria while giving the hope of moral redemption. By identifying with the oriental victims of the 'Whites', and indeed with Holocaust victims, Franza

effects a neat double gesture: she responds with moral repugnance to racist atrocities, while herself avoiding any association with 'White' ideology, historically exemplified in fascist thinking.

In the figure of Franza, a woman whose identity is founded in victimhood, deceit, and idealization, many of the characteristics of post-war Austrian identity manifest themselves. In his article on education and national identity in post-war Austria, Robert Knight shows how a similar constellation of features served the attempt to construct an identity in opposition to Germany.[21] The major parties of the Second Austrian Republic made the claim that the difference between Austrians and Germans was both national and ethical; the Austrians were not members of a Greater German Nation, and Austrians had been resisting victims of National Socialism. Felix Hurdes, secretary of the People's Party, and Education Minister from 1945, emphasized an Austrian Nation that was capable of reconciling East and West, was purged of German traces and was based on a distinct ethnic identity involving intermarriage with Slavs and Magyars. He argued that 'Durch eine Geschichte von Jahrhunderten . . . eine wesentlich andere Blutmischung und eine Erziehung, die an anderen Sternen orientiert war, Österreich längst eine eigene Nation geworden [ist] und mit Deutschland nichts als die Schriftsprache gemein [hat]'.[22] (As a result of centuries of history, . . . an essentially different mix of blood, and an upbringing that has been oriented to quite other stars, Austria has long become her own nation and has only the written language in common with Germany.) Hurdes may not have been expressing the view of all his government colleagues here, but there was certainly agreement between the People's Party and the Socialists to insist to the outside world that Austria had been the victim of German aggression, and to deny or ignore the fact that there had been widespread support for the *Anschluß* of 1938.[23]

Austria's acknowledged status as victim was central to its self-definition, and continued to be generally accepted until the Waldheim affair of the 1980s forced public discussion and acknowledgement of Austrian support for the Nazi regime and anti-Semitic policies.[24] The denial that sustained this image was profound, as Jean Améry stated so clearly: 'Österreich jedoch, von seinen Politikern der Welt als ein Opfer Hitlers vorgestellt, steht vor der unerträglichen Nötigung, sich selbst ganz und gar zu verleugnen.'[25] (Yet Austria, presented to the world as a victim of Hitler by its politicians, is faced with the unbearable need to deny itself absolutely.) And as Gerhard Botz argues, while anti-Semitism continued to be rife, Austria benefited financially from its 'victimhood', first by having Allied reparations substantially reduced, then by refusing compensation payments:

Im Gegensatz zur Bundesrepublik Deutschland lehnte Österreich als 'Opfer des Nationalsozialismus' Entschädigungszahlungen an Israel ab und verzögerte bzw. erschwerte solche an einzelne Juden lange Zeit . . . Die österreichische Regierung versuchte immer wieder, die Vermögensrückstellungen an Juden aus Grundbesitz, Betrieben, Wohnungen, Kunstgegenständen, Aktien etc. möglichst einzuschränken. (Zigeuner sind im übrigen erst ab 1981, Zwangssterilisierte und Homosexuelle bis heute nicht voll als Opfer des Nazismus anerkannt worden, während Dienstzeiten und erlittene Schäden durch Tätigkeit im NS-Staatsapparat und in der Wehrmacht voll kompensiert wurden.)[26]

(In contrast to the Federal Republic of Germany, Austria rejected compensation payments to Israel, claiming to be a 'victim of National Socialism', and for a long time delayed, or obstructed, such payments to Jews . . . The Austrian government repeatedly attempted to limit as much as possible the restitution to Jews of property, businesses, flats, artworks, shares, etc. (Incidentally, gypsies were only recognized as full victims of Nazism in 1981, and those who were forcibly sterilized and homosexuals have still not been recognized. In contrast, a period of service and damages incurred whilst working in the NS state machinery and in the Wehrmacht, were fully compensated.))

It is in the processes at work in constructing identity that strong parallels emerge between the individual woman Franza and the public discourse of post-war Austria. Botz concludes that in terms of her representation of National Socialism, Bachmann was 'more modern' than other contemporary historical analyses, but goes on to argue that there is a tension, if not a contradiction, between that and the traces of the official 'victim' discourse and her mourning for the loss of the Habsburg Empire.[27] Yet in his analysis Botz gives little attention to the narrative strategies of Bachmann's fiction, using the themes present in her prose as ready, unmediated evidence. This failure of vision is repeated in an article by Hans-Ulrich Thamer, in which he argues that in Bachmann's public comments 'Österreich ganz im Sinne des im Österreich der Nachkriegszeit lange dominanten Geschichtsbildes lediglich aus der Perspektive des Opfers [erscheint].'[28] (Austria is presented in a way which is fully in keeping with the historical conception of Austria that was so long dominant after the war, which was simply from the perspective of the victim.) He then cites 'Unter Mördern und Irren' and *Malina* as further evidence, without first considering questions of narrative perspective, thus too easily aligning authorial statement with fictional expression. I would like to argue, however, that although Bachmann may share 'das verbreitete österreichische Gefühl der Nostalgie und des Verlustes'[29] (the widespread Austrian feeling of nostalgia and of loss), her prose work serves as a complex critical response to nostalgia and idealization. To take further Botz's comment on Bachmann's modernity, her fiction is evidence that she

was not only ahead of her time in her depiction of National Socialism, but that she thematizes the many processes involved in the construction of identity, and then goes on to appraise them critically. The narrative perspective is so important because it crucially transforms sympathy for the protagonist from being an apologia for victimhood and deceit to being a critical appraisal which is nevertheless founded upon comprehension of the protagonist's real suffering. The tension that Botz identifies is one arising from the narrator's profound sympathy with Franza and her views, and her concurrent refusal to condone Franza's position. And by extension, through the parallels established with Austrian identity, the tension reflects the narrator's sympathy for Austria, but also her refusal to simplify what post-war Austria is through idealization or deceit. Similarly, the eager demonization of Germany, lurking in *Das Buch Franza* but more obviously thematized in *Requiem für Fanny Goldmann* and the *Goldmann/Rottwitz* novel, is not advocated but criticized as a necessary bolster for Austrian idealization.

Franza's suffering cannot be seen in isolation from the process of submission and self-deception that not only facilitate but actively contribute to her death. Just as in her relationship with Jordan it is her willingness to identify with him as a moral authority which prevents her thinking about and questioning her responsibility, so too her tendency to conceive of political issues solely as moral instances results in attitudes based on idealized generalizations in which she fails to reflect upon her own role. So although Franza may powerfully and evocatively articulate the voice of the wronged, she is a figure who, in her failure to differentiate critically, provides the conditions, even the support, for the wrongdoing.

The 'Heimkehr nach Galicien' itself already signals the impossibility of Franza's ideals. As the name of the place in which Franza and Martin grew up, Galicia is also the name of the province that belonged to Austria before 1918, after which it was ceded to Poland. The return home to Galicia thus represents both the futile attempt to recapture the imagined comfort of a large and protecting Empire, 'das Haus Österreich' (170) (the House of Austria) and the fantasy of an imagined childhood idyll with its profound and unexploitative sibling love. For Martin it was a time when his bare-legged sister looked after him, and when they were so close that she instinctively knew when he was drowning and ran to rescue him; for Franza it was the time before illness, of the coming of peace and 'Sire', of her love for her brother and the English Captain, unmarred by the manipulative objectification of her relationship to Jordan. The narrator confirms the power of the desire for Galicia, for a return to an uncorrupted pre-history,

remarking 'Wie unwiderstehlich ist Galicien, die Liebe' (149). (How irresistible Galicia is, love is.) That Galicia assumes this function of unsullied idyll, a place with an untarnished pre-history, relates too to the fact that it was a province which, before the Second World War, had a large Jewish population. The desire to return here is thus also the desire to turn away from a present that is dominated by the knowledge of genocide.

Martin, however, is himself aware of the impossibility of returning to what was: 'Es war alles ganz sinnlos geworden, was er gedacht . . . und was er erinnert hatte, das war nicht mehr die Franza von früher . . . und von Galicien war auch nichts mehr übriggeblieben' (157). (It had all become pointless, what he had thought . . . and what he had remembered, that was no longer the Franza of before . . . and nothing was left of Galicia either.) 'Der ganze Mythos einer Kindheit . . . und eines Wiederfindens' (158) (the whole myth of a childhood . . . and of a rediscovery) as Martin recognizes his yearning to be, is not, however, merely a personal myth, but carries with it the association of a greater past. Martin and Franza's cottage becomes representative of the lost Habsburg Empire, within which one could identify with a part or with the whole, now modernized but with no name. The cottage is 'Überbleibsel eines imposanten Besitzes . . . wo man auch zu den Großen oder den Kleinen gehören konnte, und das hier in Galicien war einmal groß gewesen, ein Reich und ein Name, und jetzt gab es das nicht mehr, dafür elektrisches Licht und fließendes Wasser' (158) (a small remnant of an imposing property . . . where one could belong to the great or the small, and this place in Galicia had once been great, an empire and a name, and now it no longer existed, but instead there was electric light and running water).

Although both siblings share this yearning for the past, their relationship to that yearning is quite different. This becomes evident in their responses to the names on the gravestones at Maria Gail that Franza has insisted upon visiting. The names are a mixture of Germanic and Slavic, and the first names are endlessly repeated in a circle. The importance of the names lies not only in the fact that some, like Gasparin, belong to relatives, but that they represent a political system that was:

Nicht nur die Ranner und die Gasparin hatten sich so immer im Kreis gedreht, und dazu um ihre Hausnamen . . . damit sie doppelt getauft waren wie das Haus Österreich, das sich mit seinen dreidoppelten Namen immer im Kreis gedreht hatte bis zu seinem Einsturz und davon noch an Gedächtnisverlust litt, die Namen hörte für etwas, das es nicht mehr war. (170)

(It was not only the Ranners and the Gasparins who had repeated their names like this, and also revolved around the name of their house . . . so that they became

doubly christened, like the House of Austria, which had turned itself in a circle with its three double names until its collapse; an event it failed to remember, still hearing names for something that no longer existed.)

This political ailment of looking to the past for a name that is now obsolete, of thus seeking to define oneself anachronistically, is, in Martin's view, what Franza is suffering from. In her new faked passport she has once again assumed her maiden name of Ranner, so attempting to regain the past through a name. Martin observes 'daß auch Franza von einem Einsturz mitgerissen wurde und daß sie durch ihre Krankheit noch an der Krankheit des Damals litt, viele Merkmale auch dieser Krankheit trug. Sie schaute zurück, drehte sich in ihren wirklichen alten Namen' (170) (that Franza was also swept along by a collapse and that through her illness she was suffering from the 'in-those-days' disease and displayed many of the characteristics of this illness: she looked back, wrapped herself in her real old names). The problem is that this old name 'bedeckte sie nicht mehr ganz, nur noch die Blößen' (171) (no longer fully covered her, only her nakedness). Whereas Martin perceives Franza to be looking back to an idealized past, refusing to recognize that these old names are effective disguises for 'die Monstrosität des Besitzenkönnens und Besitzenwollens' (171) (the monstrosity of ownership and the desire to possess), he is determined to reject the myth, the 'veralteten Schmerzen und Verhängnissen' (171) (obsolete pains and disasters). Although he soon rejects the notion, it occurs to him that not only Jordan is a 'Fossil' in his ways of thinking, but his sister is too, as someone not prepared to look forward and develop: '[Fossil] galt mit für alle Zumutungen, die von langher kamen, für alle diese Erpressungen, für die Erpresser wie Jordan und die Erpreßten wie Franza' (171–2). (The term 'fossil' included all the demands that stemmed from long ago, all this blackmail; it included the blackmailers like Jordan and those blackmailed, like Franza.)

This view of Franza is from Martin's perspective. However, just as his analysis of Franza's subservience to Jordan is later confirmed by Franza's own analysis and the narrator's 'Vorgeschichten' (pre-histories), so too is his judgement of her idealization of the past in 'Heimkehr nach Galicien' consistent with the changing perspectives of the following sections, even though the emotional and political context differs. In two of the versions of 'Jordanische Zeit' Franza's idealization manifests itself in a different and disturbing form. Here it is not projected onto the lost Habsburg past, but onto exploited and victimized races and groups whose very existence has been threatened by 'Whites', and with all of whom Franza fully and undifferentiatedly identifies. She dreams a dream in which she is in a gas-chamber and Jordan turns on the gas, a dream which is all the more terrifying because

for Franza it represents her conscious experience: 'es [ist] nichts Fremdes, es gehört zu mir' (229) (it's nothing strange, it belongs to me). Her self-positioning as a Holocaust victim is confirmed when she calls herself 'ein einziger Spätschaden' (215), a term referring to the long-term psychosomatic effects of Nazi persecution.[30] And on the occasion of her visit to Dr Körner, who had been a Nazi doctor involved in euthanasia killings, she establishes an immediate relationship between her own suffering and the anguish of the witness B., a victim of Nazi experiments, by, like him, saying to the oppressor, 'Verzeihen Sie' (forgive me). Franza says it to Körner, the witness said it to the court: 'Verzeihen Sie, daß ich weine . . .' (306) (forgive me for crying). Her surprise at the fact that Dr Körner is Austrian is telling: 'Sie hatte automatisch angenommen, er sei Deutscher' (298). (She had automatically assumed he was German.) Just as in her relationship with Jordan she avoided what had been perpetrated in the past, thereby becoming complicit through passivity, here she repeats the process by assuming that the perpetrators were German; as an Austrian woman identifying with victims while accepting German guilt, she can avoid the question of Austrian involvement in persecution, until so shockingly confronted with evidence to the contrary.

Franza's identification is not only with the Holocaust victims, but more generally she defines herself as 'von niedriger Rasse' (230) (belonging to an inferior race), or indeed as an inferior class, 'denn ich [bin] ausgebeutet, benutzt worden, genötigt, hörig gemacht' (230) (for I have been exploited, used, compelled, enslaved). She draws many comparisons between her own plight and gradual death and that of the aboriginal Australians, the Papuans, the Incas, the Murutes of North Borneo, the Blacks in general, until she finally asserts 'Ich bin eine Papua' (232). (I am a Papuan.) Jordan's exploitation of her is, in her view, like the White exploitation of 'lesser races', and there is no doubt that Franza articulates the despair of victims of oppression and exploitation powerfully and with a moral outrage that is effective and easy to sympathize with:

Er hat mir meine Güter genommen. Mein Lachen, meine Zärtlichkeit, mein Freuenkönnen, mein Mitleiden . . . er hat jedes einzelne Aufkommen von all dem ausgetreten, bis es nicht mehr aufgekommen ist. Aber warum tut das jemand, das versteh ich nicht, aber es ist ja auch nicht zu verstehen, warum die Weißen den Schwarzen die Güter genommen haben. (231)[31]

(He took my goods from me. My laughter, my tenderness, my gaiety, my sympathy . . . he erased each one when it appeared until it never appeared again. But why does someone do that, that is what I do not understand, but then it is impossible to understand why the Whites took the Blacks' goods away from them.)

In the final section, Franza's idealization and its necessary opposite, demonization, find expression in the opposition of the desert and the Whites, and, as Moustapha Diallo points out, between the desert and Cairo.[32] I have already shown how the desert signifies for Franza the final moral absolute; it is the place where she feels she can no longer be oppressed, and where she can finally attain a subjectivity that does not depend on victimhood: 'Ich werde nie mehr auf die Knie fallen, vor keinem Menschen, vor keinem Weißen' (255). (I will never fall to my knees again in front of any person, in front of any white person.) The law of the desert affirms the right of all to have access to water, a law in which Franza sees the guarantee for this new subjectivity: 'Du siehst, sagte Franza, es darf auch mir hier etwas nicht verweigert werden. Ich komme zu meinem Recht' (264). (You see, said Franza, even I cannot be refused anything here. I am coming into my own.) The desert represents the authenticity and respect that the White cultures have lost; it is they who desecrated the ancient Egyptian graves in their search for knowledge and categorization, a desecration that continues in the form of the stream of eagerly photographing white tourists in the museum, the 'Breughelfiguren aus Holland, aus Deutschland, aus Dänemark, mit sonnverbrannten Unterarmen und glühenden Nasen' (289) (Breughel figures from Holland, Germany and Denmark, with sunburned underarms and glowing noses). Franza is repulsed by the tourists' behaviour and vomits. She considers it, though, a just response: 'Ich habe euch, euch Leichenschändern wenigstens vor die Füße gespien' (290). (At least I have been sick at your feet, you grave-desecrators.)

It is at this point that we come up against the problem of the increasing confluence of the narrator's and Franza's voice in the final section, for it would seem to lend authority to the protagonist's identification with the desert and criticism of the Whites. There are certain passages where the Whites are criticized and the desert acclaimed as a place where authenticity of perception can be regained, which can be read from the perspective of either Franza or the narrator or both, but are not specifically ascribed to Franza, even if they are congruent with her view:

Wer fürchtet hier die von den Weißen katalogisierten Bakterien. Wer wäscht einen Becher aus, wer kocht das Wasser ab, wer laust die Salatblätter, wer nimmt den Fisch unter die Lupe? Hunger, Durst, wiederentdeckt, die Gefahr, wiederentdeckt, die Ohren, die Augen geschärft auf die Außenwelt gerichtet, das Ziel wiedergewußt. (259)

(Who fears the bacteria that have been catalogued by the Whites here. Who cleans out a cup, who boils the water, who washes the salad, who examines

the fish under a magnifying glass? Hunger and thirst are rediscovered, danger is rediscovered, ears and eyes are sharply trained on the world, the goal is again known.)

Here, the view of Whites as petty and divorced from basic and authentic human sensation appears to be condoned by the narrator, as is the accusation that their presence is ubiquitous, to the point of colonizing others' psyches:

Die Weißen kommen . . . Und wenn sie wieder zurückgeworfen werden, dann werden sie noch einmal wiederkommen . . . sie werden mit ihrem Geist wiederkommen, wenn sie anders nicht mehr kommen können. Und auferstehen in einem braunen oder schwarzen Gehirn, es werden noch immer die Weißen sein, auch dann noch. (278)

(The Whites are coming . . . And when they are repelled, then they will come once again . . . they will come with their spirit if they can no longer come another way. And even when they are resurrected in a brown or black mind, they will still be the Whites, even then.)

Now the critical potential of this position is undoubtedly considerable. As the debates in contemporary post-colonial theories reveal, colonialism and white supremacy are achieved and maintained not just through political and economic dominance, but through language and the privileging of certain modes of thinking and Eurocentric philosophies. But as contemporary debate also reveals, the reduction of the discussion to generalized binaries within which one pole dominates the other, forecloses on the possibility of a more complex analysis and fails to recognize the dynamic and often ambiguous relationships of power, resistance, hybridity and complicity. This, for all the critical potency encapsulated in Franza's attack on the Whites, is precisely the reduction that she makes. Lennox describes just this double effect of critique and reinscription of imperialist discourse. She points to Franza's fantasy of the desert as the place of healing that can rescue her from Europe, her conceptualization of and identification with it as 'Other' that is, like her, oppressed and exploited by European man. Such fantasies, Lennox concludes, have little to do with the desert, or with the real places of Egypt and Sudan, but are themselves typical of the way in which European identity – here the identity of a European woman – constitutes itself through projection onto a racialized Other. The question remains, however, of whether these simplifying fantasies are Franza's alone or whether the narrator is lending authority to her view. This is the question that concerns Albrecht in her close analysis of the historical veracity of Franza's assertion about the Papuans, Incas and Aborigines. She argues that Franza's statements are historically wrong, simplified and that they

have the effect of undermining the centrality of violence in the process of colonization: 'Und auf diese Weise hat sie mit verblüffender Logik den Zusammenhang zwischen ihrer individuellen Lebensgeschichte und der Weltgeschichte hergestellt.'[33] (Thus, with stunning logic, she establishes the link between her own personal history and world history.) She argues that Franza's view is worryingly similar to the mentality in the 1960s which sought to justify colonialism by seeing historical events as inevitable for the development of civilization, and that the narrator does not adequately relativize Franza's position, but leaves her free to construct dubious parallels. Albrecht does not ascribe Franza's views to Bachmann, but concludes by asking whether the novel achieves more than the confirmation of Franza's world view. I wish to suggest that it does, first by arguing that the narrator is more critical than Albrecht avers, and secondly by considering the importance of the textual emphasis on irresolution.

There are undoubtedly certain passages where the narrator's voice seems to be at one with her protagonist's. However, because enough has already preceded these passages to point to the limited and self-destructive process of Franza's compulsion to idealize, even at the point where the narrator's sympathy for her protagonist leads to the occasional convergence of voice, this is not equivalent to privileging Franza's views. The reader is invited to sympathize with Franza's despair without neglecting the critical perspectives that have already served to relativize her judgements (those of the narrator, Martin and, of course, Franza's own acknowledgement of self-deceit). The moments of confluence are not enough to argue that the narrator adopts Franza's perspective even while she does accept, and wishes the reader to accept, the profundity of her protagonist's suffering. Indeed, the text makes clear that Franza's conceptual model is questionable, not least by depicting the disparity between her idealized or demonized types and the reality she confronts.

In 'Heimkehr nach Galicien' Martin questions the way in which he refers to the 'Jordans of this world', asking himself (in the form of an internal monologue) 'Was meint er bloß mit den Jordans dieser Welt, er machte da aus einer Person viele, bloß weil die eine ihn ärgerte und ihm von Anfang an verdächtig gewesen war' (150). (What did he mean, the Jordans of this world. He turned one person into many, just because that one individual annoyed him and he had been suspicious of him from the start.) But unlike her brother, Franza is never shown to question the process of her own generalization, be it either to idealize or demonize. Just as was the case with her confrontation with the sea cucumber; this then results in reality causing shock, devastation and enhanced trauma, not as an opportunity

for reflecting upon her own preconceptions and assumptions. Thus her idolization of the desert and its imagined authenticity, in contrast to the rationality of the West, bears little relation to the authenticity of the customs she experiences and the revulsion they provoke. There are three obvious examples of this, all occurring on the occasion of the wedding feast. She is totally disconcerted by the children present there, children who for her are not children, for 'sie warfen Liebesblicke, hatten Liebesgesten' (275) (they gave loving looks, made loving gestures). Her reaction is extreme, for they do not conform to her expectation of 'normality':

Weil sie sich nicht zu helfen wußte, sagte sie zu Martin, die Kinder hier sind nicht normal, siehst du das nicht. Das sind eben andere Kinder, sagte Martin . . . Das sind doch gar keine Kinder, wiederholte Franza immer wieder. Sie fing zu weinen an und wiederholte den Satz ein paarmal. (275–6)

(Because she could not help herself, she said to Martin, the children here aren't normal, can't you see that. They are just different children, said Martin . . . But they just aren't children, Franza repeated continuously. She started to cry and repeated the sentence a few times.)

The degree of repulsion and horror that Franza feels when she sees the slaughtered camel and the cretin makes manifest her inability to approach the cultural realities of her abstract desert. The killing of the camel, the bridegroom's gift, appears as a type of sacrilege, both against the camel, and the sand, drenched in its blood: 'Ich kann nicht weiter . . . ich will nicht durch das Blut, durch diesen Sand, der von seinem Blut . . . sie watete durch den blutenden Sand' (280). (I cannot go on . . . I don't want to go through the blood, through this sand, drenched in its blood . . . She waded through the bleeding sand.) When she sees the dead camel she can go no further, and similarly the cretin's extreme deformities appal and incapacitate her; she cannot look at him, cannot move when he touches her, but can only stare at the belly-dancer. Yet what is also crucial to note here is that just as her excessive idolization of Jordan was based in her eagerness to see in him the embodiment of something more, here too the figures provoke such an excess of horror because Franza projects onto them more than they are, seeing in both the camel and the cretin aspects of herself. Of the camel she comments, 'Ich weiß, wie ich aussehe. Ich sehe aus wie das Kamel, das mich ansieht' (280). (I know how I look. I look like the camel that's gazing at me.) Of the cretin she says, 'Das ist alles schon in mir. Er fährt in mich, deswegen kann ich nicht hinschauen' (281). (That is all already in me. His presence is penetrating me, that's why I can't look at him.) By relating to others and the Other solely in terms of embodiments of her own moral

yearnings or anxieties, she moulds them, albeit inadvertently, to her own image. So Franza, while idolizing the desert and demonizing the culture that is familiar to her, is constantly limited by her own preconceptions. She treats the desert as an object of her own desires and projections, and is thus caught up in the very process of objectification that she is constantly criticizing.

Bachmann wrote that 'Auf das Opfer darf keiner sich berufen. Es ist Mißbrauch. Kein Land und keine Gruppe, keine Idee, darf sich auf Ihre Toten berufen.' (No one should appeal to the victims. It is an abuse. No country and no group, no idea should appeal to its dead.) Yet precisely this is so difficult to articulate, as she goes on to state: 'Die Schwierigkeit, das auszudrücken'[34] (The difficulty in expressing this). She also wrote that '[Der Faschismus] fängt an in der Beziehung zwischen Menschen. Der Faschismus ist das erste in der Beziehung zwischen einem Mann und einer Frau.'[35] (Fascism begins in the relationship between people. Fascism comes first in the relationship between a man and a woman.) Hans-Ulrich Thamer is unhappy with this loose use of the word 'fascist', remarking:

Auch wenn man diesen Gebrauch des Faschismusbegriffs als 'Metapher' versteht, so bleibt unübersehbar, daß die Schriftstellerin damit der zeitgenössischen Inflationierung des Faschismus-Begriffes folgt, die der Historiker als wenig erkenntnisfördernd und gar als potentielle Verharmlosung der tatsächlichen Vernichtungspraxis des Nationalsozialismus kritisieren muß, was freilich nicht in Ingeborg Bachmanns Absicht gelegen hat.[36]

(Even if we understand this use of the term 'fascism' as a 'metaphor', we cannot overlook the fact that the author is going along with the contemporary inflation of the term. The historian is obliged to be critical of this, since it does little to further our comprehension and potentially even undermines the actual destructiveness of National Socialism, which certainly was not Bachmann's intention.)

Although it is undoubtedly true that Bachmann's use of the term here is limited, I would nevertheless argue that her fictional explorations of the personal roots of what she terms fascism do not undermine the atrociousness of National Socialism itself. For she is concerned with a causality that is too rarely deemed the prerogative of the 'historian', although it is crucial for the successful functioning of power. What she reveals are the mechanisms through which individuals, in this case a woman, willingly become subservient to power, and comply with it by mistaking it for or choosing to see in it a moral authority. Franza is certainly a victim of the unscrupulous and ambitious exercise of power by Jordan, but it is she who has empowered him by projecting on him her need for a moral certainty and ideal. The

narrator makes it perfectly apparent that Franza is determined to disregard the discrepancy between ideal and man from the first, writing of one of their first meetings, 'Es klaffte etwas zwischen Jordan und Franza, und was klaffte, wollte sie schließen' (242). (Something gaped open between Jordan and Franza, and she wanted to close the rift.) Franza is a crucial part of this process, does not learn, but continues to seek her ideal, comparing herself and identifying with the dead in just the way Bachmann denounced, thereby reinscribing the phallocentrism and colonizing discourses she believes she is escaping. This is a protagonist who on the one hand tells Martin that Jordan is no fossil, but 'ist heutiger als ich . . . er ist das Exemplar, das heute regiert' (230) (is more contemporary than I am . . . he is the type that governs nowadays), and on the other goes to the ex-Nazi and is surprised that he is Austrian. In her search for an idealized moral authority in response to her dissatisfaction with her contemporary society, she is instrumental in the perpetuation of power that she abhors, and indeed does not realize until too late that she has become its victim.

THE RIGHTEOUS SERVANT

Through her narrative technique, here still in a form which she found unsatisfactory, Bachmann allows us to sympathize with suffering without being overwhelmed by it. She points to the destructive potential that idealization has, be it the projection of a moral ideal onto individuals, or onto national identity. The person of Franza herself, therefore, does not suggest the hope of a utopia, feminist or any other, but the modes of death that result from aspiring to one. It is, however, important to return again to the question of the narrator's sympathy for her protagonist. This sympathy may be used by critics to demonstrate Bachmann's own embeddedness in the oppressing discourses of her time; indeed, the tension between the criticism of the protagonist and the sympathy for her may be cited as evidence for the author's inability to extricate herself from those discourses while yet recognizing their destructive effects. As was discussed earlier, this is Lennox's position; while recognizing that through the figure of Franza Bachmann attempts to expose the fact that racist, imperialist fantasies are constitutive elements of the European psyche. Lennox nevertheless argues that the author herself fails to escape racist structures of thought by using a real non-European country to explore the European psyche. Although Lennox fully acknowledges the complexity of the text, I wish to argue that the contradictions it manifests are more than a symptom of Bachmann's being a product of her time. The nature of the narrator's sympathy for

Franza and the narrative context within which it is expressed urgently point to the tension between critique and sympathy as being a positive and ethically constructive irresolution.

The narrator draws attention to the nature of her relationship to her suffering protagonist by means of one early moment of explicit narrative intervention in the text, when the narrator both quotes and gives the reference for Matthew 12. 20: 'Das zerstoßene Rohr wird Er nicht brechen, und den glimmenden Docht wird Er nicht auslöschen' (149). (He will not break a bruised reed nor quench a smouldering wick.) In quoting Matthew's Gospel here the narrator indicates that her own concern with the nature of suffering and victimhood constitutes a critical dialogue with the predominantly Old Testament debate about suffering and innocence. Although the reference is to the New Testament, Matthew's Gospel is the most 'Jewish' of the four, his aim being to establish that Christ is the fulfilment of the Old Testament prophecies and is therefore the Jewish Messiah.[37] This is one of the points in Matthew's narrative where he cites Isaiah in order to confirm the continuity of the tradition by suggesting that in Christ can be seen the figure of the Righteous Servant. Matthew's citation comes from the first of the four 'Servant Songs' in The Book of Isaiah,[38] songs which articulate a response to the question raised by the exile of the Jews in Babylon. Whereas in the Book of Kings this exile is presented as the punishment decreed by a righteous God because of the sins of his people, the Book of Job and then of Isaiah confront the difficult issue of how a righteous God can punish the innocent and make them suffer for the sins of others. This leads in the Book of Isaiah to the concept of the 'Righteous Remnant' (those returning from Babylon), or the Righteous Servant, who suffers almost because of his righteousness; he is divinely appointed, and reveals the way in which God uses people to achieve his purpose. Thus the suffering of innocents is theologically justified as having a redemptive effect for all.[39] The four songs describe the servant, his rejection, his abjection, his silence and his gentleness. Furthermore, in the course of the songs there is a movement from the depiction of a corporate concept of the servant as Israel, the Jewish Nation, to the individual suffering figure; a relationship between corporate and individual identity consistent with the narrator's emphasis upon the interaction between national and individual identity.

I do not wish to suggest that by invoking the tradition of Jewish thought in which suffering is redemptive the narrator is seeking to persuade the reader that Franza herself is the figure of the Righteous Servant, or that she is ascribing to Austria the role of the new Israel. Indeed, the point at which the narrator makes her reference is carefully chosen to undermine any simple

parallels between the symbolic figure of the servant and any one of the protagonists. The reference is linked to the concept of Galicia and with it, of love: 'Heim nach Galicien, Matth. 12. 20. Wie unwiderstehlich ist Galicien, die Liebe' (149). (Home to Galicia, Matthew 12. 20. How irresistible Galicia is, love is.) Thus the Righteous Servant becomes equated with an ideal, Galicia, that no longer exists, and is presented as being part of a yearning for a past and a past love which is now lost. By implication, therefore, the Righteous Servant, as corporate or individual identity, is an ideal which can also only be yearned for but not attained. Crucially, however, and as the text of *Das Buch Franza* goes on to demonstrate, it is the process of idealization itself and the attempt to see ideals lived as moral absolutes that results in deceit and destruction. By invoking the Righteous Servant where she does, the narrator admits to her own yearning, but recognizes it as an unlivable ideal, as unattainable. The myth of the sinful and the righteous cannot be translated into a clear-cut reality of guilt on the one hand and innocent suffering on the other; on the contrary, the Righteous Servant is a personification of ideals that may be momentarily glimpsed, not wholly replicated. Thus it is no accident that the narrator's reference is incorporated into the description of Martin's long journey to find his sister, and it is perfectly possible to see the biblical 'he' as referring to Martin. For Martin does not attempt to break his bruised sister with his recriminations when he finds her, and it is he who so silently bears his sister's grief. It is a similar glimpse that we are offered in the narrator's relationship to Franza, for, far from depicting her from a position of detached critical analysis, as Jordan was doing, she unquestioningly sympathizes with Franza's suffering, while being fully aware that Franza belongs neither to the righteous nor to the innocent. 'Die Liebe aber ist unwiderstehlich' (149). (Love, however, is irresistible): if anywhere, it is in the examples of irresistible love for inadequacy that the redemptive moments of the text should be sought. The narrator maintains the tension between critique and sympathy, thereby neither objectifying her protagonist, nor subsuming her otherness through identification and idealization. The narrator does not follow Franza's fatal lead ('was klaffte, wollte sie schließen' (she wanted to close the rift)), and, by sustaining ambiguity, she does not condone her reader's attempt to close the gap. In this narrative ambiguity is thus more than an expression of the fact that Bachmann was a product of her time. It is a refusal of the murderous effects of grand ideals, of idealization and of the simplification of the Cold War rhetoric; it is also a refusal of the murderous effects of objectifying or assimilating the Other.

CHAPTER 2

On sharks and shame

The purpose of my examination of *Das Buch Franza* was to counter critical trends based on an acceptance of Franza's perspective as privileged and
authorized by the narrator, and by extension therefore, in some critics'
view, by Bachmann. My study has emphasized crucial gestures of irony,
judgement and analysis offered by the narrator in response to her protagonist. These act to negate the interpretative cogency of any textual readings
which fail to consider the significance of the narrator's critical viewpoint.
Indeed, I argue that the ethical thrust of the text lies not in the attempt
to ascribe to Franza's suffering an innocence and redemptive function so
evidently lacking, but in the narrator's ability to combine her critical voice
with sympathy. In this chapter I focus on two further fragmentary texts
by Bachmann and continue to draw attention to the narrators' critical and
questioning roles. For, through her narrative perspective, Bachmann not
only ensures that ambiguity is recognized as fundamental to the formation
and understanding of identities, but also reveals its potentially disturbing
presence beneath any moral assertion to be a necessarily positive safeguard.

REQUIEM FÜR FANNY GOLDMANN

Bachmann first referred to the Goldmann story in a letter in 1966, although
Albrecht and Göttsche indicate that she may already have been working
at it earlier than this, in parallel with *Das Buch Franza*. She abandoned
work on the story at the latest at the end of 1966, about the same time
as she abandoned the Franza tale, and began work on a new novel, the
Goldmann/Rottwitz-Roman, in which the Goldmann story still plays a major
role, but does not constitute the whole novel. *Requiem für Fanny Goldmann*
is the story of a beautiful actor, her first marriage with Harry Goldmann
and her later dependence on and exploitation by the young writer Anton
Marek. She becomes bloated and alcohol-dependent, but most important,
filled with a hatred that consumes her, and which therefore appears to

her 'wie ein Todesurteil' (322) (like a death sentence): 'Ihr ganzer Körper war angefallen, ihre Hirne, ihre Leitungen waren eingespannt von dem Haß' (322). (Her whole body was assailed, her brain and her nerves were consumed with hate.) She thinks of her hate as a mortal illness. However, as is the case with Bachmann's other protagonists, the narrator not only points to the inadequacy of a simple victim/oppressor framework for understanding Fanny's plight, but also relates the ambiguities present in sexual relationships to the public sphere and questions of national identity.

In the early drafts for the Fanny Goldmann and Marek characters of 1964 that are ascribed to the *Todesarten* novel, greater emphasis is laid on Marek's exploitation of Fanny as an object for his writing, comparable to Jordan's study of Franza. This aspect of the story again becomes central in the context of the *Goldmann/Rottwitz-Roman*, but in *Requiem für Fanny Goldmann* Marek's crime is to seek a relationship with Fanny in order to use her as emotional and financial support, to use her social position in Vienna to advance his own, and to use her connections to help publish his work. The narrator of this story is a conventional omniscient third-person narrator, whose sympathy undoubtedly lies with Fanny, and who does not like Marek.[1] She candidly informs the reader of Marek's calculating behaviour, commenting that Fanny 'schien [Marek] der Schlüssel zu sein zu dem Wien, in das er nicht hatte eindringen können . . .' (305) (seemed to Marek to be the key that would open the doors to the Vienna that he would otherwise not have penetrated . . .). She agrees with Martin Ranner's assessment of Marek: 'Er war, in mancher Hinsicht, was Martin Ranner von ihm sagte, ein gerissener kleiner Verbrecher, von einer Skrupellosigkeit, die sich noch die Skrupel der erstrebten Gesellschaft einverleibt' (305). (He was in some respects, as Martin Ranner said of him, a cunning little crook, so unscrupulous that he assimilated the scruples of the social circles he sought to be part of.)

The narrator is not only candid in relation to Marek, but makes clear the extent of Fanny's naive and gullible dotage: 'Kurze Zeit später [war] Fanny ihm hörig' (304). (A short time later Fanny was in his thrall.) Fanny starts to show an interest in literature because of him, but is equally keen to ignore the fact that despite being a writer he does not share that interest: 'Sie hatte ihn im Verdacht, daß er faul sei, aber sie ließ sich sofort überzeugen, daß das seine Arbeit hemme, das Selberlesen' (306). (She suspected that he was lazy, but she immediately convinced herself that reading would inhibit his ability to work.) The narrator may not like Marek, but Fanny's conventional and simplistic response to Marek provokes her sharp irony. So when Fanny attempts to reassure herself after being rejected by Marek

by telling herself 'er kann nicht immer an meiner Schürze hängen' (325) (he can't always be tied to my apron strings), the narrator remarks, 'In solchen Bilderbüchern dachte diese Fanny, die nie eine Schürze getragen hatte' (325). (Fanny thought in such clichés, never having worn an apron.) The narrator's depiction of Fanny points to her narcissism as a driving force in her self-destructive dependence. The narrator analyzes in detail the process whereby her exploitation by Marek gives her a false idea of her importance to him, even enables her to idealize herself. So when she realizes that he is repeating her opinion of Italo Svevo, she thinks he must be doing so in innocence:

er wisse selber wohl nicht mehr genau, was er von ihr habe, und dies kam ja einer Vertiefung gleich, es war nicht zu sagen, wo das Denken des einen anfing und des andren aufhörte, so wollte Fanny es, und wenn Fanny etwas wollte, richtete die Welt sich danach, und was Fanny dachte, hatte Gültigkeit, und so, unmerklich, wurde die ganze Person Marek einem Prozeß unterzogen, [aus dem] sie immer bedeutender, reiner, vollkommener und fabelhafter, anbetungswürdiger hervorging. (306)

(he probably did not know himself any more exactly what he had from her, which was like consolidating what they had, since it was impossible to say where one of them started thinking and the other stopped. This is what Fanny wanted to believe and when Fanny wanted something, the world complied, and whatever Fanny thought gained validity. And so, imperceptibly, Marek underwent a change and emerged all the more important, purer, more complete, magnificent and adorable than before.)

Fanny's sense of affirmation is illusory, resting upon her self-deluding belief that she is important to Marek even after he begins a relationship with Karin Krause. He flatters her by claiming that she is the first and most important judge of his work, that he will throw it away if she disapproves – flattery under which she thrives. Yet what she thinks of as flourishing is nothing but self-deception. Fanny does slowly realize that she is being destroyed by this relationship, that Marek 'sie ängstlich und älter machte mit jedem Tag' (308) (made her older and more anxious by the day), and she sees in her sister a domesticated version of her own role. She tells Maria Pilar 'du läßt dir von der ganzen Familie auf der Nase herumtanzen, und dann schwieg sie beschämt, denn die Wischnewski-Töchter waren einander so unähnlich nicht' (318). (You let your whole family mess you around, and then she was silent, ashamed, because the Wischnewski daughters were not so dissimilar.)

The Wischnewski daughters' tendency towards subservience is a pattern that is already established early within the context of their family. Once

again it is the fragments of the protagonist's 'pre-history' which point to her responsibility for and contribution to her own destruction. Fanny's mother and two aunts criticize and idealize her even into adulthood, berating her for trivial lapses in manners, demanding apologies under threat of never seeing her again, then offering solace by belittling her sister. Fanny is able neither to distinguish between flattery and praise nor to recognize the shallow emotional manipulation inherent in the treatment of the sisters. Instead, she 'fühlte [sich] geschmeichelt, daß nur auf sie, Fanny, Verlaß war und sie ihrer Familie Freude und Ehre machte' (302) (felt flattered that only she, Fanny, was dependable and that she was a credit to her family and gave them pleasure). Her narcissistic compulsion to feel indispensable is also in evidence in her relationship with Goldmann. When after their divorce she visits him and finds his flat full of travel paraphernalia, she is unable to listen to what he tells her about his new interest in Judaism, since it has nothing to do with her.

I argued that in *Das Buch Franza* Franza's need to idealize, to seek a higher moral authority, is instrumental in causing her death. In *Requiem für Fanny Goldmann*, the role played in a woman's self-destruction by her tendency to idealize is also explored, although in this fragment the form of that idealization is different, involving both the protagonist's image of herself as an ideal type, and stereotyped images of Austria. Albrecht and Göttsche comment that, unlike the earlier drafts for the figure of Fanny, the Fanny of *Requiem für Fanny Goldmann* 'nicht mehr allein Österreicherin ist, sondern Symbolfigur eines untergegangenen Österreich und seines eigentümlichen Wertsystems' (572) (is no longer simply an Austrian woman, but a symbol for a lost Austria and its curious value system). Whereas their comment implies that Fanny is an anachronistic symbol of an Austria that did indeed once exist, I would argue that the text is more suggestive of her representing an imaginary Austria, an idealized cliché. This becomes even more evident in the Goldmann/Rottwitz novel, as I shall show later, but is already present in this fragment.

Fanny has constructed an image of herself that does not allow for negativity, 'weil sie schön und schuldlos und großzügig sein wollte und sein mußte, sie vertrug keine Beschädigung der idealen Fanny, sie verzieh es sich nicht, von Mißgunst entstellt zu sein' (296) (because she wanted to be and had to be beautiful and innocent and generous, she did not tolerate the ideal Fanny being sullied, she could not forgive herself for being distorted by resentment). It is for this reason that she is destroyed by her hatred for Marek, for a hating Fanny does not fit with the ideal image of herself with which she identifies. The destructive effect of that later hatred is prefigured in the

scene when Goldmann teases her about her dislike of the rival actor Maria Malina, asking whether her gesture of throwing away a gift from Malina is an example of Christian 'love-thy-neighbour'. Fanny's response seems extreme, and she needs him to reconfirm her in her untainted image of herself: 'Sie zitterte vor Beschämung und brachte ihr Zittern in seinen Armen unter: . . . Ich bin doch sonst nicht so gräßlich. Verzeih du es mir, dann ist es gut' (296). (She trembled with shame, and buried her trembling in his arms . . . I'm not usually so horrible. Forgive me, then it will be fine.) What is interesting here is that Fanny's dependence upon a perfect image for her identity is inseparable from an idealized picture of Austria with which the text associates her; Fanny's identity is constructed through ideal images at both a personal and national level. The narrator is, however, quick to ironize the superficiality of the perfect and unsullied vision of beautiful Austria. Presenting herself at her best in the summer, Fanny wears a dirndl 'in dem sie lächerlich schön aussah, man hätte sich Marzipanschweine und Schoko-ladenmisthaufen um sie vorstellen können und eine Ansichtspostkarte mit tiefblauen Salzburgerseen' (303) (in which she looked laughably pretty; one could have imagined marzipan pigs and chocolate cowpats surrounding her, and a picture postcard showing the deep blue lakes around Salzburg).

The comparison that seems to be invited through the parallel of Fanny's self-idealization as beautiful and innocent, and the similar idealization of Austria through such a constructed marketing image, finds confirmation in Fanny's own insistence on the importance of manners as a form which sustains the impression of order, an image of behaviour with which she can continue to maintain her self-image. Manners are equated with acting, so when she is introduced to Karin, Marek's new lover, Fanny's manners are impeccable and she offers a response worthy of her role in *Thank you for the Roses*, and which 'aus dem zweiten Akt hätte sein können' (313) (could have come from Act II). However, crucial here is that manners are not only equated with role-playing and deceit, not least self-deceit, but are seen by Fanny as something that defines her as Austrian. Karin is German, and Fanny is anxious that Karin will therefore not know how to behave: 'Und wenn [die Krause] an Stelle von Manieren etwas wie Gutmütigkeit oder sonstwas Diskutables haben sollte, dann würde Fanny mit der Angele-genheit zurechtkommen. Hoffentlich benimmt sie sich anständig, seufzte Fanny' (312). (And if instead of having manners this Krause was good-natured or something else debatable, then Fanny would come to terms with the matter. Hopefully she will behave herself properly, Fanny sighed.) Her fear of Maria Malina fades into insignificance in the face of this German woman, for Malina 'war wenigstens aus demselben Land und kannte die

Spielregeln' (312–13) (was at least from the same country and knew the rules). The 'Bilderbuch' (picture-book) naivety of her faith in manners as a manifestation of national identity is sorely undermined by Marek's *faux pas* of offering her a seat in her own home. Fanny hastily dismisses the notion that he, an Austrian, could possibly be without manners as sacrilege.

The precondition of Fanny's 'death', without denying the abuse she suffers at the hands of Marek, is her full identification with ideals and therefore her dependence upon sustaining them in untainted form. She thus lives in continual self-deceit, a situation in which acknowledgement of anything that is not the stuff of story-book fantasy must lead to her collapse. Complexity and ambiguity, let alone manipulation or hatred, do not exist for Fanny, and this is why her relationship with Goldmann appeared to sustain her. For he enabled her to feel confirmed in her ideal image, encouraging her to view herself as an antique, her shoulders unrivalled in this modern age. Goldmann seeks to authenticate their value by searching through the paintings of Watteau and Boucher, until they both finally decide that Fanny is 'settecento' (321) (seventeen-hundreds). But when Goldmann compares her to the Karlskirche, Fanny's mistake is to overlook a fairly basic distinction; the church is old, is of another time, whereas she and Goldmann construct an image of her according to their contemporary picture of a previous age, something that is stressed further in the later version. Fanny is neither an antique 'Möbelstück' (320) (piece of furniture) nor a postcard, but would like to be, and would like Marek to sustain her in that belief. Fanny does not symbolize a past Austria, because there never was an Austria that existed in the perfectly mannered and innocent form of her imagination, just as she does not represent an innocent woman destroyed by the betrayal of her optimistic faith in her lover. *Requiem für Fanny Goldmann* may yearn for the repose of Fanny's soul, and it certainly succeeds in winning our sympathy for her, but it does not deny her responsibility in her own destruction.

THE *GOLDMANN/ROTTWITZ-ROMAN*

The *Goldmann/Rottwitz-Roman* is the name given by the editors of the *'Todesarten'-Projekt* to the unnamed book which Bachmann worked on during the period from the winter of 1966 to 1970, if not longer, and which they argue was intended to be the next novel after *Malina*. Like the other texts examined in this chapter, it remained unfinished, but the drafts are extensive, recounting the stories of one beautiful woman, Fanny Goldmann, and one important woman, first named Eka Kottwitz, but who

in later drafts becomes Aga Rottwitz, the political journalist referred to in *Malina*. The editors have identified four writing phases, all of which have in common a framework narrative set in the present world of writers, and the central women's stories, which emerge from conversations between writers: the first phase, consisting of only one fragment, was in the summer of 1966; the second, from the winter of 1966–7, concentrating on the Goldmann story and its framework narrative; the third, around 1967–8, with drafts for both the Goldmann and Kottwitz stories and for their frameworks; and the fourth, from 1967–8 until at least 1970, with further drafts for the stories and framework. Although there are variations between the four writing phases, these variations do not entail contradictions, with the narrative framework and the stories of two women largely consistent in the themes they address and issues they raise.

The Goldmann and Rottwitz/Kottwitz stories are, of course, concerned to explore the way in which the women are destroyed, ostensibly by their menfolk, but also through their own compliance and self-deceit, with a major theme being the specific exploitation and betrayal of a woman used as material by her writer husband. This is a theme which is detectable in very early drafts for the Fanny Goldmann story, but which in this novel is associated more specifically with the figure of Kottwitz/Rottwitz and her husband, first named Kuhn, then Jung. Another major theme is the relationship of Austria and Germany; the juxtaposition of the Austrian Fanny and the German Karin presented in *Requiem für Fanny Goldmann* has now developed into the figure of the Austrian actress and the German journalist, two figures who are not directly linked. Just as important for the exploration of these themes as the stories of the two women is the narrative framework of the novel, which is extensive enough to stand independently as its own story. The framework narrative is shared by a third-person narrator and Malina, whose voices seem close, if not identical, in terms of their judgement and moral attitude. Within the framework the main themes are themselves not only developed and appraised, but are considered in relation to questions of narrative perspective, motivation and interpretation. I shall return to a detailed discussion of the significance of the framework after an initial analysis of the Goldmann and Rottwitz/Kottwitz stories.

MORE ON FANNY GOLDMANN

If anything, these later versions of the Fanny story are clearer and more forthright in emphasizing her responsibility, and consequently do have the effect of slightly undermining the sympathetic response to her decline which

was so evident in *Requiem*. So when Marek starts seeing another woman, Fräulein Böllinger, narrative distance is retained in the statement 'Fanny kam sich wie eine Märtyrerin vor' (356). (Fanny felt like a martyr), and judgement is evident when Fanny's gesture of making a gift of earrings to her rival is described as 'eine[e] Aufwallung von Masochismus' (356) (a surge of masochism). The extent of the masochism only becomes evident when we learn that the same Christl Böllinger also had an affair with Goldmann, (although that lasted only three days and not eight), but that Fanny still responds to Marek with servile adoration, ringing him to ask for forgiveness and reciting a litany of praise even after he has hung up. She expresses her desire to be dependent on a man to Goldmann, when she regrets that he did not tie her to him, commenting 'Das wäre aber besser gewesen' (447). (That would have been better.)

The heightened critical response to Fanny is achieved in part by emphasizing her masochistic dependence on Marek to the point of presenting her as stereotyped, as the narrator does when he generalizes from the examples of Fanny and Böllinger, referring to 'das Betragen solcher Frauen von der Art' (356) (the conduct of that type of woman). However, a critical context is also achieved by means of establishing textual parallels between Fanny and other figures to whom less sympathy is attached. One such parallel is suggested in phase two, shortly before the story of Fanny begins with the familiar 'In einer längstvergangenen Zeit' (353) (In a time long ago). Malina is relating a story of an author accused of plagiarism. His conclusion functions as a preliminary comment on the causes of Fanny's hatred for Marek, which is more a response to her own poor behaviour than a reaction to him. Fanny has undermined her good opinion of herself:

Der Haß von Personen, die es übernehmen, jemand zu verfolgen, rührt ja meistens daher, daß sie sich selber einmal schlecht benommen haben und nun nach andren Gründen suchen und sie auch finden, um den zu vernichten, der ihnen ihre gute Meinung, die sie von sich selber haben, stört. (352)

(The hatred of people who undertake to persecute someone usually stems from the fact that they have behaved badly themselves. And now they are looking for, and find, other reasons to destroy the person who interfered with the good opinion they had of themselves.)

That Malina's comment is so apt for Fanny is confirmed in a later draft from phase four, where we are told that 'Was sie sich zuletzt nicht vergab und warum sie todkrank wurde, das war ihr Fall, daß sie unter ihr Niveau gefallen war und einem kleinen ehrgeizigen Streber aus Mattersburg . . . Dinge erzählt hatte . . . die sie nie sagen hätte dürfen' (450–1). (In the end what she could not forgive herself for and why she became mortally ill, was

that she had lowered her standards and had told an ambitious little social climber from Mattersburg . . . things that she never should have done.) Thus Fanny's hatred for Marek is clearly depicted as a consequence of the fact that she has behaved badly in her own eyes; Marek may be an ambitious social climber, but the responsibility for her self-consuming shame lies with Fanny herself.

A further development from *Requiem für Fanny Goldmann* is the now explicit and unfavourable parallel between Fanny and her father, made in the latest phase of Bachmann's work on the book. It is not new to the reader that Oberst Wischnewski's suicide was not a heroic death as his wife would like to believe, but a consequence of his fear that his involvement in Dollfuß's assassination would become public knowledge when the Germans invaded Austria. What is new is the narrative excursus on those who commit suicide, people who overrate their own involvement in events or their own importance, who are 'sensibel . . . und [für das], was sie für eine Schande halten, wenn es aufkommt, aber nicht für eine Schande, wenn es geheim bleibt, bereit sind, sich zu erschießen' (450) (sensitive . . . and willing to shoot themselves for what they consider a disgrace if it becomes public, but which they do not consider a disgrace if it remains a secret). The narrator considers it sublime cowardice, not far removed from sublime pride, which leads people to suicide, unable to accommodate shame with their self-image. The excursus applies as much to Fanny as to her father; she cannot live with the public shame of having lowered her standards with Marek, an author who reshapes some of the anecdotes she has told him about her relationship with Goldmann. But as the narrator makes clear, suicide is not a necessary step, since public exposure would have been only temporary, and someone other than Fanny might not have been bothered at all. She is like her father because both hold values which are 'eigentümlich' (450) (curious), both overestimate their own importance and cannot tolerate the relativization of their ideal image.

The third parallel suggested in the text and which focuses on the question of Fanny's responsibility is again to be found in the latest phases of writing. It is made by Fanny herself when she meets Goldmann years after their divorce, when she is already aware of the course of her destruction and failure of the relationship with Marek. Fanny speaks of her own and others' death in relation to the sudden death of Maria Malina, the actor who was professionally and personally her rival. We learn the details of this death from the framework narrative; Maria Malina, Malina's sister, went swimming from a boat off the coast of Greece where she was on holiday with a male companion, and the next thing this companion knew when he turned round was that there was a pool of blood on the water; Maria had

been eaten by a shark. Within the framework, this version of her death is surrounded by doubt and suspicion, but from Fanny's point of view, it is the shark that is crucial. Admitting to Goldmann that both Maria's and her life was a misery, she asserts that everyone has their own shark lurking, and that although Maria's death was painful and fast, 'Für uns ist der Hai nicht so sichtbar unser Mörder, es geht langsamer und er kommt verkleidet und ist grausamer, die verkleideten Haie tun es langsamer mit uns' (448). (In our case the shark is not so obviously our murderer, it's a slower process and the shark comes disguised and is crueller; the disguised sharks take their time with us.) The obvious implication here is that Marek has been her shark. More generally, her interest in the figure of the shark fits with her desire to understand her failed relationships in the simple terms of victim and vicious predator. But in a rare moment Fanny's thoughts wander towards, and then skirt around, the possibility that in another context she too might be a shark. She asks Goldmann 'Wer ist dein Hai, das sehe ich nicht? Ich bins doch hoffentlich nicht gewesen, ich habe dir doch nichts angetan, oder doch, manchmal ja, aber das kann nur etwas vorbereitet haben, was ich dann nicht getan habe' (448–9). (I can't see who your shark is. I hope it wasn't me, I didn't do you any harm, or maybe sometimes I did, but that can only have paved the way for something I didn't do.)

   The text offers no answer to Fanny's brief speculation other than by implication. It does, however, again confirm the importance of the build-up to the kill, so to speak, the period of the 'etwas vorbereitet haben' (having paved the way), which allows for the later success and ease of the predatory attack. So although on the one hand the narrative voice speaks of Goldmann as 'der einzige Mann, der gut zu ihr gewesen war' (449) (the only man who had been good to her), it also makes explicit the contribution he makes to Fanny's narcissistic idealization, by constructing her in his image of the perfect Viennese woman:

sie wiederum wußte nicht recht, was Wienerisch war und österreichisch, und sie lernte es von Harry Goldmann, der sich in Hollywood eine so genaue Vorstellung davon bewahrt oder erst gemacht haben mußte, daß es ihm gelang, aus einer etwas inkoloren Fanny den Inbegriff einer Wienerin zu machen. (444)

(She, on the other hand, did not really know what was Viennese and what Austrian, and she learned it from Harry Goldmann. He must have brought with him, or first formed, such a precise idea from Hollywood, in order to succeed in making of a somewhat colourless Fanny the epitome of a Viennese woman.)

This is a moment when the banality and superficiality of generalizing notions is ironically and poignantly exposed. More broadly, the irony here

works as a criticism of the pervasiveness of Hollywood in establishing and then perpetuating national stereotypes. Specifically, Fanny comes to depend upon the perfection of an image that is no more than a Hollywood projection by the only man who was good to her. And if we remain with Fanny's shark metaphor, being the only-man-good-for-her is a perfect disguise for a shark, for neither Goldmann nor Fanny comprehends the damage consequent upon such image-making. The inverse may also be the case; without consciously being Goldmann's shark, Fanny may nevertheless have caused disastrous consequences of which she herself is unaware.

EKA KOTTWITZ/AGA ROTTWITZ

The drafts of this second central story of the novel depict the relationship of a highly successful German political journalist, Eka Kottwitz (who in the later stages of phase four becomes Aga Rottwitz), and the Austrian writer Jung (first, Kuhn). Again, there is slight variation in the plot of the drafts, but the crux of the story is as follows. Eka is an intelligent and critical woman, and comes from an extensive aristocratic family – a combination which makes Jung feel permanently insecure. Whereas she loves him, he is ambitious and finds their liaison socially useful because of his association with the well-known name of Kottwitz. He is well aware of his lover's critical intelligence, but finds the extent of her knowledge of literature intimidating. Although aware that Eka's response to his work is more constructive than that of previous lovers, who merely sought to flatter him, he nevertheless feels belittled by her astute comments, since they do not constantly affirm him as the best writer in the world in her eyes. For him, 'Eka war schuld dran, daß er sich relativiert vorkam' (419) (it was Eka's fault that he felt relativized), and the result is a relationship resting on a fundamental misunderstanding: 'Was für ihn ein Machtkampf war, das war in Ekas Augen ein schönes, nie langweiliges Beisammensein' (419). (What for him was a power struggle was in Eka's eyes a nice, and never boring, companionship.) The consequences for Eka are devastating, for Jung attempts to undermine and demean her, both privately through sexual disregard – 'er [fiel] gelegentlich über sie her' (420) (he fell upon her occasionally) – and publicly, by spreading rumours of his martyrdom at the side of an egocentric and ambitious woman, thus preparing the way for leaving her without being tainted with the blame. Finally, she hurls herself from a window, but survives, permanently confined to a wheelchair.

Kuhn/Jung is unpleasant, calculating and manipulative; undoubtedly of a type with Marek, he is 'wie alle Männer von Format, die keines haben'

(421) (like all men of stature, who do not possess any), and the narrator's sympathy lies firmly with Eka. But in keeping with the by now familiar pattern of Bachmann's female protagonists, Eka/Aga's suicide attempt has as much to do with the dreadful recognition of her own self-deception as with a man's studied oppression. The discrepancy between her astute mind in relation to politics, history and literature and her simplistic understanding of her own relationship is profound: 'Sie hatte, nicht anders als jede kleine Gans, an Liebe und Nichtliebe geglaubt' (393) (She, like any other silly goose, had believed in Love and Not love), and far from being aware of complexity or ambiguity, 'sie bewegte sich in einem Einmaleins' (393). (She moved according to formulas.) She certainly does not consider that Jung might have motives other than those of love for being with her: 'Er nahm . . . eine Frau her, bei deren Namen sofort alle Leute aufstanden' (401). (He got himself . . . a woman at whose name people immediately stood up.) The gulf between her theoretical knowledge and her personal ignorance takes on almost comic proportions when it comes to sex. She is a woman who 'kannte . . . in blühender Geläufigkeit das ganze Vokabular der Psychopathologie, der Sexualogie' (419) (was remarkably fluent in the whole language of psychopathology and sexology), who even knows the approaches of different schools of thought to all types of perversion, but who at the same time recoils at the most simple of words and who does not know what an orgasm is. Her tragedy is that 'In ihr schieden sich also papierene Vorstellungen, in denen alles erlaubt und verstanden war, von einem so schmalen erfahrenen Bereich, daß ihr [niemand] über diesen Abgrund helfen konnte' (419). (In her, the gulf between the theory, in which everything was allowed and understood, and the very limited practice, was such that no one could help her over this divide.)

Eka is perfectly aware of the discrepancy. She knows that Jung is doing nothing to facilitate her discovery of orgasm, and has been aware of this even in the 'good years' of the relationship. He throws himself on her and treats her like an object while concurrently asserting that he knows a lot about women. But Eka nevertheless chooses to ignore this contradiction:

[Sie] war so entschlossen, keinen Widerspruch zu dulden, ihre Beziehung vollkommen zu finden und im übrigen zu denken, daß eine so tiefe geistige Freundschaft wie zwischen ihr und Jung unmöglich in einer banalen körperlichen Anziehung einen Ausdruck hätte finden können. (420)

(She was intent on tolerating no contradiction, on finding her relationship perfect and, furthermore, on thinking that such a profound spiritual friendship as that which existed between her and Jung could not possibly find expression in banal physical attraction.)

Once again it is the protagonist's desire for perfection, for simple wholeness, that leads her willingly to ignore the mechanisms of her oppression and so exacerbate her humiliation.

The process of Eka's self-deception is given one final twist in two of the later drafts. For not only has she by now had to confront her humiliating role in her relationship with Kuhn/Jung, but rather than becoming more self-reflexive as a result, she then responds to a new oppressive situation in similar manner, still hoping for the redemptive wholeness that has hitherto eluded her. This new situation is the episode in which she is suddenly and violently raped by a Somalian student. Rape is always a thorny problem for feminist criticism, unless it is unambiguously depicted as violence against women, the physical manifestation of their abuse and oppression at the hands of men. In Bachmann's work there is no such clarity. As Albrecht and Göttsche point out, the rape episode is thematically linked to the slap in the story 'Rosamunde' and the orgy scenes in the *Wüstenbuch* and *Das Buch Franza*, and seems to confirm what the Self says to Malina, 'Daß eine normale Frau ganz normal vergewaltigt werden möchte.'[2] (That a normal woman quite normally wants to be raped.) They feel unable to reach a conclusion about Bachmann's possible intentions in developing this theme, suggesting that perhaps 'Ingeborg Bachmann bei der Behandlung dieses Motivs auf die Diskrepanz zwischen Tagträumen dieser Art einerseits und dem tatsächlichen Wunsch nach Realisierung dieser Phantasien andereseits abzielte' (585). (In her treatment of this motif, Bachmann was pointing to the discrepancy between this type of daydream on the one hand, and the actual desire to fulfil such fantasies on the other.) They also feel that the draft of 1969 referring to Eka's rapist as Abdu, the same name occurring in the *Wüstenbuch* and *Franza*, seems to echo utopian aspects of those earlier texts. In keeping with her criticism of *Das Buch Franza*, Lennox argues that the treatment of Eka's rape depends upon the employment of a racist vocabulary which reduces the African man to the pervasive stereotype of black man as sexual predator. Referring to the work of Frantz Fanon and Mary Ann Doane, she avers that Eka represents the typical 'White Lady', for whom the attainment of adult female sexuality (masochistic in nature) relies upon the repression of aggression. In a racist society the black man becomes the projected source of this aggression, and the fantasy of the white woman being raped by a black man is thus both a centrally constituting element of female sexuality and a device for white men to justify their control over white women and Blacks. Eka, like Franza before her, is unable to transcend the racist discourses which structure her identity as a white woman.

Scrutiny of the narrative voice is vital for any assessment of whether the protagonist's views are being condoned or held up for criticism. Even within the Rottwitz/Kottwitz drafts the narrator's approach is not consistent in tone. So when Eka/Aga responds to the prolonged and painful assault with revulsion, but at the same time feels dramatically altered by the bestiality of the rape, it is difficult to know whether the narrator is confirming the protagonist's view of events, or merely reporting from her perspective. Thus in the brief paragraph relating the rape of Aga Rottwitz, the narrative tone is authoritative, and would seem to confirm that the rape has changed her into a woman: '[Abdu machte] in einer einzigen Nacht aus [der] Aga dieses Jung eine Frau' (440). (In a single night Abdu made a woman of Jung's Aga.) On the other hand, the extensive descriptions of the rape of Eka Kottwitz, although largely in the third person, tend to relate her perspective. Eka herself 'merkte . . . daß sie nicht zerstört war, sondern völlig verändert' (427) (noticed . . . that she was not destroyed, but totally changed), and if the narrator takes the opportunity to refer to her time with Jung as 'Kleinmädchenspiele' (425) (little girls' games), it is Eka who tells her brother 'ich war plötzlich eine Frau' (429) (I was suddenly a woman). And, to return to the draft describing Aga, it is clearly she who considers the rape as a rebirth: 'Sie dachte einen Moment, daß es weniger war wie vergewaltigt werden, sondern wie eine Geburt, eine Tortur' (440). (She thought for a moment that it was less like being raped than being born, an ordeal.)

A clear distinction between protagonist and narrator in these scenes is difficult, and ambiguity lingers in terms of the formative, even enlightening, function the rape has on the protagonist. Nevertheless, there is enough narrative distance and evidence of Eka/Aga's ongoing self-delusion for a critical reading of her response to the rape to be sustained. In a process similar to that of Franza's confrontation with the extremes of the desert, Eka experiences the rape as an extreme which both shatters her Self and allows for its reassertion; an extreme that is once again represented by Africa and its supposed otherness:

Sie hat nicht eine Erschütterung ihres Körpers erlebt, sondern eine Gehirner-schütterung, ihr Ich ist ausgestrichen worden, sie schüttet, während das Somaliland diese Erschütterung bewirkt, noch ein paar Gedanken aus . . . Ein paar Tage später ist Eka noch immer dabei, ihr Ich widerherzustellen. (430)

(She did not experience a shock to her body, but to her mind; her ego was erased. While Somalia was still having this shocking effect upon her, she shook out a few ideas. . . . A few days later Eka was still trying to re-establish her ego.)

It is through his flippancy in this last sentence that the narrator communicates his distance to and reservations about Eka's new self. For, in a way which is reminiscent of Franza's story, a gulf is revealed between the protagonist's belief that something has changed in the confrontation with the extreme, and what emerges as no more than the manifestation of previous patterns of self-deceit in another guise. For, while believing that she is totally different, Eka imagines a new beginning with Jung, wishes to show him how different she is: 'Ich kann ihn jetzt wirklich lieben' (428). (Now I can really love him.) The narrator's irony manifestly conveys the impossibility of her fantasies: 'Es wird etwas Wunderbares sich zwischen ihnen beiden zutragen, diese Langeweile, diese Knechtschaft der Gewöhnlichkeit, dieser Dualismus wird verschwinden' (430). (Something marvellous will take place between the two of them; this boredom, this slavery to normality, this dualism will vanish.) Indeed, her optimism allows her to anticipate that 'sie wird ihn und sich erlösen' (430) (she will redeem them both). Caught up in her own desire for change, Eka fails to recognize that the 'real' love she now has for Jung, her belief that perfection exists, is not an escape from previous dualities, but another form of the desperate relationship that she is as determined as ever to consider perfect. In fact, she never sees Jung again.

The identification of moments of irony and distance in the narrator's response need not, and for Lennox does not, dispel the anxiety that Bachmann herself is instrumental in reproducing racist assumptions in her exploration of female identity. Lennox feels that despite the complexity of the narrative structure of the fragment and because there are other instances in Bachmann's œuvre of stereotypical representations of Blacks, Bachmann cannot escape the criticism that she directs at her figures. This conclusion does much to rescue Bachmann from the fate of perpetual idealization. Yet I would not wish to leave the matter here. For if a complex narrative technique is recognized as being central to a text, its function is greater than to make critics' decisions more difficult.[3] The interpretative ambiguity generated by the narrative technique is fundamental to how we understand the text. So, while acknowledging that the tension between critique and reinscription, the concurrent challenging and perpetuation of discourse, relates to the historically specific situation of Bachmann as author, we must also recognize that a text which insists on tension and ambiguity as governing aesthetic modes is actively exploring the significance and value of ambiguity as a response to, not only as a reflection of, its time.

Eka's suicide attempt is not simply the result of being abandoned by Jung, but is a consequence of recognizing her own complicity with that relationship, of becoming aware not only of the nature of the relationship, but of her

faith in it. So in retrospect she feels that she would have been better served by being with an illiterate man or worker, rather than in this 'Krampfzustand mit Jung über Jahre der Hypokrisie und andauernden Heuchelei und auch noch selber dran zu glauben' (421) (desperate situation with Jung, the years of hypocrisy and ongoing deception and then even believing in it oneself). But as is the case with Fanny, the humiliation and suicide has a public dimension, specifically linked to Kuhn/Jung's vocation as writer. Although in the later versions the textual emphasis is on the rape episode and the theme of self-deceit in the immediate build-up to the suicide attempt, this does not deny Eka's fear of public exposure as a central cause for her leap. Her terrible personal confrontation with her own gullibility is inseparable from Kuhn/Jung's willingness to exploit the relationship for writing purposes, which for her is tantamount to a public shaming. Again, though, she must acknowledge that she is helpless against the machinations of her former lover, a fact that further compounds the cycle of humiliation. This interweaving of private and public shame emerges in a conversation with her brother Hajo, when she admits to him that Jung is blackmailing her:

er hat mich in der Hand, wenn dus genau wissen willst, und ich habe das zugelassen. Er hat mir gedroht, daß er meine Briefe veröffentlichen wird. Hajo sagte mit offenem Mund, und das hast du geglaubt. Ja, sagte Eka, das ist es eben, ich habe es geglaubt. Und es war da auch ein Zusammenhang. (414)

(He's got me in a corner, if you really want to know, and I allowed it. He threatened to publish my letters. And you believed him, Hajo said open-mouthed. Yes, said Eka, that's the point, I believed him. But it was in connection with other things.)

The idea that public exposure is a form of murder is emphasized in the framework narrative. It is the framework, with its explicit discussion of the themes of women as victim, the murderousness of the literary world and the fiction of national identity, that I shall now discuss.

THE FRAMEWORK NARRATIVE AND THE ROLE OF MALINA

As was mentioned earlier, the framework to the stories is narrated by both an omniscient third-person narrator and Malina; their voices and opinions are close, even overlapping. Although the various drafts are not consistent in terms of who narrates what, Malina's main role is to narrate Fanny's story. (An exception is the brief fragment from the first phase of writing in which the narrator depicts Malina as a writer whose protagonist is Martin Ranner, an idea that Bachmann did not develop.) However, at times the distinction between the narrator's voice and Malina's is a difficult one to make; in phase

four, for example, Malina also becomes the narrator of the Kottwitz story, yet part of the story is told once Malina and his interlocutor Jonas have separated, implying that the narrator is now taking over. The variation among the fragments as to who narrates which of the women's stories prevents any one pattern emerging, although it is precisely this inconclusiveness that leads Albrecht and Göttsche to make the following comment:

Zu bedenken ist jedoch, daß Malinas Erzähler-Rolle in keinem Stadium der Arbeit an dem *Goldmann/Rottwitz-Roman* letztgültig festgelegt [*sic*] wird; im Gegenteil ist durchgehend erkennbar, daß der autoriale Erzähler und Malina im Hinblick auf das Erzählen der Figurengeschichten miteinander konkurrieren, so daß der Gedanke naheliegt, daß dieses Konzept auch beibehalten werden sollte. (586)

(It is worth considering that Malina's role as narrator is not finally decided at any stage of work on the Goldmann/Rottwitz story. On the contrary, it is discernible throughout that the authorial narrator and Malina are in competition with one another to narrate the women's stories, which suggests that this idea was going to be retained.)

The narrator and Malina may vie to tell the stories, but they do not represent different approaches or reactions to the women, and are unified in their moral response to what they depict. Indeed, the narrator is very concerned to present Malina as trustworthy and a man of principle. We are explicitly told that, when at a gathering in Munich Fanny Goldmann becomes the subject of gossip and dispute between a drunken Marek and a Herr Ertel, Malina silently leaves the room, despite not even knowing her. He is an observer who is not defined by others' gossip or by a particular role in society, and so carries a certain authority for the young writer Jonas:

Da Malina offenbar nicht drauf aus war, hier Geschäfte zu machen oder Erscheinung zu machen, auch nicht klar war, wer ihn überhaupt eingeladen hatte und wer ihn brauchte in Frankfurt, aber auch niemand Anstoß an seiner Person nahm und niemand über ihn redete, er also nicht einmal in die Gegenwart oder die Zukunft hinübergetratscht werden konnte, blieb Jonas nur seine abstruse Gymnasiastenrolle übrig. (380–1)

(Since Malina was clearly not intent on doing business here or making an impression, and was not even clear who had invited him and who needed him in Frankfurt; since no one took offence at his presence or talked about him, and he could not be made the object of gossip now or in the future, Jonas was left only with his abstruse schoolboy role.)

Malina's authority as an independent and uncommitted observer is not disputed by the narrator. Indeed, the narrator is happy for Malina to assume his own omniscience in those fragments in which Malina narrates either

the Fanny Goldmann or the Rottwitz/Kottwitz story. So although there may be competition in terms of which of the two is heard and at what stage of the story, both voices are closely identified.

The context of the framework is always the world of writers: in phase one Malina is researching the background for his story about Martin Ranner; in phase two, a party is being given by the publisher Gernreich; and in phases three and four, the location is the Frankfurt book fair. The central stories then emerge from conversations Malina holds with a young and talented Austrian writer, first named Jörg Maleta, later Jonas, and are offered as living examples of the destructive effects of the manipulative and exploitative behaviour of writers. The balance of themes between the framework and the two central stories is thus a complementary one: in the women's stories, it is the personal aspect of the story that dominates, their dependence on and exploitation by their male lovers, and the ongoing self-deceit with which they attempt to sustain themselves. The public dimensions of the story, the betrayal of confidence by their lovers, who publish intimate details which expose the women to the public gaze, as well as the theme of national identity, are crucial, but receive more explicit attention in the framework. In contrast, the framework narrative does not explore, but merely confirms the importance of the complex and painful subject of a victim's complicity in her victimhood through brief, generalized comments. So Malina, harsh in his judgement of indiscretion or 'Hochverrat' (361) (high treason), is equally clear that 'Frauen werden immer so töricht sein und sich blenden lassen von dem jungen Genie . . . Dies sind die wahren Hintergründe unsrer Literatur' (361) (women will always be this foolish and let themselves be blinded by the young genius. . . . This is the true background of our literature), a comment that applies to Fanny and Franza. His sympathy for the victims is unwavering and he warns against the ease with which fame and money effectively smokescreen the murders that take place in private, claiming that any decent enough man 'sich leicht überzeugen lassen [wird], daß hier der Ermordete schuldig ist und nicht der Mörder' (362) (will easily let himself be convinced that in this case the murder victim is to blame and not the murderer). Nevertheless, he refuses to simplify, and also refers to victims as 'Opfer . . . in ihrer Verblödung' (362) (victims . . . in their stupidity). Simple, generalized and provocative comments such as this, made within the framework, are then explored with sensitivity in the main stories.

The framework sets the tone of a sustained moral critique of writers and their methods, of their personal ambition and their willingness to sacrifice integrity in order to achieve it. Malina takes on the role of temporary mentor to the young and suddenly successful Maleta/Jonas, determined

to make him aware of the gulf between public fame as a good writer, and private crimes committed in the process of attaining status. Writers pursue a life of 'Grausamkeiten, Abscheulichkeiten, Bloßstellungen' (360) (cruelty, atrocity, exposure), objectifying the women they live with. The publishing world is a lion's den in which the most powerful will themselves one day be deposed from their supremacy. Malina has no illusions that Jonas will be any different, and he cynically summarizes Jonas' future crimes:

Sie werden Briefe abdrucken, erpressen, Sie werden Ihre Freunde bloßstellen, und die werden kuschen . . . Sie werden eines Tags von einer Frau geschieden sein, die sich nicht mehr auf die Straße wagt . . . und Sie werden sich darüber lustig machen. (363)

(You will copy letters and blackmail people, you will expose your friends and they will submit to you . . . One day you will be separated from a woman who no longer dares to leave the house . . . and you will make a joke of it.)

The narrator intimates that Malina is right, for the next day Jonas cannot really remember what Malina has said. And when Jonas later meets the third wife of the peace-prize-winning author, he does his best to convince himself that she cannot possibly have slit her wrists, although there is no reason to doubt the fact.

Malina describes publishing as a world 'in der der Buchhandel zum Menschenhandel ausgeartet ist' (367) (in which the book trade has degenerated into human trade). 'Die Literatur ist ein schmutziges Geschäft, so dreckig wie der Waffenhandel, und wenn es niemand bemerkt – *tant mieux*' (373). (Literature is a dirty business, as dirty as the arms trade, and if no one notices, so much the better.) He points to the irony that in a world where fiction dominates, it is the limitations of people's fantasies that prevent them from suspecting the degree of cruelty and murder lying behind people's 'true' stories, despite the fact that 'jeder doch im Hintergrund mit einer monströsen Geschichte lebt, oder eines Tags leben wird' (386) (everyone lives with a monstrous tale below the surface, or will one day). In one dramatic sentence Malina describes the hypocrisy, criminality and profit- or ambition-driven unscrupulousness that constitute the literary world; he wanders through that world

wie durch ein Schlachthaus, und während [man] unter anmutigen Nekkereien, Witzeerzählen, Abmachungen, Artigkeiten und Bosheiten alle gleichzuwalzen scheint, vergesse ich doch [nicht] das nackte Entsetzen, die Schreie, das Schluchzen, der brutale Handel, die Fußtritte, die die Opfer der Literatur haben einstecken müssen, unter dem Druck der Zahlen, der Summen, der Auflagen, des Prestiges, des skrupellosesten Ehrgeizes. (353)

(As though through a slaughterhouse. And while it seems as though all are made one by the charming banter, the jokes, the deals, the wit and the bitchiness, I do not though forget the naked horror, the screams, the sobs, the brutal trade, the kicks that the victims of literature have had to endure as a result of the pressure of numbers, of sums, of editions, of prestige and of unscrupulous ambition.)

The moral indignation directed against both the literary establishment and the immoral behaviour of individual writers is also extended to encompass the prevailing views among the writers on national identity, specifically manifested in anti-German sentiment.[4] Allegiance to Austria and things Austrian is revealed to be part of a writer's strategy of self-confirmation. In the example of the young Maleta in phase two, his identification with Malina as a fellow Austrian helps him to feel as though he is an exception within the publishing industry, an individual who can see through the machinations and political dealings of that world, who can retain a certain authenticity, while, at the same time, being able to see through it all. Happy to be present at a party given by the publisher Gernreich in Frankfurt, he thinks that the publishing industry, dominated by the German publishing houses, typifies everything that is German: 'es ist doch zum Kotzen, die Deutschen' (341) (the Germans make you sick). In contrast, Maleta's own Austrian identity, here manifested in his assumption of a common bond and shared opinions before he has even spoken to Malina, rests upon the association of maternal love and quiet. Yet the narrator is sharp in his irony, making it clear that Maleta's national identity rests upon an opportunistically defined polarization of Germany and Austria to suit his own purpose; Maleta is dependent upon simplistic thinking and, more importantly, on his convenient amnesia regarding his own active participation in the German publishing world, the world that offers him the success he aspires to:

Denn der junge Revoluzzer dachte natürlich nicht, jetzt nicht, an seinen Vertrag mit dem Haus Gernreich . . . nicht an die Beklemmung in dieser Gesellschaft, die ihn unmerklich korrumpieren würde, sondern er dachte noch wie ein Kind . . . an dieses Nichtverstehen, das seinem Zynismus und seiner prächtigen Intelligenz keine Ehre machte, an etwas, das Mama heißen konnte oder bitte Licht auslöschen oder . . . bitte mehr Diskretion. (341)

(For naturally the young revolutionary was not thinking now of his contract with the Gernreich publishing house, of the sense of social oppression that would imperceptibly corrupt him. Instead, like a child . . . he still believed in something that could be called 'mummy', or 'lights out now' or . . . 'more discretion please'.)

In phase two Jonas has similar firmly developed ideas about the Germans: 'Jonas [war] schon dahinter gekommen, daß die Deutschen meist weit

weniger wußten, aber was sie wußten, plakatierten sie, man sah sie förmlich herumlaufen mit Kenntnissen und Theorien' (348). (Jonas had already found out that the Germans knew much less, but they showed off their knowledge, you could see them literally walking around with their theories and ideas.) Although Jonas' views are not specifically ironized here, generally any stereotyping of either Germans or Austrians is criticized. Thus Malina is shown laughing to himself about the three Austrian authors Jonas, Marek and Benedek, who with nothing else in common, all attempt to give themselves greater credence as Austrian by refusing on principle to admit 'daß sie irgendetwas von diesen Deutschen gelesen hatten, oder gar [von] deren Wichtigkeit etwas wüßten [oder] doch nur vage' (375) (that they had read something by these Germans, or even knew that they were important, or maybe only vaguely). When Benedek launches into an anti-German tirade, calling them cheats and hypocritical scoundrels, he seems more accurately to be describing himself; he stands there 'finster mit einem stereotypen Lächeln' (378) (darkly, with a stereotypical smile), a man so self-controlled, 'wie einer, der befürchtet, im nächsten Moment irrsinnig zu werden' (378) (like a man who fears he will go insane at any moment), and who refuses to respond to Malina when addressed, only looking through him. Any credibility attaching to his views is thoroughly undermined.

Malina, that perspicacious and authoritative figure, is quick to point out to his young aspiring colleague that the cruelties and crimes of the publishing world are not just of German making, but also occur in the quieter Vienna. The story of Fanny is his immediate example; the story of Eka follows. And like his Austrian compatriots at the book fair, Jung too resorts to the fictitious construct of national identities to bolster his status in his own eyes, affirming himself in relation to Germany, which is for him represented by his German lover and her whole extended family. Jung is eager to dismiss the signs of her aristocratic origins, for example, the way in which she enters a room or her poor style of dress, as North German, but the narrator is firm that it 'hatte nichts mit Barschheiten und Härten zu tun, sondern wäre ebenso in Wien . . . abgelaufen' (435) (had nothing to do with being curt or hard, but would have happened in just the same way in Vienna). The fact that Eka/Aga is German does nothing to lessen the degree of her suffering, nor her culpability; she, like Fanny, is a victim of an ambitious Austrian writer, and for neither of them is national identity a help.

Indeed, as has been shown, Fanny's faith in herself as the epitome of the Austrian woman is a contributory factor in her demise. It is a fiction with

which she deludes herself, an identity to which she conforms and which she believes is somehow real, rather than imaginary. And in her case too, national identity is combined with the art of fiction – Goldmann's Hollywood idea, a script he has written for Fanny and which she subsequently so 'authentically' performs. The link between the literary world and national identity is a crucial one, for national identity is exposed as one more of these writers' fictions, one more narrative to help them in their spurious self-definition, to sustain them in the belief in their own innocence despite the contracts they have signed and the ambition they harbour. Like Fanny's exaggerated postcard appearance, Austria becomes for them the idealization of what never was, and Germany and the Germans become in their eyes the corrupting agents of this idealized image.

In this text the concept of national identity is revealed to be no more than a totalizing and stereotyping fiction, a narrative sustained by belief but confounded by facts, and implicated in the process of self-deceit. As a totalizing narrative, one that seeks to impose definition, a simplifying understanding of national identity is subject to further criticism in relation to questions of narrative perspective; for repeated emphasis is placed on the importance of unfinished narratives, stories in which ambivalence lingers. Causes cannot be systematically explained and analyzed, because so often they lie in unnoticed, transitory moments, fleeting flashes of tactlessness. Malina (possibly the narrator) comments 'daß selbst einfachere Vorgänge als die zwischen Fanny und Marek für immer ein Dschungel von Fragen bleiben werden' (358) (that even simpler events than those occurring between Fanny and Marek would remain a jungle of questions for ever), for it remains impossible to tell of the apparently inconsequential moments that are the origins of later death: 'Allein, was ein Freund mit einem besorgten Gelächter einem Freund antun kann, dem er zu helfen meint damit, das ergibt eine unabsehbare Geschichte' (358). (Even the effect that one friend's sympathetic laughter can have on another friend that he thinks he is helping results in an unforeseeable story.) Knowledge of a person is always incomplete, so to think that one knows a person limits the possibilities of their individuality within a relationship, for it defines them, imposes an identity upon them: 'Nichts ist darum verwerflicher als die Freundschaft, die meint, den andren zu erkennen' (359). (So nothing is more reprehensible than the friendship that believes it knows the other.)

It is Malina's distance from the stories he tells, his inability to provide all the answers and refusal to speculate in order to fill the gaps which leads him to say that 'meine Geschichten sind wahr. Sie haben den Vorzug dieser Unvollkommenheit' (365). (My stories are true. They have the advantage of

such imperfection.) He quickly further qualifies his comment by admitting that 'ich von [dem] Ausdruck wahr nicht viel halte' (365) (I don't think much of the expression 'true'), thus disclaiming his version of events as the definitive one. In stark contrast to Malina's methods are those of Jung: 'Er beobachtet wohl genau, deswegen [wird] jede Person zur Karikatur. Er beobachtet jeden zuende, man kann aber jemanden nicht zuende beobachten und deswegen nicht zuende beschreiben' (416). (He observes exactly, that is why every person becomes a caricature. He observes everyone completely, but it is not possible to observe someone completely and therefore is not possible to describe them completely.) The eagerness to explain, describe, totalize and define, be it by writers, psychiatrists, historians or friends, objectifies both people and peoples to caricatures or types, and excludes the wider truth of what cannot be known in favour of the simpler truth of what can be narrated or reported.

But Malina goes yet further. He does not content himself with simply equating what is not said with what is not known. He is concerned to make the point that what is not said is inextricably linked to the narrator's own limitations or abilities, the narrator's blind spots or moments of penetration. A story does not exist in and of itself, and its areas of obscurity or incompleteness do not necessarily derive from the narrator's ignorance, but from the obscurity and incompleteness within the narrator himself:

Malina erklärt Jonas, warum nicht an jeder Stelle genau gesagt wird, was jeder tut oder sagt oder denkt oder begreift oder fühlt etc. Es hängt nicht damit zusammen, daß Malina an dieser Stelle weniger weiß, sondern daß das Erzählte, am Erzähler haftend, seine Dunkelstellen, seine Obskuritäten hat, wenn ich sage, es war unklar, was Jung in dieser Zeit dachte, während ich anderswo behaupte, es genau zu wissen, so ist das so zu verstehen: in uns selber ist es taghell bis dunkel mit allen Schattierungen, oder in die Dunkelheit dringt ein Scheinwerfer, und dem entsprechend haben die Vorgänge, alles betreffend, ihre [sonnigen], hellen, [naheliegenden] Stellen bis zu ihren tiefen Verwirrungen, ihrem Halbgewußten, nicht Gewußten. (432)

(Malina explained to Jonas why he did not describe at every point exactly what each character was doing or saying or thinking or comprehending or feeling etc. It had not got to do with the fact that at these points Malina knew less, but that the story which is dependent on the narrator has shadowy moments of obscurity. If I say it was unclear what Jung thought at this time, whereas I claim somewhere else to know exactly, this is what I mean: within us it ranges from being as clear as day to obscure, with all the shades between, or a spotlight penetrates the gloom. In the same way all events, whatever they relate to, have their [sunny], bright spots through to their moment of deep confusion, of what is half-known or not known.)

It is therefore inappropriate to speak of perspective, because there exists only 'die Totale' (the total) of the narrator and the narrated.

This brings us to the final remarkable twist in this text, the last irony through which the text celebrates the incompleteness of narrative. This irony rests with the figure of Malina. It is important to ask why, if the narrator's and Malina's voices are so close, and their judgements similar, the narrator assigns to Malina such an important narrative role in the text. Why does Malina narrate and what lies behind his distanced, moral stance? The obvious reason given is that he is motivated by the episode of his sister's death. The violent shark attack gives rise to gossip and suspicion; in the absence of witnesses, as Jordan points out, 'Das ist entweder ein perfekter Mord oder eines von den Unglücken, die so unwahrscheinlich sind, daß eben niemand sie glauben mag' (382). (Either it's the perfect murder or one of those accidents that are so unlucky that just no one can believe them.) The death remains ambiguous; neither the narrator nor Malina offer privileged insights that might confirm whether it was indeed an accident or murder. It does, however, offer a motive for Malina's sensitivity to other women's suspicious deaths; as the narrator remarks in phase one: 'Das ist nun einmal ein neues Motiv, Rache' (338). (So that is a new theme: revenge.) But this is not all, for crucially the figure of Malina brings with it the memory of another ambiguous death, never referred to, but alive in the reader's association: the death of Malina's alter ego, the Self in *Malina*. We are aware that in another context Malina is implicated in a death, even though that 'murder' too remains ambiguous. So when at a dinner party it is Jordan who casts doubt on the credibility of a shark attack, an unnamed guest, evidently aware of Jordan's own sullied record, thinks to himself 'grade dieser Jordan habe es nötig, solche Bemerkungen zu machen' (398) (it would be Jordan who feels the need to make such remarks). It is not difficult to be reminded of Malina in this passage, the man who in a different context has been more than the enlightened narrator of this text. As Fanny remarks to Goldmann, there is a shark for each of us, and Malina is no exception. We do not know for certain whether and for whom he has been the shark, although we entertain a lively suspicion. But that is the point: we cannot know, but we can learn from him that the authority he carries as a narrating figure in the context of this book does not exclude other relationships and other roles in which his appraising distance is destructive.

If the narrator were left to tell the stories without Malina, we would not bring with us the knowledge of another arena where Malina was a more dubious protagonist. Yet through the narrator's close association with Malina he is able to combine a convincing moral appraisal of oppression and

a refusal to relativize judgement with the constant reminder that even moral rectitude is built on shifting sand, and should not become the renewed object of the (reader's) urge to simplify and idealize.

In these first two chapters on Bachmann's prose I have focused on Bachmann's narrative technique as a complex critical form. With it she suggests that ambivalence, ambiguity and not knowing, in combination with critical sympathy, constitute an ethically responsible mode of reply to (self-) destructive identity founded upon deceit, suffering and victimhood. Indeed, through her narrative practice, which also aims ambiguity at the reader, she extends this insight beyond the historically specific reaction to post-war Austria to an astute and incisive analysis which continues to interrogate notions of identity. The textual ambiguity, while certainly reflecting Bachmann's own 'Dunkelstellen' (shadowy areas) and 'Obskuritäten' (moments of obscurity), is also explicitly presented as an ethical mode of response, real and aesthetic, which guards against the objectification of the Other. Bachmann's narratives refuse the notion of a cohesive identity and the conceptual apparatus that depends upon such a notion. Her texts richly articulate precisely that for which Homi Bhabha later calls: 'To write the story of the nation demands that we articulate that archaic ambivalence that informs modernity. We may begin by questioning that progressive metaphor of modern social cohesion – *the many as one* – shared by organic theories of the holism of culture and community.'[5] Bachmann's challenge to contemporary debates is the subject of the next chapter, in which I analyze *Malina* explicitly in relation to feminist theory.

CHAPTER 3

Malina: *experience and feminism*

The critical emphasis in the previous chapter on narrative technique is also central to my approach to Ingeborg Bachmann's novel *Malina*. It is a book which lends itself to interpretations which are based on the dichotomy of male and female. The text is itself structured around this opposition; the narrator is a woman, and the three chapters focus on her relationship to three male figures: her lover Ivan, the father and Malina, her companion and alter ego. The narrator expresses the suffering which these relationships cause her, finally describing her disappearance into a crack in the wall as 'murder', with Malina standing as the obvious perpetrator, but with Ivan and the father implicated as other men who have failed to understand her. Not surprisingly, *Malina*, written in 1967–70, has become one of the major works of the women's writing canon.

The confrontational structure of *Malina* has encouraged feminist criticism which emphasizes the oppression of the female narrator by the male figures. Her emotional stance, her difficulty in articulating her subjectivity and her debilitating relationships with the egoistic Ivan, her cruelly analytic alter ego Malina, and the sadistic father-figure are seen as testifying to the impossibility of the existence of 'woman' in patriarchy. As a writer, the narrator represents female creativity, which is threatened and finally eradicated by the three men. Karen Achberger, for example, views the narrator's own fairytale of the 'Princess of Kagran' as a feminist utopia, arguing that it offers hope of women's sovereignty in the future, as it existed once in the past. Similarly, she points to the emphasis on the colour gold in the narrator's imagined women: 'Einmal werden alle Frauen goldene Augen haben, sie werden goldene Schuhe und goldene Kleider tragen, und sie kämmte sich ihr goldenes Haar' (140). (One day all women will have golden eyes, they will wear golden shoes and golden dresses, and she combed her golden hair.) Achberger argues that with the colour gold there is the suggestion of queenship, hence the possibility of a future golden age.[1]

The acceptance of the text's binary oppositions by no means leads to readings which are as literal as Achberger's, and many are subtle, fruitful and thought provoking. In her imaginative and detailed analysis Gudrun Kohn-Waechter sees the opposition between female protagonist and male alter ego as representing the confrontation between pre-modernist and modernist writing,[2] and Monika Albrecht and Jutta Kallhof see it as two diverging narrative positions, that of the self attempting to tell an untellable past and Malina, who represents the position of the omnipotent narrator.[3] In a recent article, Elizabeth Boa points to the historical context of the book, arguing that *Malina* is a study of a woman intellectual of the mid-twentieth century. She argues that the figure of Malina can be seen as

a moment in the history of relations between the sexes in Europe, an effect of women's admission to education and the entry of middle-class women intellectuals into the public sphere. The murder of *Ich* in this view conveys the insufficiency of liberal emancipation to change deep-rooted (but not unchanging) gender conditioning. Seen in this light, *Malina* is the work of an author in much the same position as Beauvoir, a well-known writer respected by a male cultural establishment, but highly conscious of the limits to that respect and of the hard choices to be made in order to succeed in the institution of literature.[4]

These interpretations are highly instructive and add considerably to the understanding of Bachmann's work. There is, however, one fundamental issue which they do not confront: the male–female polarity itself. Underlying most feminist critical readings of *Malina* is a tacit acceptance of the juxtaposition of male Malina and female protagonist as the narrator herself presents it. The opposition, although leading to different interpretations, is accepted at face value, with the narrator as the (representative) figure which is oppressed within the male, rational symbolic. The narrator's perspective is thus privileged over that of Malina, and her suffering does not itself come under critical scrutiny.

The active or underlying acceptance is expressed by many critics. Thus Boa comments on the conclusion of the book, 'On the most pessimistic reading, *Ich*'s murder suggests that it is impossible to intervene in the public sphere, here symbolised in the act of writing "I", without donning a male persona and impossible to write *as a woman* outside of the patriarchal definitions.'[5] Sigrid Schmid-Bortenschlager, critical though she is of attempting to see ideals of the feminine in the 'Kagran' tale, accepts that there is a distinct repressed mode of female expression lurking in the semiotic, but that Bachmann uses the male language of the symbolic order to represent

female suffering.[6] Angelika Rauch comments on Bachmann's work as a whole that 'durch die Anschauung einer weiblich-toleranten Lebensform wird die männliche Eroberermentalität der Zivilisation entblößt und in Frage gestellt' (through the perspective of a tolerant female persona the dominating, male mentality of civilization is exposed and thrown into question), but feels this particularly applies to the *Todesarten*.[7] And Christa Bürger argues that the 'Princess of Kagran' is a parable of femininity; a woman experiences separation through meeting a man, followed by alienation and death.[8]

My argument with these interpretations is that they too readily accept the binary opposition of male and female at two levels. First, at the textual level, they accept the narrator's perspective, privileging her position as female and hence not allowing for the possibility that the narrator collaborates in her own destruction. The feminist critics identify with the narrator's account of her suffering as a woman and do not scrutinize the reliability of her account. Secondly, the male–female opposition is accepted at the level of feminist theory; most of the interpretations are informed by French post-structuralist feminist theories. These theories, although they differ from each other in emphasis and in their positioning of woman within the symbolic order, are usually used in the service of arguments which fundamentally accept oppositional structures of male and female. It is not my purpose here to discuss the relative merits of Luce Irigaray or Julia Kristeva, nor indeed of certain uses of Lacanian feminism. The point is that these theories are neither discussed nor challenged by the critics, so they do not bring to their analyses an awareness of the theoretical challenges to binary polarities presented by, for example, deconstructionist feminists. Thus the male–female opposition in *Malina* too easily goes unchallenged at the two levels of text and theory, and readings often fail to do justice to the complex self-reflexive nature of the book.

Two recent criticisms have in different ways highlighted the difficulties of interpretations which accept oppositions at face value and which privilege the female element. In her review of the feminist reception of Bachmann, Sara Lennox is critical of the way in which the author has been appropriated by 'eighties feminism'.[9] She calls for new feminist readings which take into account Bachmann's historical context and which do not attempt to perpetuate 'wishful thinking' about Bachmann's politics. Erika Swales, sceptical of the legacy of French feminist thought, shows how Bachmann's story 'Ein Wildermuth' relativizes the polarities which it depicts, and thus self-consciously questions the validity of such oppositions. In relation to

Malina she asks the crucial question of whether it too is a text which consciously reflects upon its central male–female opposition.[10]

I wish to argue that if we do not accept the privileging of the female perspective over that of the male in *Malina*, it is possible to see the text as a complex study of the effects of different responses to historical experience, and how these different modes of responding are central to definitions of the female subject.[11] The female narrator and Malina represent alternative ways of responding to experience, and both reveal strengths and weaknesses in that response. Bachmann is exploring the tension between an approach to history which insists upon the centrality of the subject and its perceptions, and one which emphatically denies experience as an adequate foundation for meaning. However, where Albrecht and Kallhof maintain that *Malina* is less concerned with the battle of the sexes as with opposing modes of existence that are irreconcilable, I would argue that irreconcilability is itself a comment on the inadequacy of structuring experience around gendered polarities. The tension between the two modes of responding to experience is of central importance to feminist discourse and questions of identity politics. I will argue that there is ambiguity in the text and that tension is not resolved, but that it is precisely in both recognizing and complementing such irresolution in a reading of the text that the critical momentum of the text and of feminist enquiry is sustained. Thus in this chapter I develop the analyses of the previous chapters, in which I argued that Bachmann's complex narrative strategies ascribe an ethical function to ambiguity as a safeguard against destructive moral simplification, and specifically consider the implications of this vision for a feminist hermeneutics.

THE FIRST-PERSON NARRATOR

The trouble with first-person narrators is that their perspective dominates, identification and sympathy are facilitated and it can be difficult to maintain critical distance. The desire to read *Malina* as a feminist text has often meant that rigorous scrutiny of the reliability of the narrator has been neglected as a result of identification with her as the female element. Yet failure to question the narrator's perceptions must affect the critical assessment of the status of the binary opposition of male and female. It affects whether the narrator must be viewed as the inevitably oppressed half of that polarity, thus effectively letting it stand unchallenged, or whether she is revealed as complicit in the performance of the polarity, thus undermining notions of its fixity.

I would argue that there is ample evidence in the text for maintaining distance from the perceptions of the narrator. Crucially, it becomes clear already in the prologue that her recollections are not always accurate; at one point she states 'Es war auf der Glanbrücke. Es war nicht die Seepromenade' (22). (It was on the Glan bridge. It was not the lakeside promenade) and two paragraphs later: 'Es war nicht auf der Glanbrücke, nicht auf der Seepromenade, es war auch nicht auf dem Atlantik in der Nacht' (23). (It was not on the Glan bridge, not on the lakeside promenade and nor was it at night on the Atlantic.) Her memories are often governed by what she would have liked to have happened: 'Im Café Musil habe ich vielleicht doch nicht das Stück Torte nach der Aufnahmsprüfung bekommen, aber ich möchte es bekommen haben und sehe mich mit einer kleinen Gabel eine Torte zerteilen' (21). (Perhaps I did not have that piece of cake in Café Musil after the entrance exam, but I would like to have had it and see myself cutting up the cake with a little fork.) It is clear that what is important for her is that memory is not limited to fact but that it is governed by emotional perception. The past, experience, is felt; its reality is not limited to the analysis and definition of science. The narrator describes her attraction to astrology in similar terms: 'Weil ich mir die Zusammenhänge hoch oben über uns einbilden darf, wie ich will, weil mir keine Wissenschaft dabei auf die Finger sehen und draufklopfen kann' (23). (Because I may imagine the relations high up above us as I like, since no science can look over my shoulder and rap me on the knuckles.)

The world as felt experience reaches its apotheosis in her relationship to Ivan, and again it is significant that in the structure of the novel this episode should come first. For in the narrator's deification of Ivan, her clichéd behaviour in relation to him, and her self-deception that 'für Ivan habe ich nichts zum Schein' (37) (I don't pretend to Ivan), the reader is presented with evidence that the narrator is gullible, naive and dominated by feelings which can clearly have a negative effect. That her relationship to Ivan reduces the narrator to conventional images of the desperate mistress has been commented upon amply by critics, but it rarely results in a questioning of her perspective as a whole. However, it is crucial to see this episode as an important indication of the narrator's inadequate modes of perception, not just in relation to Ivan, but in relation to what follows with Malina. The fact that the prologue's thematization of the importance of emotion in reacting to experience is followed directly by an illustration of how the protagonist's feelings lead her into stereotypical patterns of behaviour is a textual invitation to be aware of the limitations of her viewpoint and not to privilege her perceptions in the book. For the text is concerned to explore

two differing modes of responding to experience, not simply by setting up a simple opposition, but by systematically exposing the devastating implications of remaining trapped within opposition.

EXPERIENCE

'Und wenn ich zum Beispiel in diesem Buch "Malina" kein Wort über den Vietnamkrieg sage, kein Wort über soundso viele katastrophale Zustände unserer Gesellschaft, dann weiß ich aber auf eine andere Weise etwas zu sagen – oder ich hoffe, daß ich es zu sagen weiß.'[12] (And if, for example, I don't say anything about the Vietnam War in this book *Malina*, or anything about the umpteen catastrophic conditions in our society, I do, though, know how to say something in another way – or I hope that I know how.) Bachmann's novel is certainly no naturalistic exposition of global catastrophe, but a history of abuse and how it can be lived with is her central theme, and one which cannot be treated by recounting events: 'Denn ich glaub' nicht, daß man, indem man zum hundertsten Mal wiederholt, was an Schrecklichem heute in der Welt geschieht, es geschieht ja immerzu Schreckliches, daß man das mit den Platitüden sagen kann, die jeder zu sagen versteht. In den Träumen weiß ich aber, wie ich es zu sagen hab'.'[13] (I don't believe that you can express the terrible things happening in the world today, and terrible things are constantly happening, by repeating them hundreds of times, or by talking in platitudes that everyone can say. But in dreams I know how I have to say it.) This book is very much about history and experience and their effect on the individual; more specifically, it is about their effect on the female subject, how she is able to respond and how this response defines notions of subjectivity. The narrator reacts to experience emotionally, investing events with feeling and also with the desire to feel absolutely. She does not relativize through analysis and forms judgements based on the immediacy of the feeling which events provoke. In contrast, Malina remains emotionally distant and insists upon constant questioning of facts, causes, the meaning which might lie behind the appearance of an event. He insists on constant enquiry, she on the immediacy of the felt instant: 'Dieses Gleichgewicht, dieser Gleichmut, der in ihm ist, wird mich noch zur Verzweiflung treiben, weil ich in allen Situationen reagiere, mich an jedem Gefühlsaufruhr beteiligen lasse und die Verluste erleide, die Malina unbeteiligt zur Kenntnis nimmt' (261). (This equilibrium, this equanimity that is in him is going to drive me to despair, because I react in all situations, I let myself get involved in all emotional turmoil and I suffer the losses that Malina disinterestedly takes note of.)

Far from removing *Malina* from the arena of feminist debate by seeing it as a text primarily concerned with interpretations of experience, I
would argue that it in fact pinpoints one of the most crucial and controversial issues of the feminist discourse: the status of experience. For
many areas of feminist theory, women's experience is regarded as central
to the claim for emancipation. The very existence of feminism as a political programme depends upon women's feeling of being oppressed and on
founding an identity politics based on the generalized concept of woman.
Women's historical experience of oppression and exclusion is used to justify
the existence of a female subject as different and as Other, with different
modes of perception and response. Experience thus becomes the foundation of feminist ontology, whereby women's status as marginalized in
patriarchal society is equated with a different subjectivity. So in the face of
post-structuralist denials of the subject and Foucault's question 'What matters who's speaking?',[14] women, it is argued, do care, for it is only now that
they are able to articulate the subjectivity which has hitherto been negated
or denied, and assert that subjectivity as different, but as equally valid.

Feminist ontologies based on experience are by no means uniform, with
some theorists more obviously ascribing innate characteristics to women
than others. In her article on the problem of experience for feminists in the
natural and social sciences, Marnia Lazreg describes the alternative methodology espoused by certain feminist thinkers in response to the methodological requirements of objectivity and to concepts which failed to 'tap
women's experience'.[15] This new methodology requires a 'feminine cognitive style – in the positive sense of artistic, sensitive, integrated, deep, intersubjective, empathic, associative, affective, open, personalized, aesthetic
and receptive'.[16] ('Anything else?' I am tempted to ask.) In contrast to
this somewhat simplistic equation, the French feminist philosopher, Luce
Irigaray, offers a sophisticated critique of women's experience in what she
terms the 'between-men culture'.[17] She too, although refraining from defining 'woman' through a list of characteristics, sees the appeal to experience
as crucial in her discussions of female subjectivity. She writes that

Most women's experience tells them, on a cultural level, that they are first and
foremost asexual or neuter, apart from when they are subjected to the norms of
the sexual arena in the strict sense and to family stereotypes. The difficulties they
face in order to enter the between-men cultural world lead almost all of them,
including those who call themselves feminists, to renounce their female identity.[18]

Similarly, Irigaray discusses female subjectivity in relation to women's experience of their body and of childbirth: 'How can women's health be defined?

Hardly anything, in our present society, enables women to be *female sexed subjects* . . . How can the natural suffering a woman experiences during childbirth be separated from the artificial suffering society imposes upon her?'[19]

In contrast to this insistence on the importance of experience, certain strands of feminist philosophy refuse to accept it as an adequate basis for identity. Deconstructionist feminists question the whole relationship of experience and female identity, arguing that women's experience tends to be approached as though it is intrinsically significant, with the concomitant assumption that merely recounting it must therefore be beneficial for women. Instead, they see the emphasis on experience as a way of reinscribing existing structures of domination; experience becomes a new foundation and source of truth, and, repeating the pattern of all foundationalist myths, one in which primary premises and presumptions are not questioned. In terms of women's writing, in both fiction and women's history, this leads to the universalization of identity based on the shared experience of the female writer/historian and her readership, and it results in the naive assumption that the mere recounting of lived experience is a form of resistance to oppression. Consequently, the discourses within which gender is constructed are not analyzed. As Joan W. Scott argues, 'such an understanding of shared experience closes down inquiry into the ways in which female subjectivity is produced, the ways in which agency is made possible, the ways in which race and sexuality intersect with gender, the ways in which politics organize and interpret experience – the ways in which identity is a contested terrain, the site of multiple and conflicting claims'.[20]

Scott does not call for the abandonment of the word 'experience', but calls for its historicization, by which she means making it the object of enquiry: 'Experience is at once always already an interpretation *and* is in need of interpretation. What counts as experience is neither self-evident nor straightforward; it is always contested, always therefore political.'[21] Any attempt to unite women on the grounds of their common experience as 'women' is thus effectively to elevate experience to the position of a new truth and so to impede the analysis of what structures that experience in the first place. It also means that the term 'woman' is taken as self-evident and is not itself challenged as part of an already existing discourse. Deconstructionist feminists insist upon the questioning of all received terms, including that of 'woman', since, like other terms, it too acts to inhibit the radicality of the feminist challenge. In agreement with Derrida, Gayatri Spivak regards adherence to the term as unacknowledged masculinism, and she points out that to use 'woman' is to reinscribe phallocentrism:

The claim to deconstructive feminism (and deconstructive anti-sexism – the political claim of deconstructive feminists) cannot be sustained in the name of 'woman'. Like class consciousness, which justifies its own production so that classes can be destroyed, 'woman' as the name of writing must be erased in so far as it is a necessarily historical catachresis . . . It should be a lesson to us that if we do not watch out for the historical determinations for the name of woman as catachresis in deconstruction, and merely seek to delegitimize the name of man, we legitimize what is diagnosed by Nietzsche and acted out by Foucault.[22]

These two approaches to experience and identity lead to considerable tensions and rifts within feminist debate. Deconstructionist feminists are seen as denying female subjectivity just as it is emerging historically. Thus Margaret Whitford avers

that the move from the masculine subject to the disseminated or multiple subject bypasses the possibility of the position of woman-as-subject . . . Women . . . have never had a subject to lose. The problem for women, then, is that of acceding to subjectivity in the first place. Its dissemination is not an exhilarating or perilously heroic adventure, but an alienating and familiar condition.[23]

Theorists who maintain that some universal concept of 'woman' is crucial for effective political action fear that the abandonment of such a term would weaken the political efficacy of feminism. Naturally, feminists who are sympathetic to strategies of deconstruction deny this, claiming that the most radical change can only come through releasing a term from historical constraints. Judith Butler argues that 'to deconstruct is not to negate or dismiss, but . . . to open up a term, like the subject, to a reusage or redeployment that previously has not been authorized'.[24]

The validity and inadequacies of these two very different approaches to experience are held up for scrutiny in *Malina*. Each approach is exemplified in the figures of the narrator and Malina; one in which the female subject is defined by the immediately felt effect of experience on the self, and one which persistently seeks to analyze what lies behind experience. However, the contrast is not a simplistic one. For each type of response is shown to entail both positive and negative aspects, and, despite the temptation to identify with the narrator, neither response is evaluated as better than the other.

THE NARRATIVE SELF

For the narrator the meaning of an experience lies in the immediacy of its emotional effect upon her and she seeks to comprehend the hidden truths of experience in this perceived effect. Her absolute involvement in

emotion is coupled with an active resistance to questioning or analyzing this involvement. Yet although she herself is shown to privilege this form of perception above reflexivity, it is not privileged in the text as a whole, where the devastating and negative effects of her responses are exposed. It is these I shall concentrate on first.

The narrator elevates her feelings to the status of absolutes which she never challenges. Her relationship with Ivan takes on religious fervour; she describes him as 'mein Mekka und mein Jerusalem!' (41) (my Mecca and my Jerusalem!) and the 'Du' (you) with which she will one day be able to address Ivan will be 'das Vollkommene' (130) (perfection). She does not reflect about her own perceptions, for this would detract from the immediacy which for her is life enhancing. She constantly emphasizes her existence in the present, for to exist in the here and now precludes a reflexive stance, a distance from which to start analyzing. She admits to Malina, 'Es muß einfach alles gleichzeitig aufkommen und auf mich Eindruck machen' (307) (Everything simply has to arise at the same time and make an impression on me), and she suppresses knowledge in order to persist in a particular emotional reaction: 'Nie wollte ich denken, wie es im Anfang war, nie, wie es vor einem Monat war . . . Ehe gestern und morgen auftauchen, muß ich sie zum Schweigen bringen in mir. Es ist heute. Ich bin hier und heute' (154–5). (I never wanted to think about how it was in the beginning or a month ago . . . Before yesterday and tomorrow appear I must silence them within me. It is today. I am here and today.) The narrator perceives the effect of Ivan upon her as life itself, so to relativize that experience or cast doubt upon it by questioning it would for her be life threatening. This response to Ivan is typical of her perceptions generally, whereby she derives her identity from her emotional reaction to experience and is therefore fundamentally threatened by the concept of analytical thought and self-reflexivity. She must defend herself against anything that can threaten her perceptions, for to question them would be to question her subjectivity.

Consequently the narrator considers absolute concepts and secrecy as intrinsic virtues. She conducts her affair with Ivan behind closed doors, not in order to hide the fact, 'sondern um ein Tabu wiederherzustellen' (30) (but in order to re-establish a taboo). She is so struck by the 'Briefgeheimnis' (confidentiality of mail) because a letter cannot truly convey the authenticity of the moment; the present becomes the past once the letter is received. She comments in the prologue, 'denn vernichten müßte man es sofort, was über Heute geschrieben wird, wie man die wirklichen Briefe zerreißt, zerknüllt, nicht beendet, nicht abschickt, weil sie von heute sind

und weil sie in keinem Heute mehr ankommen werden' (8–9) (for one should destroy what has been written about today immediately, just as one tears up real letters, scrunches them up, does not finish them or leaves them unsent, because they are today's and they will no longer arrive on a today). What remains of an unopened letter is a secret which eludes any type of definition and analysis. Allied to the narrator's emphasis on secrecy is her dismissal of thought and of thinkers, and Ivan is not alone in being attractive to her because he does not seek explanations. Her weakness for road labourers is based on her reduction of them to their physique, and her delight in the Roman car mechanic similarly idealizes his manual labour and his apparent stupidity. How unlike Einstein, Faraday, Freud or Liebig this mechanic proves to be, 'denn das sind doch Männer ohne wirkliche Geheimnisse' (for they are men without real secrets). The narrator describes her visits to this mechanic as a pilgrimage, once again elevating her emotional response to him to a religious plane, a response which she neither wishes to explain nor have understood: 'Aber man will ja nicht verstanden werden. Wer will das schon!' (292). (But of course one doesn't want to be understood. Who wants to be!) Her idealization of the male body is part of a broader rejection of thought which also forms part of her utopian visions: 'Wir werden aufhören zu denken und zu leiden, es wird die Erlösung sein' (145). (We will stop thinking and suffering, it will be the deliverance.) Again, this is explicit in relation to Ivan: 'Was habe ich gelesen bisher, wozu dient mir das jetzt, wenn ich es nicht brauchen kann für Ivan' (81). (What have I read until now and what use is it to me if I can't use it for Ivan.) And when she is lying next to him, she is 'befreit von allem Gelesenen für eine Stunde' (82) (freed for an hour from all I have read).

The consequences of the narrator's refusal to reflect upon or question her absolute identification with feeling are shown to be destructive. Her behaviour is reduced to the enactment of clichés of woman. She dresses to please Ivan, views herself in terms of film slogans, and yearns to please him with gestures of absolute love involving self-sacrifice or domestic functions: 'Aber Ivan verlangt nicht, daß ich mich aus dem Fenster stürze, daß ich für ihn in die Donau springe, daß ich mich vor ein Auto werfe . . . Er will auch nicht, daß ich . . . seine beiden Zimmer aufräume und seine Wäsche wasche und bügle' (266). (But Ivan doesn't ask me to fling myself out of the window, or leap into the Danube for him, or throw myself in front of a car . . . He also doesn't want me to clear up his two rooms or wash and iron for him.) Although the 'Prinzessin von Kagran' (Princess of Kagran) story has been seen in terms of the *Ich*'s exploration of new language or of a lost matriarchal ideal, I would agree with Schmid-Bortenschlager that figures

like the Princess and the women with golden hair point to traditional ideal images of women as found in fairytales and reproduced in trivial literature.[25] This would certainly concur with the narrator's tendency to mould herself to formulaic patterns of female behaviour in order to please.

For all that the narrator is so devastated by different levels of experience, personal and political, she is so absorbed in her feeling of devastation that she becomes dominated by narcissism, which results in the marginalization of whatever concern for victims she might feel. When she meets the Bulgarian with Morbus Buerger, her reaction is one of overwhelming panic. Her horror certainly drives her to make the necessary arrangements for his travel to Itzehoe, but the victim of the disease becomes an object of revulsion from whom she must escape, the personification of the disease itself: 'der Morbus ist da' (117) (the morbus has arrived). Similarly, after sitting with someone with leprosy, she is desperate to rid herself of the knowledge of the disease. She wants to wash her hands 'nicht um die Ansteckung zu vermeiden, sondern das Wissen von Lepra' (119) (not in order to avoid infection but the knowledge of leprosy). She asks herself 'warum solche Leute meinen Weg kreuzen' (119) (why such people cross my path), but in fact she finds contact difficult even with 'healthy' people: 'Warum habe ich bisher nie bemerkt, daß ich Leute fast nicht mehr ertragen kann?' (175). (Why haven't I noticed before that I can barely tolerate people any longer?) In a move of remarkable self-aggrandizement the narrator shortly afterwards compares her suffering with that of Christ. Her body 'bewegt [sich nur noch] in einem ständigen, sanften, schmerzlichen Gekreuzigtsein auf [Ivan]' (179) (can now only move in a constant, gentle, painful process of crucifixion towards Ivan), and the short route from Ivan's flat to hers is 'de[r] Weg meiner Passionsgeschichte' (179) (my way of the Cross).

The individual is all too often lost to the narrator because of the domination of her own feelings. The shouting of a child is so painful for her, 'eine marternde Belastung für mein Gehör' (a tormenting burden for my ears), that she is resentful of Malina's interest in it: 'Malina muß etwas anderes daraus hören und meint nicht, daß man sofort die Ärzte oder die Kinderfürsorge verständigen müsse' (262). (Malina must make something else of the shouting and doesn't think that the doctors should be called immediately or the child welfare services informed.) She says of Malina: 'Ich habe nie daran gedacht, daß Malina Bronchien haben könnte' (280). (It has never occurred to me that Malina could have bronchial tubes.) Likewise, political events are secondary to the importance of emotion, and her politics, be they personal or political, are governed by what symbolizes absolute emotion: Ivan. He is at once lover and symbol, everything is 'von der Marke

Ivan' (27) (of the brand Ivan) in comparison to which 'Washington und Moskau und Berlin sind bloß vorlaute Orte, die versuchen, sich wichtig zu machen. In meinem Ungargassenland nimmt niemand sie ernst' (25).[26] (Washington and Moscow and Berlin are simply impertinent places which try to make themselves important. In my Ungargasse land no one takes them seriously.) In Ivan she finds escape from the outside world and can immerse herself in the apolitical world of the senses: 'In dieser animierten Welt einer Halbwilden lebe ich, zum ersten Mal von den Urteilen und den Vorurteilen meiner Umwelt befreit, zu keinem Urteil mehr über die Welt bereit, nur zu einer augenblicklichen Antwort, zu Geheul und Jammer, zu Glück und Freude, Hunger und Durst, denn ich habe zu lange nicht gelebt' (76). (For the first time in this animated world of being half savage I live freed from the judgements and prejudices of my environment, no longer eager to judge the world but eager only for momentary answers, for howling and wailing, for happiness and joy, hunger and thirst, because for too long I haven't lived.)

However, although the narrator may wish to view her withdrawal into the personal realm as positive, as living, it is nevertheless revealed as intrinsically debilitating and self-destructive. She is rendered helpless by the impact of events upon her and is dependent on Malina for both maintaining the household and retrieving her from moments of extreme despair and collapse. She can do nothing to help herself because her identity is so utterly defined by the emotions of the moment, which dictate her response. The narrator, although she can in one way be seen as passive, is nevertheless complicit in her own destruction precisely because she actively insists upon the supremacy of emotion. Nor is she blind to the destruction it involves, and there are occasions in the text where the protagonist prefigures her death. Early in the book, when she does not answer the telephone, she comments, 'es kann nur Ivan gewesen sein, und ich will nicht gestorben sein, noch nicht' (39) (it can only have been Ivan, and I don't want to have died, not yet), and shortly after she says, 'Ich lebe in Ivan. Ich überlebe nicht Ivan' (43). (I live in Ivan. I will not survive Ivan.) Frau Senta Novak's analysis is astute when she describes the opposition between Malina and the narrator as 'der Verstand und das Gefühl, die Produktivität und die Selbstzerstörung' (261) (understanding and feeling, productivity and self-destruction).

The narrator's complicity in destruction does not relate only to self-destruction, but also to the question of enabling destruction to occur without offering effective opposition. There is a revealing exchange between the narrator and Malina in one of their dialogues in the central chapter,

in which Malina asks her why she sought to protect her father from the police. Her reasons are based on feelings of the moment: 'Meine Absicht war es . . . das Schlimmste im Moment zu verhindern. Malina: Warum hast du das getan? Ich: Ich weiß nicht. Ich habe es getan. Damals war es richtig für mich, es zu tun' (217). (It was my intention . . . to prevent the worst at that moment. Malina: Why did you do it? I reply: I don't know. I did it. Then it was right for me to do it.) This indicates that although the narrator figures in the dream sequences as a victim of the crimes of the father, she is not herself uninvolved in their perpetuation. Similarly, her emotional perception of past crimes means that although the narrator is able to recall the crimes in dream images, she at the same time represses the implications of those images when they become emotionally overwhelming. In this way her mode of response functions both to expose the horror of the crime but also to resist examining her relationship to the perpetrators.

So when Malina questions her about the compromises needed in order to survive, the narrator is evasive: 'Malina: Wie einverstanden aber muß man sein? Ich: Ich habe zu sehr gelitten, ich weiß nichts mehr, ich gebe nichts zu, wie soll ich das wissen, ich weiß zu wenig . . .' (233). (Malina: But to what extent must one be in agreement? I reply: I suffered too much, I no longer know anything, I won't admit anything, how should I know, I know too little . . .) On another occasion she speaks of the four murderers, and again she gives the impression of refusing to recognize what she must know: 'Von dem vierten kann ich nicht reden, ich erinnere mich nicht an ihn, ich vergesse, ich erinnere mich nicht' (297). (I cannot speak of the fourth, I can't remember him, I forget, I can't remember.) Although on quite a different scale to the events recalled in the dream sequences, the narrator's relationship with Ivan nevertheless depicts how it is possible for her to be implicated in perpetuating patterns of oppression as a direct result of her emotional involvement.

That the issue of complicity is not merely incidental to the text, but a theme which must be considered in any appraisal of the figures is made clear by the repeated references in the central chapter, 'Der dritte Mann' ('The third man'), to the mother. She, like the narrator, suffers at the hands of the father's violence in the dream sequences, but her role in the violence is ambiguous. The mother is identified with a dog 'der sich voller Ergebenheit prügeln läßt. So haben meine Mutter und ich uns prügeln lassen, ich weiß, daß der Hund meine Mutter ist, ganz Ergebenheit' (197) (that totally submits to being beaten. That's how my mother and I let ourselves be beaten. I know that the dog is my mother, totally submissive). The mother, and by implication the narrator, as the use of the verb 'lassen'

(to let) indicates, could resist, but does not: 'Ich denke, der Hund habe keine Ahnung, daß er meinen Vater nur ein wenig ins Bein beißen müsse, damit die Prügelei ein Ende hat, aber der Hund heult leise und beißt nicht' (198). (I think that the dog has no idea that he only needs to bite my father in the leg a little for this beating to stop, but the dog cries quietly and does not bite.) As the dreams progress, the mother is increasingly interchangeable with the father, so the narrator 'weiß nie genau, wann er mein Vater und wann er meine Mutter ist' (244) (does not even know exactly when he is my father and when he is my mother), and she asks Malina 'Warum ist mein Vater auch meine Mutter?' (243). (Why is my father also my mother?) The mother's behaviour imitates the father's, and like him, she evades the narrator's questions:

Ich trete zu meiner Mutter, sie hat die Hosen meines Vaters an, und ich sage zu ihr: Heute noch wirst du mit mir sprechen und mir Antwort stehen! Aber meine Mutter, die auch die Stirn meines Vaters hat und sie genauso wie er hoch zieht in zwei Falten über den müden, trägen Augen, murmelt etwas von 'später' und 'keine Zeit'. (244)

(I go to my mother, who is wearing my father's trousers, and say to her: today you will speak to me and give me answers. But my mother, who also has my father's brow, which she draws up just like him into two lines above the tired, lethargic eyes, mumbles something about 'later' and 'no time'.)

In her excellent discussion of subversiveness and complicity in Bachmann's work, Sabine Hotho-Jackson rejects the possibility of a positive reading of the mother–daughter relationship as it is suggested by Kristeva and Irigaray.[27] She argues that the narrator is seeking autonomous femininity by breaking the bondage of the Freudian family, but admits that

she lives in a . . . dynamic tension between complicity and rebellion. Like Franza, *Ich* realises that she too has squandered the potential to undermine the structure of her prison when, instead of setting fire to the house of patriarchal history, she stamped the fire out: 'ich wollte nicht, daß ein Brand entstünde, ich habe mit den Füßen auf der Glut herumgetreten' (III, 306f.) (I didn't want a fire to start. I stamped on the embers with my feet) – or, in other words, I did not seize the power but annihilated myself.[28]

The question of complicity cannot be divorced from the persona of the narrator and must be taken into account in any critical assessment of her narrative of suffering. Otherwise the complex tensions of the text are ignored, and the questions posed by feminist criticism are simplified.

However, I do not wish to stress only the negative aspects of the narrator's mode of responding to experience. They have been emphasized at length

so far because they are often underplayed in order to privilege her perspective. These negative aspects are, though, inseparable from the empowering qualities of the narrator's identity as oppressed female subject. It is to these qualities that I shall now turn, albeit briefly.

Despite what has been described as her rejection of reflexive thought and her own admission that 'die Abstraktion . . . ist vielleicht nicht meine Stärke' (92) (abstract thought . . . is perhaps not my strong point), it is the immediacy with which the narrator experiences events which enables her to adopt a critical stance towards society. Her attachment to absolute values gives her a yardstick with which to judge complacency and battle against silence. Her interview with Mühlbauer is a prime example, in which she refuses to give the expected and acceptable answers and leaves Mühlbauer angry, embarrassed but marvellously exposed as 'ein Sklave [seines] Blatts' (102) (a slave of his paper). In the interview she makes explicit the importance of remembering the past in a country like Austria, precisely because nothing else happens there:

von hier aus gesehen, wo nichts mehr geschieht . . . muß man die Vergangenheit ganz ableiden . . . man muß die Dinge ableiden, die anderen haben ja keine Zeit dazu, in ihren Ländern, in denen sie tätig sind und planen und handeln, in ihren Ländern sitzen sie, die wahren Unzeitgemäßen, denn sie sind sprachlos, es sind die Sprachlosen, die zu allen Zeiten regieren. (98)

(seen from here, where nothing happens any more . . . we have to atone for the past . . . we have to atone for things, for the others don't have time to in their countries, where they are active and plan and act. They sit in their countries, the truly outmoded people, for they are speechless, it is the speechless people who have always ruled.)

Relating to experience emotionally enables her to react with indignation to injustice, to recognize hypocrisy and to challenge the detachment and cynicism of contemporary society. Much comes under criticism. The high society of which she herself is part is exposed as superficial and cruel, but sophisticated in its manipulation of individuals: 'Es gibt Worte, es gibt Blicke, die töten können, niemand bemerkt es, alle halten sich an die Fassade, an eine gefärbte Darstellung' (291). (There are words and looks that can kill. Nobody notices, everyone sticks to the façade, to a biased account.) The media's reporting of events is 'ein unglaublicher Betrug' (270) (an unbelievable deceit), with news items being chosen according to mood. The narrator criticizes consumerism as an extension of the black market, and in a parody of marketing language she berates what she sees as the commodification of values through advertising: 'Der Augenblick der

Wahrheit kommt . . . VIVIOPTAL . . . Nehmen Sie morgens . . . und der Tag gehört Ihnen! Ich brauche also nur Vivioptal' (265). (The moment of truth is coming . . . VIVIOPTAL . . . Take it in the morning . . . and the day will be yours. So all I need is Vivioptal.) She points to the silence surrounding the first post-war years in Austria: 'Diese Zeit ist aber aus ihren Annalen getilgt worden, es gibt keine Leute mehr, die noch darüber sprechen. Verboten ist es nicht direkt, aber man spricht trotzdem nicht darüber' (289). (But this period has been erased from its annals, there are no longer people who speak of it. It is not exactly forbidden, but nevertheless it is not spoken of.)

The narrator concludes that 'Die Gesellschaft ist der allergrößte Mord-schauplatz. In der leichtesten Art sind in ihr seit jeher die Keime zu den unglaublichsten Verbrechen gelegt worden, die den Gerichten dieser Welt für immer unbekannt bleiben' (290). (Society is the biggest murder scene of all. The seeds of the most unbelievable crimes have always been quite easily sown in it, crimes which will remain unknown to the courts of this world for ever.) This quotation serves as a neat example of the combina-tion of the negative and positive aspects of the narrator's responses; on the one hand she is empowered to stand back and criticize the hypocrisy of society, and the destructive and primitive relationships formed within it; on the other hand the comment is a universalizing condemnation behind which the narrator is able to ignore her own participation. Nevertheless, her criticism is a real one.

Finally, in relation to the past, and indeed to the continued violence of the present, it is the narrator's emotional perception of history that enables her to recount the horrors of war and murder in a manner which is unmediated and powerful. Through the medium of the narrator's dreams Bachmann starkly illustrates her comment 'In den Träumen weiß ich aber, wie ich [Schreckliches] zu sagen hab.' (But in dreams I know how to speak of terrible things.) The dream sequences convey cruelty, fear, brutality and desperation, and, through the narrator's refusal to accept a distanced position, reveal the devastating effects of events on the psyche.

It may appear contradictory to stress the inadequacies of the narrator's mode of perception, its destructive aspects, narcissistic domination and involvement in perpetuating structures of oppression, while concurrently affirming the critical stance with which the narrator is empowered. But it is precisely this double aspect which the text is concerned to reveal and refuses to simplify. Her emotional response to experience is both positive and negative; it at once empowers her and continues to deform her. And in relation to Malina, whose response to experience is that of the questioning

analyst, a similar ambivalence is depicted – one that is destructive and constructive.

MALINA

Malina responds to experience in a manner reminiscent of that outlined by Scott, refusing to accept it as self-evident and constantly demanding that it be interpreted. For him, experience needs to be contested, as do the concepts with which experience is articulated, and herein lies the threat to the narrator. The negative effects of the unremitting refusal to accept a subject's experience as a basis for identity is taken to a logical extreme in this text when the narrator perceives herself as murdered by Malina. He denies her identity by denying her experience and the emotional importance to the narrator of that experience. Hence the constant theme throughout the book that Malina is distant, does not like listening to her stories and is concerned only with analysis. As the narrator comments, 'Sein Zuhören beleidigt mich tief, weil er hinter allem, was gesprochen wird, das Unausgesprochene mitzuhören scheint, aber auch das zu oft Gesagte' (263). (His listening deeply offends me, because he seems to hear what remains unsaid behind what is said, and also what is said too often.) He actively ignores her experience and does not listen to the narrator's stories as she would like, whereas questions would always be appropriate: 'Was sich noch ereignet, was er meine kleinen Geschichten nennt, darf nie besprochen werden . . . Fragen dürfte ich nach den unmöglichsten Sachen' (131–2). (The things that still happen, things which he describes as my little stories, may never be talked of . . . But I would be allowed to ask about the most impossible things.) The narrator is adamant: 'Es ist Malina, der mich nicht erzählen läßt' (279). (It is Malina who does not let me tell my stories.)

The narrator says of Malina that 'er [wird] immer Distanz halten, weil er ganz Distanz ist' (315) (he will always keep his distance because he is distance itself), and later describes him as 'unmenschlich' (336) (inhuman). I would argue that just as the narrator structures her identity upon the immediacy of experience, so Malina's identity is governed by the denial of emotional involvement and the privileging of analysis. His identity is thus shown to be threatened on the occasion when the narrator cites moments in the past when he has been close to death by crushing, drowning and electrocution. His reaction is emotional and violent and he attempts to deny the episodes. However, most crucial in his reaction is his denial that the narrator was present, for to acknowledge her presence in those moments

would be tantamount to admitting the unavoidable emotional impact of those events. The ambiguity of the narrator about whether she was there or not, whether it was she who nearly drowned or Malina, is a device which emphasizes the co-existence of the narrator and Malina as modes of responding to experience, a co-existence which in this case it is in Malina's interest to deny. His distance is thus revealed to involve active repression of emotional effects of experience on him; his identity depends on denial of the immediacy of experience, just as the narrator's depends on the denial of self-reflexivity. The consequence is destruction and self-destruction.

The negative effect of Malina on the narrator has been amply examined in studies of *Malina*, but it is vital to balance this with the recognition that Malina's analytic mode is also given considerable positive value in the text. The narrator herself is aware of the importance of Malina's questions for attaining a greater comprehension of herself, saying 'er soll nach allem fragen' (181) (he should ask about everything), 'er soll mir meine Worte erklären' (200) (he should explain my words to me), and 'Malina sollte mir helfen, nach einem Grund für mein Hiersein zu suchen' (264). (Malina should help me search for a reason for my existence.) The narrator depends on Malina to help her when she is overcome, and, as the central chapter reveals, is concerned to comprehend her suffering. However, although Malina is often hailed as the embodiment of male rationality, aspects of his mode of analyzing experience are far from antithetical to deconstructionist feminist discourse, which insists on challenging all concepts and values. Malina too challenges normative values, is critical of assumptions and rejects absolutes: 'Malina wendet sich allem mit einem gleichmäßigen Ernst zu, auch Aberglauben und Pseudowissenschaften findet er nicht lächerlicher als die Wissenschaften, von denen sich in jedem Jahrzehnt herausstellt, auf wieviel Aberglauben und Pseudowissenschaftlichkeit sie beruht haben' (261). (Malina approaches everything with equal seriousness, he doesn't even find superstition and pseudo-sciences more ridiculous than the sciences, which are themselves based on so much superstition and pseudo-scientific knowledge, as becomes clear each decade.) He infuriates the protagonist by refusing to judge with the ideology-laden terms 'good' and 'bad': 'Ich glaube, daß Malina Änderung und Veränderung in jeder Hinsicht kalt lassen, weil er ja auch nirgends etwas Gutes oder Schlechtes sieht und schon gar nicht etwas Besseres. Für ihn ist offenbar die Welt, wie sie eben ist, wie er sie vorgefunden hat' (262). (I think that change and alteration leave Malina cold in every way, because he doesn't see good or bad anywhere, let alone something better. The world is for him obviously as it is, as he has found it.)

In thus objecting to the amorality that such a stance can involve, the narrator resembles those feminist theorists who reject post-modernism because it denies the unified subject just when women are finding a voice. And indeed, Malina's approach does entail the denial of the female subject as represented by the narrator, as is most starkly portrayed by her disappearance into the wall. Malina no longer recognizes her validity, her subjectivity and this causes her death: 'Ich stehe auf und denke, wenn er nicht sofort etwas sagt, wenn er mich nicht aufhält, ist es Mord' (354). (I stand up and think, if he doesn't say something straight away, if he doesn't stop me, then it is murder.) However, from the point of view of feminist deconstruction, the denial of a female subject is a necessary step to real radicalism and the dismantling of binary opposites, and in the figure of Malina the potential of this position is also represented. Thus Malina does not accept that a reversal of hierarchies is adequate for real change. When the narrator expresses the hope that 'es wird nämlich so enden, daß ich über alles verfügen kann' (you see it will end . . . that I can determine everything), Malina responds, 'So kommst du nur von einem Wahn in einen anderen Wahn' (328). (That way you go from one delusion into another.) From Malina's point of view, the destruction of the self can also be positive: 'Ich: Ich müßte mich ja selber beseitigen! Malina: Weil du dir nur nützen kannst, indem du dir schadest . . . Es wird dir sehr nützen. Aber nicht dir, wie du denkst' (328). (I reply: I would have to get rid of myself! Malina: Because you can only be of use to yourself by damaging yourself . . . It will help you considerably. But not you yourself as you think.) Malina emphasizes the possibility of fighting differently: 'Du sollst jetzt weder vor- noch zurückgehen, sondern lernen, anders zu kämpfen' (329). (You should now neither go forward nor back, but learn to fight differently.) Whereas the narrator can only contemplate victory in relation to a symbol, Malina sees victory beyond both the ideological sign and the insistence on the female subject: 'Ich: Siegen! Wer spricht denn hier noch von siegen, wenn das Zeichen verloren ist, in dem man siegen könnte. Malina: Es heißt immer noch: siegen. Es wird dir ohne einen einzigen Kunstgriff gelingen und ohne Gewalt. Du wirst aber auch nicht mit deinem Ich siegen' (330). (I: I win! Who is still talking of winning here, when the sign is lost in which one could win. Malina: It is still called winning. You will succeed without a single trick and without violence. But nor will you win with your Self.)

Malina views the narrator's experience-related identity as a hurdle to change: 'Wenn man überlebt hat, ist Überleben dem Erkennen im Wege' (233). (If one has survived, survival obstructs understanding.) Far from being complacent, he is concerned to disrupt the existing order and the

unchallenged acceptance of concepts within it. In answer to the narrator
about what can be done, he comments, 'Ruhe in die Unruhe bringen.
Unruhe in die Ruhe' (327). (Bring peace to unrest. Unrest to peace.) It is
within this context that his challenge to the opposition of war and peace can
be read, his assertion that there is only war and that individuals themselves
are this war. For Malina there is a constant struggle against normalization
and the acceptance of dominant ideology, and the narrator's division of
life into war and peace reveals individual internalization of norms and
the successful deception that there can be times at which the subject can
afford to be complacent. As Malina says to the narrator: 'Du mußt nicht
alles glauben, denk lieber selber nach' (192). (You don't have to believe
everything, it's better to think for yourself.) On one level Malina is well-
integrated into society, unlike the narrator; he works at the Army Museum,
an institution 'documenting the blood-stained history of male intellectual
curiosity, which continues apace in the age of technology',[29] and, according
to the narrator, he mixes easily in Viennese society. Yet his conformity is
external, and thus largely illusory. The narrator describes how he causes a
rupture in Viennese society: 'Er webt nicht an dem großen Text mit . . . das
ganze Wiener Gewebe hat ein paar kleine Löcher, die nur durch Malina
entstanden sind' (315). (He doesn't help to weave the large text . . . the
whole Viennese fabric has a few small holes that have come about solely
through Malina.)

THE UTOPIA PROBLEM

So far I have been concerned to show that two different modes of responding
to experience each have negative and positive features, and that the mode
of response represented by the narrator is not privileged in the text. This
carries important implications for the question of feminist utopias, for any
reading of the book which seeks a utopian moment solely in relation to the
narrator's perspective necessarily accepts and privileges the emotional and
non-reflexive aspects of the narrator. It ignores the text's emphasis on these
characteristics as *also* negative and as traits which facilitate complicity. It is
worth returning to Hotho-Jackson's article here, for she is careful to discuss
the negative implications of the narrator's complicity while still linking a
moment of feminist utopia to the figure of the narrator. Hotho-Jackson
sees in the stereotypical feminine behaviour an echo of Irigaray's call for
the subversive strategy of mimesis, whereby subordination is turned into
affirmation. Rather than arguing for this view of the narrator's femininity,
Hotho-Jackson argues that 'it is, however, part of Bachmann's more radical

project of subversion to show the failure of the strategy'.[30] She views the narrator's will to say no as the counterbalance to complicity, and links the narrator's entry into the wall with Bachmann's insistence on the artist's moral responsibility in her *Frankfurter Vorlesungen*: 'It is a movement away from Ivan's escapist project and away from narrating a utopian fable towards writing *Todesarten*, the book which does not suppress pain and destruction, the quintessential ingredients of history.'[31] The narrator's entry into the wall does not mean she is silenced; she seizes the initiative, and through the self-reflexive nature of the text the story of her annihilation is heard. The reader will gaze at the wall, where the narrator should be, 'thus communicating with *Ich* and collaborating with her in the quest for a "neue[n] Geist" (new spirit) and a "neue Sprache" (new language)'.[32]

Hotho-Jackson's argument is convincing, but I would nevertheless distance myself from her conclusion. Collaboration with the narrator in a search for a new language involves collaboration with the negative as well as the positive aspects of the figure. The negative aspects *are part of* the annihilation upon which the reader gazes, and collaboration therefore implies acceptance of the narrator's whole position. Furthermore, such a conclusion disregards the positive traits which Malina represents (again, alongside the negative ones), and so still rests upon and perpetuates the acceptance of the male–female polarity. In contrast, I wish to argue that it is this very polarity which is the object of Bachmann's criticism, criticism which prevents locating utopia with the figure of the narrator.

The destructive conclusion of the novel comes about precisely because of the maintenance of the male–female opposition. The few utopian moments in the book are at those points where the narrator and Malina are shown to be in a relationship of mutuality and exchange, even if only fleetingly, and can be found in 'Der dritte Mann'. In this chapter, Malina does indeed listen to and accept the importance of the narrator's perceptions of experience at their most devastating, and she is concerned for Malina to question that experience and its meaning. The moments are brief, but depend on this mutuality, and reinforce what the narrator later says to Malina, that 'was du und ich zusammenlegen können, das ist das Leben' (308) (what you and I can merge together, that is life). Thus through Malina's enquiry the narrator is enabled to speak of her perceptions more easily, without having to deny them: 'Wie leicht wird es, darüber zu reden, es wird schon viel leichter. Aber wie schwer ist es, damit zu leben' (243). (How easy it becomes to speak about it, it is already becoming much easier. But how difficult it is to live with it.) But similarly, when Malina holds her, the narrator comments: 'Wir kommen nicht voneinander los, denn seine Ruhe

ist auf mich übergegangen' (246). (We do not let go of one another, for his calm has passed over to me.) She has accepted his calm, but he has also accepted and acted upon the need for an emotional response to the narrator's suffering.

As has been emphasized, these moments are transitory. The subsequent destruction becomes inevitable as a consequence of the rigidity with which the narrator and Malina are fixed within the male–female polarity. But this polarity is not thereby being confirmed as inevitable and untransmutable. On the contrary, the opposition is thus exposed as spurious, as reductive, and not as a basis upon which change can be effected. The polarity is set up in order to reveal its inadequacy and its potency as a tool of oppression. Bachmann is pointing to the need for the interaction of both modes of responding to experience in the formation of identity. Neither mode is shown to be superior to the other, but it is the intransigent and ultimately inhibiting labelling in terms of gender which is the basis for (self-) destruction.

Yet here comes the final insoluble difficulty, a difficulty which the text does not shirk. Each mode of response does necessarily remain irreconcilable with the other; a female subject defined by the experience of oppression cannot at the same time question the very notion of the subject and refuse the universalizing signifier 'woman'. The narrator and Malina co-exist in one woman, but an exchange between them can always be only momentary, for each must deny the other. But Bachmann is not attempting to offer a utopia based on reconciliation. She is in this text acknowledging that conflict is part of the discourse surrounding the question of the female subject, while at the same time exposing the futility of fixed polarities. Furthermore, this conflict, if it is not reduced to fixed opposites by those themselves involved in it, can be a productive clash or tension, as suggested by those brief moments of exchange between the narrator and Malina. Momentum for change is produced not by the triumph of one way of conceiving the subject over another, but by the acceptance of conflict which would itself then undermine the destructive efficacy of fixed polarities. As Butler rather cryptically writes: 'I would argue that the rifts among women over the content of the term ["woman"] ought to be safeguarded and prized, indeed, that this constant rifting ought to be affirmed as the ungrounded ground of feminist theory.'[33]

The question which it is still important to address is why the book is written from the perspective of the female and in the first person, if her perspective is not to be read as privileged. I would suggest that the text itself thereby places the reader into the very position of perceiving the two

modes of responding to experience and of conceiving of the subject at once. On the one hand the first-person narrator elicits reader identification with the protagonist and her suffering; on the other hand the reader is in his or her role as reader distanced from the text and concerned to comprehend it. Consequently the reader shares the same internal conflict which the text is depicting, and is left with a sense of tension and ambiguity. Yet it is Bachmann's portrayal of unresolvable ambiguities which is fundamental to the creative momentum in which the search for change and utopia lies. In the text's refusal to provide resolution, either emotional or theoretical, the arguments of feminism continue to be thoroughly questioned.

AUSTRIAN IDENTITY AND THE HOLOCAUST

The importance to feminist criticism of recognizing the co-existence of negative with positive traits in the figure of the narrator, and of retaining a critical distance to her perspective, becomes particularly acute in relation to the theme of Austrian identity, which in *Malina* is linked to the narrator's identification with Holocaust victims. The parallels between this narrator and the protagonists of the other *Todesarten* texts are strong. As became clear in the analysis of *Das Buch Franza*, idealization, deceit and victimhood are not merely characteristics of individual identity, but are fundamental to the formation of post-war Austrian identity.[34] The narrator of *Malina* is highly critical of contemporary Austria, as is clear in her interview with Mühlbauer, but seeks solace from the 'Mordschauplatz' (murder scene) in fantasies that depend on idealistic images of the imperial past. So when she dreams of borderless expanses of land, this cannot only be read in relation to female subjectivity, but as an expression of desire for an empire that did indeed extend beyond borders. When she so nostalgically dreams of the day when all women will be princesses, this is a reminder of the Habsburg Empire's kingdoms, lost in 1919. The narrator gives metaphoric and serious expression to what H. C. Artmann articulates in his witty poem, 'Mein Vaterland Österreich':

> Österreich bestand ehedem
> aus den folgenden Ländern:
> dem Erzherzogtume Österreich,
> dem Herzogtume Steyermark,
> der gfürchteten Grafschaft Tyrol
> nebst Vorarlberg,
> dem Königreiche Böhmen,
> der Markgrafschaft Mähren,

dem österreichischen Anteil an Schlesien,
dem Königreiche Illyrien,
dem Königreiche Galizien und Lodemerien,
dem Lombardisch-venezianischen Königreiche,
dem Königreiche Ungarn mit seinen Nebenländern
Slawonien, Kroatien und Dalmatien
und dem Großfürstentume Siebenbürgen.

Heute besteht Österreich
aus den Ländlein:
Wien,
Niederösterreich,
Oberösterreich,
Salzburg,
Tirol,
Fahrradlberg,
Kärnten,
Steiermark
und dem Burgenland.

Tu, felix Austria, juble und jodle![35]

Transforming the lost past into the yearned-for future, the narrator is not restricted in her idealistic images by reference to fact, but invests those images with immediacy by experiencing them emotionally. However, the intensity of her emotional idealization is by no means only manifested in her fantasies. As an Austrian woman, her affair with the Hungarian Ivan represents a miniature reconstruction of the Austro–Hungarian bond, and her 'Ungargassenland' is for her the geographical reminder that Hungary and Austria belong together. The narrator's gaze is turned away from the major world players in Washington, Berlin and Moscow, since it is in the idealized relationship with Ivan, the historical connection with the Magyar, that she finds affirmation of herself; her assertion that she can 'live in Ivan' thus reflects her identification with an idealized imperial past and the concomitant reluctance to analyze the reality of its failures.

The narrator's increasing dependence on Ivan, her narcissism and her concern with her own feelings of devastation all complement and indeed enhance her status as victim. The post-war Austrian flight into myths of victimhood, which so easily combined with the reactionary dreams of the 'K und K' era, is starkly thematized in *Malina*, as it was in *Das Buch Franza*, through the narrator's willing self-alignment with Jewish Holocaust victims. In her dreams, the narrator recounts episodes of violent oppression, some of which are directly linked to the Holocaust, others of which are suggestive

of it. It is the narrator who is the victim of brutality in these scenes, thus identifying her suffering with that of the persecuted Jews, and equating the oppression of women with the genocide. Such direct identification carries with it significant implications for interpretation, depending upon whether the narrator is viewed as part of a complex critique of gendered oppositions or as the privileged voice of suffering femininity.

References to the Holocaust form part of the narrator's wider dream-experience of being abused and persecuted by her father. This is not limited to individual experience, but represents the abuse of women by patriarchy: the father is no individual, but, as Sigrid Weigel comments, the Name of the Father.[36] Patriarchy and the persecution of the Jews are thus always linked: 'Mein Vater nimmt ruhig einen ersten Schlauch von der Wand ab . . . und eh ich schreien kann, atme ich schon das Gas ein, immer mehr Gas. Ich bin in der Gaskammer . . . Man wehrt sich nicht im Gas' (182–3). (My father calmly takes the first hose from the wall . . . and before I can even scream I have started to inhale the gas, more and more gas. I am in the gas chamber . . . One does not defend oneself in the gas chamber.) The narrator dreams that she is one of the Jews waiting to be transported: 'Ich habe den sibirischen Judenmantel an, wie alle anderen. Es ist tiefer Winter . . . wir [warten] alle auf den Abtransport . . . [Mein Vater] sieht, daß ich abreise mit den anderen, und ich möchte noch einmal mit ihm reden, ihm endlich begreiflich machen, daß er nicht zu uns gehört' (201). (I am wearing the Siberian Jewish coat like all the others. It is deepest winter . . . and we are waiting to be transported . . . My father sees that I am leaving with the others, and I want to speak to him one more time, to make him understand that he doesn't belong to us.)

While some references are not explicitly to the Holocaust, they are so by implication, following as they do from the preceding unmistakable descriptions: 'Aber jetzt kommt jemand . . . es ist mein Vater. Ich zeige auf Ivan, ich sage: Er ist es! Ich weiß nicht, ob ich deswegen die Todesstrafe zu erwarten habe oder nur in ein Lager komme' (206). (But now somebody is coming . . . it is my father. I point to Ivan and say: it's him. I don't know whether I can now expect the death sentence because of that or whether I will be put in a camp.) Like the Nazi concentration camps, the narrator's prison is surrounded by electric wire, and in the attempt to run away she gets caught on the wire: 'Es ist Stacheldraht, es sind Stacheln, mit 100 000 Volt geladen, die 100 000 Schläge, elektrisch, bekomme ich . . . Ich bin an der Raserei meines Vaters verglüht und gestorben' (229). (It is barbed wire, there are barbs loaded with 100,000 volts, I get 100,000 electric shocks . . . I have burned up and died because of the madness of my father.) And a dream

in which the narrator is being turned into ice by her father is reminiscent of the 'Erwärmungsversuche' (warming experiments) at Dachau: 'Wir stehen bei 50 Grad Kälte, entkleidet . . . müssen die befohlenen Positionen einnehmen . . . Ich höre mich noch wimmern und eine Verwünschung ausstoßen' (221). (We stand naked at minus 50 degrees . . . and have to adopt the positions we are ordered to . . . I hear myself still whimpering and uttering a curse.)

The direct identification of the oppression of women in patriarchy with the persecution of the Jews is a worrying feature in the book. Not only is the oppression of women generalized in the process, with no account taken of socio-economic, ethnic or historical differences between women; but the fundamental difference between the successful and acclaimed female writer and the disenfranchized, disempowered and eventually gassed or brutally murdered Jew is also obscured. Now certainly, the degree of generalization can, at one level, be explained, even excused, by the fact that the comparison is only ever drawn in the narrator's dreams; she never consciously compares her sense of oppression to Holocaust victims in the way that the narrator of Anne Duden's *Das Judasschaf* does. Nevertheless, in terms of the status which the dream sequences have for expressing experiences of persecution which cannot adequately be articulated in the language of conventional discourse, the equation of women and Jews as common victims still stands.[37]

It is at this point that we again come up hard against the problem of how to interpret and respond to the narrator's self-definition as victim, her idealization of the Austro-Hungarian past and her eagerness to submit to anachronistic images that for her represent those ideals. It seems to me that if the narrator's perspective in the book as a whole is privileged and the binary structure of her relationships is upheld, there are then basically two interpretative strategies with which to approach the complex issue of identification through a perceived shared victimhood. First, identification is not acknowledged as presenting any problems, so the references to the Holocaust are not explicitly addressed or are seen as a variation on the narrator's emotional sensitivity. Her empathy is a positive characteristic, for it means that the suffering of others can be understood, will not be denied or forgotten, and so it also intensifies the political opposition against the oppressive patriarchy. However, in general, this view of identification fails to recognize that the assimilation of another person's experience of suffering to one's own equalizes and ignores difference, and denies the other's specificity. In particular, it fails to recognize that the flight into victimhood allows too for the flight from present responsibility, and that it sanctions the perpetuation of self-deceit.

The second strategy open to critics who accept the narrator's perspective is to acknowledge the problems surrounding the shared victimhood, but to see them as problems at the authorial and not the diegetic level. According to this view, the naivety of the universalizing sentiment reflects the time in which the book was written and of course Bachmann's own politics; the issues are not seen as being explored by the text itself, but as problems to which the text is blind. This is the position reflected, for example, in Hans-Ulrich Thamer's analysis, in which authorial statement and fictional texts are too easily equated.[38] A logical conclusion is to see the book as a whole as flawed, or as presenting a disjunction, while the narrator herself, as the character who makes the identification, escapes the brunt of the criticism.

In contrast to these interpretative strategies, I would like to argue that if an attitude to the narrator is adopted which approaches her critically throughout, and which sees her as one mode of responding to experience, then the narrator's fantasy of victimhood and her idealized and anachronistic identification with a yearned-for past does not become a weakness of the book, but is firmly part of the narrator's perspective. It is, of course, possible to argue that the narrative strategy of the book both reflects the limitations of Bachmann's politics and invites a critical response to the narrator's perspective. Such an argument is demonstrated by Lennox's interpretation of the fragmentary novels, when she suggests that there is a double gesture of critique and complicity which is a manifestation of the author's historical situation. Yet I would suggest again that the interpretative difficulties thrown up by this text are more than reflections of authorial ambiguity. These difficulties are fundamental to the text's aesthetic mode and are central to its ethical statement. As is the case with Bachmann's fragmentary texts, the complexity and ambiguity of identification is itself being explored in *Malina*, bound up as it is with questions of experience and identity. Following this method of interpretation, we can acknowledge in the figure of the narrator both the negative and positive qualities of identification. On the one hand there is the political impetus it can provide, the power of the images which are evoked through the unmediated emotion, and the expression of horror which might otherwise be silenced. On the other hand there is the lack of specificity, the narcissistic placing of the self in the centre of others' suffering, the refusal to consider one's own responsibility for and contribution to the inadequate present, and the political incapacitation caused by the generalization of oppression into a monolithic mass. The text is itself insisting upon these complexities as part of the critique of rigid polarities – they do not just emerge by default. Thus the narrator's multiple flights into fantasy, be they the images reminiscent

of a grand past, the myth of victimhood or partnership with the Magyar, are destructive in the extreme form they assume with this narrator in juxtaposition to Malina's rejection of the past and analytic rejection of its emotional importance to the present. It is the simplification involved in sustaining the polarity which is again exposed as destructive, and which is shown to prevent a more complex understanding of identity at either a national or individual level.[39]

I wish to return finally to the earlier discussion of experience. In the example of Holocaust representation in *Malina* it is possible to emphasize the ethical importance of the status of experience. The narrator's identification with the Jews is one manifestation of a subject position which depends upon investing emotions with truth, rejecting analysis and reacting with immediacy to the instant. *Malina* shows this subject position to be wanting, despite its benefits, just as it shows the inadequacy of the perpetually analytic subject Malina. The rigid definition of each as female or male results in destruction and oppression. It is the acceptance of conflict which has the potential to undermine the destructive consequences of intransigent opposition, even while it is impossible to reconcile them.

In terms of feminist methodology I would argue that the acceptance of conflict translates into the critic bringing into her/his criticism the awareness of conflicting feminist positions. To do this does not involve the critic in an absurd relativism, where one theory can never be judged as better or more justifiable than another, although this is always a danger. On the contrary, it means that the complexity of the questions that feminism is asking of subjectivity and identity is not avoided, but placed central to analysis. The relationship between tensions or conflict present in a text and the methodologies with which they can be elucidated and explored is a central focus in my analysis of Duden's work, in which the themes of female suffering, victimhood, violence and national identity are presented with astonishing vividness and immediacy.

PART II

Anne Duden: the suffering body

The short stories. Thoughts on the body and ethics

Anne Duden is a writer who has received considerable positive attention from critics interested in women's writing. A writer of short stories, essays, a novel and poetry, she explores the complex interaction of female identity, the body and national identity. She confronts, indeed emphasizes, aspects that are often ignored or repressed: despair, horror, violence and death. As in *Malina*, the female narrators in her work depict themselves as the suffering victims of a violent society, and their sensitivity to repressed atrocities, to the horror underlying daily existence, is identified as belonging to a feminine economy. The constant presence of violence in the texts and the resulting despair of the narrators seems to invite feminist interpretations which implicitly accept the female subject as a victim; the violence is an external ill inflicted upon her. It is this relationship of violence to victimhood which I shall scrutinize in the following chapters. In this first chapter on Duden I concentrate on the short stories in the volumes *Übergang* and *Wimpertier* and discuss the implications of the figure of the suffering female victim for the concept of a feminist ethics. Whereas there is little in the stories that invites exploration of how female and national identity interact, with the exception of 'Übergang', *Das Judasschaf* develops the stories' representation of femininity in explicit relation to Germanness. It is therefore in the following chapter on *Das Judasschaf* that I look in detail at the issue of victimhood, national identity and desire, and show that an examination of female complicity with Germany's past is crucial for ensuring that feminism retains its critical agenda.

Anne Duden's volume of short stories – *Übergang* – was published in 1982. *Wimpertier* was published in 1995, but many of the stories and poems had been previously published in journals during the 1980s. Most of the stories from *Wimpertier* referred to in this chapter were first published between 1982 and 1985. They are therefore close contemporaries with the *Übergang* stories, and address similar themes – those of suffering, victimhood and the body. The function of the body for expressing suffering is

of central importance for understanding Duden's prose, and it is therefore crucial to explore how the body is being figured; whether, for example, it becomes the site where repressed discourses reassert themselves, or whether the narrator depicts it as a female Other to a masculine economy.[1] It is with the depiction of the body in 'Übergang', the longest of the stories, that my analysis will start.

'ÜBERGANG'

The volume *Übergang* begins and ends with a section in italics in which the narrator succinctly and directly expresses what her stories seem to be articulating. Here, in the concluding section, she states: '*Mein Gedächtnis ist mein Körper. Mein Körper ist löchrig. Das Einzige, was nicht durch seine Maschen fällt, ist Liebe und Qual*' (141). (*My memory is my body. My body is full of holes. The only things that do not fall through its net are love and anguish.*) She goes on to describe how, when she was younger, she could fight both love and pain, especially pain: '*Ich köpfte, zerhackte, zermalmte. pulverisierte sie, schnitt sie mit meinem Gelächter ab*' (*I beheaded it, chopped and ground it up, pulverized it and cut it out with my laughter*). But rather than disappearing, pain then returned in new form, either in dreams, '*wo sie nun mich köpfte, zerhackte, zermalmte, pulverisierte*' (*where now it beheaded me, chopped and ground me up, pulverized me*), or by making her get up to go to the toilet: '*Dann richtete sie sich in mir zu ihrer ganzen Größe und Schwere auf*.' (*Then it raised itself to its full height and weight within me.*) Such a total equation of memory with the body is fundamental to the story 'Übergang'.

   In 'Übergang' the narrator has her face smashed in by a group of black American GIs as she drives out of a Berlin nightclub with her boyfriend, her brother and his girlfriend. She undergoes extensive treatment of her shattered jaw in hospital, details of which are related in often candid detail. Both the trauma and disfigurement of the attack and of the subsequent treatment lead to the narrator's confrontation with her own identity and, coextensive with it, memory; through the incorporation of memories from her childhood in the Second World War, the narrator establishes the extent to which her identity has been formed by the experience of repressing the knowledge of violent atrocities. The story begins with the narrative voice in the third person, but at the precise moment at which the surgeon makes the cut which marks the start of the treatment, the narrator speaks in the first person. For it is precisely with the broken, dangling jaw that the narrator can assert her identity honestly. She need no longer live the

masquerade whereby the whole, unified body is assumed to represent a whole, untroubled ego:

Dabei konnte ich doch von Glück sagen, daß nun endlich auch meine Anatomie einen Knacks bekommen hatte, daß der Körper aufzuholen beginnen konnte, was bis dahin allein meinem Gehirnkopf vorbehalten war, nämlich dem grenzenlosen Chaos der Welt auf allen Schleichwegen und überallhin zu folgen, wo es sich bemerkbar machte, es also auch in mich einbrechen und in mir wüten zu lassen. Im Grunde war ich erleichtert. (67)

(For I could count myself lucky that my anatomy had now finally received a blow, that the body could start to catch up with what had hitherto been reserved for my mind: namely, to follow the limitless chaos of the world surreptitiously and wherever it showed itself, thus also letting it invade me and rage within me. Fudamentally, I was relieved.)

The narrator feels relief that her body at last accurately represents the internal 'Knacks' (blow) which she perceives so profoundly; she need no longer live a lie, because her body is as shattered as her subjectivity.

The fact that it is the narrator's jaw which has sustained injury from the attack is not incidental to the story. The jaw, the mouth, is that part of the body associated with language and swallowing. It is with the mouth that the narrator has been swallowing and ingesting the horrors of the past which she witnessed growing up as a child during and after the war. The atrocities of the Holocaust are specifically, although not exclusively, referred to, as being the cause of her adult anguish, an anguish that surfaces when she is thirty-three years old, after decades of repression in which the mouth is the most important organ. The narrator recollects viewing *Nacht und Nebel* (*Night and Fog*), the French film documenting the Holocaust, and then describes how a process began in which everything she saw, felt and experienced was swallowed away:

Der Vakuummund wurde zum wichtigsten Organ. Er lernte nur eines: aufzunehmen und nach innen wegzuschlucken. Das Umgekehrte funktionierte nicht. Er war unfähig zum Ausdruck. Das einwärts Gegessene wurde zur Grammatik einer schwerzungigen, nicht zu sich kommenden Sprache, einer Sprache im Traumzustand, jenseits der Sinn- und Formenschwelle. Augenlos und dunkel. (70)

(*The vacuum-mouth became the most important organ. It learned only one thing: to take in and swallow down. The reverse did not work. It could express nothing. What was eaten became the grammar of a heavy-tongued, self-alienated language, a language in a dream, beyond the threshold of meaning and form, without eyes, and dark.*)

This act of swallowing is a one-way process, in that what she has taken in cannot be given out again through the mouth in the form of language: '*Ich tat es nur, ich hätte nichts darüber sagen können, da die Sprache ja das*

Gegessene und Verschluckte selber war' (77). (*I just did it, I could not have said anything about it, since the language was itself that which had been eaten and swallowed away.*) Fundamental to the experiences which so horrify her is the refusal by those around her to acknowledge what is occurring. The fact that war means death is ignored and the narrator is isolated as a child in seeing things which others apparently fail to observe. Nothing is said about the war and the cruelty it involves; there is a general attempt to treat it as no more than an '*Ausnahme, Unfall, zu überwindendes Hindernis auf dem Weg zur Harmonie*' (76) (*exception, an accident, a surmountable obstacle on the path to harmony*). In contrast, nothing escapes her notice and she '*schluckte ganze Schlachten weg, Leichenberge von Besiegten*' (77) (*swallowed away whole battles, mountains of corpses of the defeated*).

A society which fails to acknowledge pain and death, ignores the reality of war and murder, forgets horror, is a society in which the narrator can grow up '*als wäre nichts geschehen*' (77) (*as though nothing had happened*). '*Die Heere der Toten, die Gemordeten und so oder so Um-die-Ecke-Gebrachten wurden einfach verschwiegen; das Nie-wieder-gut-zu-Machende existierte nicht nur nicht, sondern war Hirngespinst.*' (*The armies of the dead, the murdered and others who were got rid of somehow were simply not spoken of; the wrong that could never be righted did not just not exist, it was fantasy.*) It is against such silence and erasure that the body is juxtaposed; the body is memory, it is witness to the past even though its testimony initially seems to be invisible: '*Und ich war wie eine Tafel, auf der ununterbrochen geschrieben wird, aber nie ein einziger Buchstabe stehenbleibt und nachzulesen ist: der Körper das unbeschriebene Blatt. Beweis für das Verschwinden von Kriegen*' (77). (*And I was like a blackboard which was written upon non-stop, but where not a single letter remained to be read; the body as empty page. Proof of the disappearance of wars.*) It is because the body forgets nothing that the pretence '*werde, die du nicht bist*' (88) (*become what you are not*) must fail, and '*alle einzeln niedergerungenen und abgetriebenen Momente*' (*all the individually wrestled-down and aborted moments*) of the narrator's life begin to assert themselves again.

In psychoanalytic terms this seems to be a perfect illustration of the return of the repressed, with the narrator's dreams playing a crucial role in bringing the past back to consciousness. But for the narrator the repressed is harboured in the body and the horror of its reassertion is experienced physically. Thus she describes these aborted moments of her life as having stayed '*heimlich in meinem Körper . . . Gewöhnlich . . . blieben sie ohne Konturen. Hielten sich amöbenhaft in bestimmten Körperregionen auf, vor allem irgendwo hinter den Kniescheiben, und verteilten sich nur, wenn ich*

im Dunkeln aufstand, um zum Klo zu gehen, als dickflüssiges Gift im ganzen Körper. Leichengift' (88). (*Secretly in my body . . . Usually . . . they remained without contour. They stayed like amoebas in particular areas of the body, especially somewhere behind the knee-caps, and only spread through the body as thick poison when I got up in the dark to go to the toilet. Corpse poison.*)

Awareness of the atrocities of the past is essential to the narrator's assertion of identity in 'Übergang', with her memories firmly located in the body. It is for this reason that she is able to react to her broken mouth with relief, for now her body is evidence that she is not becoming what she is not. However, her use of the term 'erleichtert' (relieved) is not combined with any suggestion that the physical manifestation of her anguished self makes the anguish any lighter to bear. Her suffering, her inability to achieve happiness and her increasing realization that *'das Geschehen wollte nicht deckungsgleich mit mir werden'* (81) (*the past did not want to become congruent with me*) is alleviated only in the sense that the effort of hiding the subjective reality can end. But the suffering cannot be escaped, resulting as it does from an identity which is rooted in the memory of the body. An honest assertion of identity must thus involve profound physical suffering as well as mental anguish, as she herself makes clear in the stark statement, 'Erinnerung – Anstrengung – Identität' (75) (memory – effort – identity). Indeed, this statement is immediately followed by a description of the build-up to and act of vomiting, which is nothing less than an assault:

[Der Druck . . .] riß den bandagierten Höllenrachen . . . mit wüster Kraft und Gewalt auf, so daß ein Stechen, Ziehen, Rukken und Schneiden die hintersten Winkel des Gehirns durchfetzte, und wälzte sich dann als schleimig schwarzrote Substanz wie Rotwein mit darunter geschlagenem Ei in eine Wanne. In der Nierenschale schwappte er eine Weile hin und her, eine Masse noch lebenden Aufruhrs. (75)

(The pressure ripped open the bandaged jaws . . . with wild strength and violence, and tore, stabbing, pulling, jerking and cutting, through the furthermost corner of the brain, until it writhed forth into a pan as a slimy black-red substance like red wine mixed with beaten egg. It sloshed to and fro for a while in the kidney dish, a mass of still-living turmoil.)

Yet it is with this violent expurgation of clotted blood that the narrator identifies herself: 'Ich war angekommen' (75). (I had arrived).

In 'Übergang' the narrator defines her individual suffering as also social. The anguish of national identity, of being aware of the atrocities committed and repressed in the name of Germany, and personal identity are articulated physically, with the body manifesting the truth of the suffering, and refusing

to let it be ignored or forgotten. In this story it is the suffering body which is the symptom of dysfunction, of the repression of violence, fear and pain, and as symptom it challenges the norms of social intercourse which depend upon the refusal to acknowledge repression. Furthermore, the physical suffering is shown to be not only the result of repressed historical atrocities, but also of the persistence of arbitrary violence into the present as part of daily existence, as is so starkly illustrated by the attack on the narrator. The assumption which is being challenged in this story is that violence is *not* part of daily life; identity itself is founded on its presence, whether it is denied or not.

Thus suffering is caused both by violence inflicted on the body and because the body articulates horrors which have been and are being denied. It is the place where the reality of external violence meets with and confirms the memory and knowledge of its inescapable centrality. The suffering body becomes equated with truths which are juxtaposed to those of the 'Alltag' (daily routine), or of conventional living. Part of the narrator's terror during recovery and convalescence is that she will return to an existence in which it becomes once again normal to deny those truths: 'Der Terror würde nachlassen in dem Maße, wie das Kaputte nicht zu flicken und die Unversehrtheit nicht wiederherzustellen war' (68). (The terror would abate to the same extent as that which had been broken could not be mended and that which was unscathed could never be regained.)

THE BODY AS VICTIM

The double movement which is so evident in 'Übergang', where the imposition of external violence on the body triggers the expression of a broader acknowledgement of injury and horror, is present in many of the short stories. It is, however, by no means depicted in the same form. In 'Übergang' suffering is linked to specific historical and social instances by retaining a realistic basic narrative of physical assault, recovery in hospital and childhood reminiscences. The narrator's identity is inextricably linked to knowledge of the German past; indeed, her heightened awareness and her positive response to her consequently heightened anguish, painful and terrifying though it is, can be seen as dependent upon references to the horror of the violent past and present. Furthermore, this story demonstrates the way in which the narrator's identity is structured in relation to ethnicity. Her Germanness is defined not only through knowledge of racist atrocities in the past, but also by the attack made on her by black American GIs. Leslie Adelson discusses the function of the GIs at length, arguing that the narrator is

giving human form to a more general 'dark presence', thus reinforcing 'the racist premise of her privileged position'.[2] At the same time, 'the racist image of the GIs points a finger at a sociohistorical context that the text does not elaborate'.[3] Thus she concludes that the story both explodes and reproduces a racist premise. There is not, in 'Übergang', the complex narrative framework that is found in Bachmann's texts; nor is there an ironic narrative voice relativizing the perspective of the protagonist. We are presented with a narrator–protagonist who privileges her present anguish at being a German woman through dependence on past atrocities and in opposition to a racialized Other. This nexus of anguish, knowledge and yet dependence on violence for sustaining present identity is complex in its implications and will be analyzed in detail in relation to *Das Judasschaf*, a text which further explores this tension. In relation to the other short stories, however, the specific reference to Germany's past makes 'Übergang' an exception, since most of the stories explore suffering and the dynamic of the double movement at the level of the individual body with remarkably little concern for contextualization or explanation. Indeed, in some, violence and the body become interlinked with fantasy. Yet if the figure of the suffering body is divorced from causality, the question of what it signifies becomes less self-evident and potentially more worrying. For it then behoves the critic to ask at what point the portrayal of anguish and injury moves from critical comment to become the indulgence of a solipsistic narrator.

In some of Duden's stories the body functions as a direct symptom of psychic unease at a very basic level. In 'Das Landhaus' (The Country House) it is a physical response which signals the narrator's discomfort in the dark house: 'Ich hatte das Gefühl, an schweren Kreislaufstörungen zu leiden' (Ü15)[4] (I had the feeling I was suffering from severe circulation problems), and in 'Chemische Reaktion' (Chemical Reaction) the narrator's sense of being engulfed by madness results in her waking up with 'überwältigender Übelkeit' (Ü54) (overwhelming nausea). In 'Arbeitsgänge' (Work Routines) the protagonist is in pain because 'Erinnerungen, Vorstellungen und Aussichten stecken als Messer Nägel Nadeln Pfeile fest in ihrem Körper' (W43) (memories, images and prospects stick fast in her body as knives, nails, needles and arrows). Such examples of a localized physical manifestation of mental pain do, however, play only a minor part in the narrators' general emphasis on the sheer physicality of anguish. Much more important is the constant sense of terror, of feeling threatened or despairing, which dominates their perceptions.

Terror, threat and despair are presented as external impositions upon the protagonists from the outside, and are often associated with imminent

violence. The whole collection of stories in *Übergang* follows the italicized pronouncement: '*Ich bin ständig auf der Flucht vor anderen Menschen. Sie haben nur eins im Sinn: mich auszubeuten oder umzubringen. Sie fangen immer mit ein und derselben Sache an. Erst reißen sie mir die Augen aus und befestigen sie an sich selbst*' (Ü7). (*I am constantly on the run from other people. They only have one aim – to exploit or kill me. They always start with one and the same thing. First they tear my eyes out and fasten them to themselves.*) This statement, which focuses only on the paranoid perception of the narrator with no explanation and no justification, sets the tone of most stories. They too concentrate on the protagonist's perceptions, her extremes of emotion, her sense of imminent or actual abuse. The stories make no attempt to explain the link between her felt response and what causes it, which has the effect of distilling her emotions into the essence of terror or anguish, while rendering the cause almost ludicrous in its mundane contrast. In 'Das Landhaus' the threat originates in the fact that the narrator cannot prevent anyone looking in at her in the house after dark because there are no curtains. Unable to hide herself from the gaze of the outside world, her fear escalates and results in physical collapse. In 'Tag und Nacht' (Day and Night) the intrusion of the noise of low-flying aeroplanes is described as a physical attack: 'Als [die Lärmwoge] unser Haus überflutet, hat sie mich schon zermatscht, alles abgedeckt, entkleidet, enthäutet' (Ü107). (When the wave of noise breaks over our house it has already mashed me, stripped, flayed and skinned everything.) And to the space through which the aeroplane flies are ascribed the qualities of a living body, so that it too reflects the wound which the narrator feels: 'Die mühsame Ausdehnung des Luftbauches, die schmerzhafte Erweiterung hat sich nicht gelohnt. Das Gewebe zerreißt, zerfetzt fasrig in alle Richtungen, macht endgültig Platz. Zurück bleibt diese Wunde . . . ein einziges aufstöhnendes und röhrendes Trümmerfeld' (Ü108). (The arduous stretching of the stomach of air, its painful extension, has not been worthwhile. The tissue tears, rips into shreds, fraying in all directions, finally making space. What remains is the wound . . . a groaning and belling site of destruction.) In the third section of the same story, the threat is posed by an initially nameless horror, 'das Kommende: diese, ihrem Wesen nach gewalttätige, Annäherung' (the approaching thing: this advance, which is violent in its very nature). This 'Ungeheuerlichkeit' (Ü113) (monstrosity) is the new day.

The textual emphasis on emotional response and the concomitant lack of interest in contextualizing the cause of distress or exploring why it should trigger such extreme responses is achieved in various ways. The story 'Chemische Reaktion' begins with the narrator firmly situating the

madness outside herself, embodying the physical threat it poses in the form of 'eine Armee im Anmarsch, nein, nicht auf mich, sondern auf all die Orte, an denen ich mich abends und am nächsten Tag aufhalten oder die ich passieren würde' (Ü50) (an advancing army, no, not advancing on me, but on all the places where I would spend the evening or the next day, or that I would pass through). By defining madness as an army, the narrator obscures the question of its origin; what is important is her perception of it as advancing from afar. Similarly, in 'Der Auftrag die Liebe' (The Task Love), the narrator personifies love in order to describe the physical attack it makes upon her. She does not know what love is, but does know the violent effect it has: 'Nur hat sie mich fest im Griff. Sie hält und schlägt mich, sie treibt mich um, sie richtet in ihrer Abwesenheit Angriffe gegen mich . . . Sie ist in allen Körper- und Nichtkörperteilen zugleich' (Ü117). (She has me firmly in her grasp. She is holding and beating me, she pushes me around, she directs attacks against me in her absence . . . She is in all body parts and non-body parts at the same time.)

The narrators' repeated insistence that suffering is externally inflicted applies also to those parts of the texts where anguish is described almost exclusively in terms of body tissue and fluids. Something, and this some-thing varies according to story, appears in the body, imposes itself, forces, pushes through, bites or ruptures the living fabric. In 'Herz und Mund' (Heart and Mouth) this thing is the bitterness which has replaced the narrator's heart, which, when she goes to bed, 'drückte irgendwie von un-terhalb meines Grundwasserspiegels . . . drückte alles hoch, bis zu den Augen und Schläfen. Zwischen Kehle und Augenhintergrund eingesper-rter heißer Schleimbrei' (Ü44) (somehow presses from below my water table . . . pushes everything up as high as my eyes and temples. Imprisoned hot slime-gruel between the throat and the back of my eyes). In 'Fleischlaß' (Flesh-letting), the narrator's sense of alienation from herself is profound, yet even here, although her trauma is personal, she depicts her anguish in terms of physical pain inflicted by others. First of all her agony is conveyed in terms of a female wolf, bear or large cat tearing her up: 'Ganze Stücke Fleisch, Muskeln, Eingeweide, Knochen riß sie heraus, würgte sie hinunter, erbrach sie in meine schlingernde Bauchhöhle . . . Schließlich kam sie bei den Nervenenden an und riß sie allesamt aus ihren Verankerungen' (W17). (She tore out whole chunks of flesh, muscle, innards and bone, retched them down and vomited them into my lurching abdomen . . . Finally she arrived at the nerve endings and tore them all out of their anchorage.) The attack on the narrator does not, however, end here. For she describes being taken to hospital, where, instead of blood-letting for her condition, the

doctor recommends flesh-letting. He advises her lover, 'Beißen Sie ihr alle zwei Tage ein großes Stück Fleisch aus ihrem Körper. Das wird sie nicht wollen, aber es ist lebensnotwendig und tut ihr gut . . . Sie wird natürlich davor zu fliehen versuchen' (W18). (Bite a big piece of meat out of her body every other day. She won't want you to but it's essential for her life and will do her good . . . She will of course try to escape.)

This section of 'Fleischlaß' is clearly in the realm of the narrator's own fantasy, yet it fits with the general pattern which presents suffering as inflicted from without, be this within a realistic or metaphorical framework. Even when this suffering manifests itself in the physical fabric of the individual female body, as it so often does, the emphasis is on the body as the victim of an external force. One final example which is worth relating is in 'Fancy Calling it Good Friday'. When the narrator is lying next to her sleeping lover after being reunited with him, Truth makes an appearance: 'Jetzt, wo ich auf dem Rücken lag, kroch die Wahrheit langsam über mich, tastete jeden einzelnen Poreneingang ab, testete die Durchlässigkeit der anderen Öffnungen' (W35). (Now that I was lying on my back the truth slowly crawled over me, carefully felt each single pore, tested the porousness of the other openings.) This truth, which remains undefined, is described as an 'enge, mörderische . . . verlogene Wahrheit' (W35) (narrow, murderous . . . lying truth), and within minutes the narrator feels 'zersetzt und zerfressen' (W35) (corroded and consumed). Once again, the narrator is having something done to her, the body is having something done to it.

The protagonists and their bodies are depicted as suffering, passive victims, but, as has already been intimated, the causes of this suffering remain either nebulous or appear out of proportion to the degree of debilitation which follows. The relationship of suffering to its origin is blurred, ignored or forgotten. Thus the cause is often an unexplained personification: madness like an army, truth or love. In 'On Holiday' the narrator's incurable pain is caused by 'kriegerische[n] Auseinandersetzungen' (Ü129) (warlike disagreements), which are, though, no further elucidated. In 'Herz und Mund', which reads in part like a condensed variation of 'Übergang', the iron pipe with which the narrator has been attacked is described in detail, but the attacker, the causes, the circumstances are irrelevant. Even in 'Übergang' it is the inflicted injury which is of central importance; the arbitrariness of the GIs' aggression is necessary to heighten the narrator's role as victim. This is similar again to the depiction of a violent attack in 'Wimpertier', which focuses on the detail of the screaming then sobbing tongue, then leaps to a capitalized but uncontextualized statement: 'Dann

Schläge von Metall gegen Holz . . . bis zu dem einen Steil ansteigenden Schrei über die starr gewölbte Zunge . . . Die Zunge legt sich zurück auf den Mundboden und fließt, verebbt, sackt ab, versickert in Wimmern, Schluchzen und Verstummen. EINE FRAU WIRD BESEITIGT' (W28). (Then blows by metal on wood . . . through to the one steeply ascending scream above the rigid, vaulted tongue . . . The tongue lies back down on the floor of the mouth and flows, subsides, falls back, seeps away in whimpers, sobs and silence. A WOMAN IS GOT RID OF.)

It is not that the narrators are attempting to hide the cause of their suffering or make it deliberately obscure. It is sometimes a mystery to them too. At a point in 'Die Jagd nach schönen Gefühlen' (The Hunt for Pleasant Feelings) when the narrator is feeling better she comments, 'Oft versteh' ich mich dann nicht mehr. Wieso habe ich so gelitten, warum hat es mich so erwischen können?' (W22). (Then often I don't understand myself any more. Why have I suffered so much, why does it get to me so much?) In 'Fassungskraft mit Herzweh' (Understanding with Painful Heart) the narrator feels that her life has contracted and that she is being pressed together: 'Ich weiß nicht, wann die Wandlung stattgefunden, über welchen Zeitraum sie sich hingezogen hat' (W31). (I don't know when the change occurred and over what period of time it happened.) Nevertheless, this not knowing undoubtedly complements the general presentation of the protagonists as being passively overwhelmed by negative forces and emotions beyond their control. In 'Die Jagd nach schönen Gefühlen', for example, the narrator claims that love is the feeling that saves her from drowning, from 'das temporäre Verschwinden meiner Selbst' (W21) (the temporary disappearance of my Self). She cannot save herself from this, though: 'ich brauche Rettung, ich muß gerettet werden, jedesmal aufs neue. Und die Rettung muß von außen kommen, denn aus mir kommt sie nicht mehr' (W21). (I need rescuing, I must be rescued, each time again. And I must be saved from outside, because I can't save myself any more.) This statement is no better illustrated in literal form than in 'Das Landhaus', in which the overwhelmed and collapsed protagonist is saved by a man – presumably one lover who took her there – after the failure of her own efforts. However, unfortunately for her, as she herself admits, once love does come to her aid it soon turns into pity, leaving her once more at the point of sinking. But what can she do? 'Aber wie man sieht, im Grunde ist mir nicht mehr zu helfen. Die tägliche Summe der Unerträglichkeiten bleibt konstant . . . Es ist ein in mich und meine Umgebung . . . eingebauter Code, ein Prinzip der Selbstregulation, das ich nicht überwinden kann' (W24–5). (But as you see, basically I am beyond help. The daily sum of

unbearable things remains constant . . . There is a built-in code in me and my surroundings, a principle of self-regulation, that I cannot overcome.)

This quotation is particularly pertinent in that it so clearly relates the narrator's passivity and victimhood to an all-encompassing resignation, also evident in other stories. There appears to be no point in attempting to be otherwise, for such is the burden of existence in the face of unbearable things. Normality is banal, futile, a trap, with nothing to offer. In 'Das Landhaus' she tries to get used to the new surroundings of the old house, but 'Am merkwürdigsten dabei war, daß ich mich für nichts interessierte' (Ü22). (The strangest thing was that I wasn't interested in anything.) 'Herz und Mund' opens with despair; the narrator lies buried in Schöneberg and Tiergarten, her heart nailed to a tree, with nothing but 'Langeweile und Überdruß' (Ü44) (boredom and weariness). In 'Chemische Reaktion' the narrator is increasingly tormented by the devastating effects of quite ordinary restaurant surroundings, a process which culminates in her being overwhelmed by the feeling that the world consists of an amalgamation of the monstrosities she observes. Her realization is to have a lingering effect: 'Von dem Schlag sollte ich mich lange nicht erholen' (Ü53). (I wasn't to recover from that blow for a long time.) In 'Fleischlaß' existence is deadening: 'Ja, also hier sitze ich, in der Todesfalle aller Tage, und finde nicht mehr zurück' (W14). (Yes, so here I am, sitting in the death-trap of every day, and I cannot find my way out.) When the narrator goes on to explain how she got into this death-trap she relates not some vile crime against humanity, but an unexceptional, albeit media-dominated and isolating, Christmas in Nottingham.

PRIVILEGING THE DARK CONTINENT

Duden's stories variously depict an unnamed woman's immersion into suffering and horror. They show the proximity of suffering to the 'Alltag' (daily routine) and its banality, and its overwhelming and debilitating domination which need bear no relation to the ostensible ordinariness of the cause or trigger. The stories are concerned to articulate the many sensations of anguish, the irrational self-absorption, defencelessness and overwhelming physical impact it has. The success of these stories is that they articulate a suffering that is not cleansed; it is repulsive, terrifying in its mental and in its physical form. It is not ennobling, it is reifying and disgusting. The suffering body is neither the sexually alluring figure of St Sebastian with his clean arrow wounds, nor that of the martyr who will be rewarded by God or fame. It is not even blood or muscle. It is 'Matschiges' (Ü45)

(mushiness), 'Schleimiges und Glitschiges' (Ü45) (sliminess and slipperiness), a 'Klumpen' (Ü47) (lump), a 'Gallertmasse' (W31) (mass of jelly), 'Medusenschrott' (W17) (Medusa-scrap).

The stories explore the possibilities of representing the sensations of suffering, where mental and physical suffering are deemed inseparable. Their intense and exclusive focus on the moment of pain or the physical effects of increasing terror is unapologetic and undiluted by detailed contextualization. Herein lies the contribution that they make, a contribution which Erich Fried describes in his review of *Übergang*. He has no doubts about the importance and value of Duden's representation of suffering or 'Angst', and writes:

Das Buch kann einen die Angst, die man meist zu vermeiden sucht, so gut kennen lehren, daß man mit seiner Hilfe vielleicht lernen kann, sich wenigstens zuweilen von Angst . . . zu befreien oder doch Abstand zu ihr zu gewinnen, wenn das in unserer Zivilisation für einen bei Bewußtsein befindlichen Menschen überhaupt noch möglich ist. Schon dies allein macht Anne Dudens *Übergang* zu einem großen Buch, das nur unerträglich scheint, solange man in Büchern bloß Zerstreuung sucht, andernfalls aber, ähnlich wie Franz Kafkas Erzählungen oder Hölderlins Gedichte um 1800, gerade dem von Verzweiflung bedrohten Leser neue Kraft geben kann.[5]

(The book can convey such a good understanding of the fear that we usually try to avoid, that with its help we can perhaps learn to free ourselves . . . from fear, at least for a while, or to gain distance to it, if that is still at all possible for a conscious individual in our civilization. This alone make Anne Duden's *Übergang* a great book, and it only seems unbearable if one is merely seeking distractions from books, but which otherwise, like Kafka's stories, or Hölderlin's poems around 1800, can give new strength precisely to the reader who is threatened with despair.)

Duden's prose is undeniably original and intense. Fried points out the beneficial effects that her powerful expression will have on the reader, effects achieved through the reader's identification with the suffering narrator. He comments that '[der Leser] braucht etwas, worin er sich wiederfindet, was ihn wenigstens die Berechtigung und Würde seiner Betrübnis versichern kann'[6] (the reader needs something in which he recognizes himself, that can at least secure him dignity and the right to his grief), and goes on to refer to two women and a man who were able to find greater dignity in their suffering as a result of being given *Übergang*. Fried is right to emphasize this achievement. Nevertheless, this is a view which, in going no further than recommending identification as a palliative, assumes that identification is in itself straightforward and positive. It also fails to question the assumptions upon which the images of suffering are founded. It is those underlying

assumptions that I shall now explore further, before turning specifically to the problems relating to identification in the chapter on *Das Judasschaf*, in which identification is actively thematized.

The intense concentration on the sensations of suffering perhaps makes it inevitable that the narrators should appear passive. Yet passivity is repeatedly identified with femininity in the stories, a worrying link that suggests that passivity, and with it victimhood, are inalienable characteristics of femininity. There is ample textual evidence for identifying suffering and victimhood with the female, not least the fact that the narrative perspective is almost exclusively a woman's. The very focus on the body makes a confrontation with questions of gender inevitable at a time when the traditional association of woman with the body is being continually questioned and reappropriated by feminist and psychoanalytic theories. There are overt references either to the suffering body as female, or to the violent imposition upon it as male. In 'Herz und Mund' the attack to the head is called a rape, and the injury inflicted by the hollow pipe is like the penetrating penis: 'Eindringen und gewalttätige Ejakulation haben zu vermehrter Schleimabsonderung geführt' (Ü46). (Penetration and violent ejaculation have led to an increase of slime secretion.) The description of the aeroplane in 'Tag und Nacht' is also represented as phallic, with its penetration and wounding of a membrane, and in 'Der Auftrag die Liebe' the familiar figure of the brave but murderous saint and archangel Michael is juxtaposed with the dead snake, with all its associations with deceitful, natural womanliness. The narrator is always a female victim, and in 'Wimpertier' (Eyelash Animal) the fact is emphasized with capitalization: 'EINE FRAU WIRD BESEITIGT' (W28). (A WOMAN IS GOT RID OF.)

Running parallel to this identification of the body and suffering with femininity is the latter's association with a heightened awareness of repressed knowledge and denied pain. These two strands are explicitly brought together in 'Arbeitsgänge', where the narrator describes herself as 'untot, weil sie es lebend ausgehalten hat' (W44) (undead, because living she has endured it). Awareness of 'das anwesende Wissen' (W45) (the knowledge that is present) is seen as more typically female: 'Einen ganzen Tag lang weiß sie . . . daß es das Wissen der Untoten, besonders der weiblichen . . . ist, das . . . ihre Existenz vereitelt' (W45). (For a whole day she knows . . . that it is the knowledge of the undead, especially of the females . . . that . . . prevents her existence.) The narrator's sense here of having greater access to this knowledge permeates the stories in various manifestations, sometimes coupled with the assumption that the narrator alone bears this suffering, effectively undermining the statement at the beginning of *Übergang*: 'Ich

glaube nicht, daß ich mehr Grund zum Klagen oder zur Freude habe als die
anderen auch' (Ü8). (*I don't believe that I have more reasons for complaint*
or joy than the others do.) On occasion others are referred to with an air
of judgement or superiority. In 'Das Landhaus' the scientists, who, as representatives of academic knowledge, are juxtaposed with 'das Wissen' (the
knowledge) and suffering of the body, are viewed with suspicion and dis-
dain. Theirs is a knowledge which can be categorized and put away, so they
cannot possibly have lives: 'Das ließ mich vermuten, daß der männliche
und der weibliche Wissenschaftler möglicherweise nichtmal miteinander
redeten, und daß alle Energie, Freude, Lust und ähnliches, aber auch alle
Traurig- und Schwierigkeit in die schon beschriebenen Karteikästen ging'
(Ü16). (That made me suspect that the male and female scientists maybe did
not even speak with each other, and that all their energy, joy, pleasure and
suchlike, but also all sadness and difficulties, were deposited in the file-card
boxes.) Needless to say, their full freezer offends the narrator's sensibilities,
described as a 'Massengrab' (Ü13) (mass grave). (Perhaps the narrator of
'Das Landhaus' is a vegetarian, unlike that of 'Chemische Reaktion', who
has chosen to eat liver in the restaurant. Although we are not told, I suspect
she is not.)

In 'Chemische Reaktion' the narrator notices that some of the leaves on
the trees have something wrong with them, but no one else notices this,
even though they could. This observation leads seamlessly into her defining
the difference between her and others:

Aber niemand nahm es wahr . . . Ich konnte deutlich erkennen, daß sie alle ein
Ziel vor den Augen hatten, damit sie in der Welt nicht irrten . . . Ich hatte das
ja nicht. Der Unterschied war einfach und logisch: sie hatten ein Ziel und sahen
nichts anderes, ich hatte kein Ziel und sah alles andere. (Ü55–6)

(But nobody was aware of it . . . I could see clearly that they all had a distinct goal
in order not to lose their way in the world . . . I didn't have that. The difference
was simple and logical. They had a goal and saw nothing else, I had no goal and
saw everything else.)

This seeing of 'everything else' includes even the awareness that the responsibility for causing destruction lies with people themselves, but as the
narrator in 'Übergang' comments, most people do not even know that they
belong to 'die Spezies der Verantwortlichen' (Ü68) (the responsible species).
The narrator, though, sees, knows, suffers.

Suffering is identified not only with the female body, but also with the
theme of darkness and the night; they are central to the experience of
anguish, as the many references testify. 'Der Terror lag ja begründet in der

Dunkelheit' (Ü34) (The terror had its roots in the darkness) the narrator
asserts in 'Das Landhaus'. In 'Herz und Mund' the description of the
bitterness and of the graveyard of her heart is followed by an awakening:
'Beim Aufwachen ist mein erster Gedanke, wo ist das alles geblieben' (Ü45).
(Upon waking my first thought is, where has it all gone.) The 'alles' is not
thereby relegated to the status of 'only a dream' and so diminished, but is
a confirmation of what the narrator writes at the end of the book: '*Nachts
hatte [die Qual] Auferstehung in neuzusammengesetzter Form*' (Ü141). (*At
night the anguish was resurrected in new-found form.*) It is often at night, in
the dark, that the narrators are confronted by the awareness of their own
or others' suffering. In 'Fleischlaß' it is every other night that the narrator
experiences the subjection of her body to something. The 'thing' moving
over and through the body is tortuous: 'Daß es sich nicht dingfest machen
läßt, daß es mich benutzt und an mir herumprobiert, als wäre ich ein
Kadaver, ein vorgefundenes Fressen, das ist die wahre Qual' (W11). (The
fact that it cannot be pinned down, that it uses me and tests me out as
though I were a corpse, a ready-prepared meal, that is the real agony.) In
many stories the narrator's awareness is coupled with a state of insomnia:
in 'Tag und Nacht' she is party to the neighbours' lurking madness; in 'Die
Jagd nach schönen Gefühlen' she lies awake and realizes 'Ich war bereits
unsäglich krank' (W22) (I was already unutterably ill), and in 'Fancy Calling
it Good Friday' it is while the narrator is waiting to fall asleep that she feels
the Truth crawling over her.

The night is by no means always the time when terror asserts itself.
In 'Chemische Reaktion' it is during the day that the narrator feels the
approach of madness, whereas the night is without dreams. And in 'Tag
und Nacht' it is the coming day that is perceived as a monstrosity. However,
there is no discrepancy in seeing the approaching day as a monstrosity when
it is at night that horror surfaces. For it is precisely the fact that night and
darkness facilitate a confrontation with the violence and suffering which
is usually denied, that they are to be welcomed: 'Im Dunkeln gibt sich
das Unsichtbare ungezwungener und natürlicher' (Ü135). (In the dark the
unseeable behaves more freely and naturally.) The dark is aligned with
clarity of vision and perception: 'Die Augen sehen wieder klarer' (Ü135)
(The eyes see more clearly again), a statement which in 'Übergang' and
'Herz und Mund' takes literal form in the emphasis on the eyes, left un-
damaged in the severely injured face.

In these stories a feminine economy is constructed, based upon suffering and images of darkness; it is an economy of acute feeling and awareness of the anguish of repression and victimhood. Crucially, although not

surprisingly, it is juxtaposed with the order and smooth running of normal life and society. Just as in 'Übergang', where the realistic plot shows suffering as a result of the violent disruption of the body's form, so too in the other stories suffering is placed in opposition to order, social order in particular. In 'Das Landhaus' the terror results in the narrator lapsing into antisocial behaviour: 'Ich hatte keine Manieren mehr' (Ü34). (I no longer had any manners.) The first section of 'Chemische Reaktion' is comic in the contrast between the madness which the narrator feels is assaulting her and her magnificent effort to hide it from her enamoured companion with his luxurious Citroën. Her success owes itself to her adherence to pre-established social norms:

als ich mit letzter Kraft den Versuch einer normalen Verabschiedung machte, indem ich mich an die Gesten und Worte vom letzten Mal und an frühere Verabschiedungsmuster genau zu erinnern suchte, schob sich plötzlich eine feste, wie mit kühlem Öl eingeriebene Zunge durch meine leicht geöffneten, wahrscheinlich lächelnden Lippen in den Mund. (Ü53)

(As I was attempting with my last bit of strength to say a normal goodbye by trying to remember precisely the gestures and words from the last time and from previous occasions, a firm tongue, which felt as though it had been rubbed with cool oil, suddenly pushed itself through my slightly parted, and presumably smiling lips into my mouth.)

The polarization of the position of suffering and darkness and that of order is stated unequivocally in 'Die Kunst zu ertrinken' (The Art of Drowning). It is in the dark that 'die Ordnung macht Anstalten, in ihre unordentlichen Bestandteile zu zerfallen' (order took measures to disintegrate into its disorderly components), and the narrator yearns for the day 'wo es nicht mehr hell wird' (Ü135) (when it will no longer get light).

THE FIGHT

The stories show a juxtaposition of woman, suffering, body and darkness on one side, and man, society, order and reason on the other. A feminine economy is depicted as the repressed, undefinable Other of the male symbolic; it exists at the point where symbolic disintegration occurs. The stories do not, however, make a direct correlation between that economy and the individual woman. We are not dealing here with a feminine economy which can be 'implemented' or inhabited by women who establish an alternative way of living, as is typically the case in Christa Wolf's work. There, it is women themselves who represent and enact an idealized feminine economy,

most obviously in the women's community outside Troy in *Kassandra*, and outside Corinth in *Medea*. In Wolf's work a feminine economy is a utopia to be striven for, a way of reattaining the humanity which has been lost to men and women in modernity. In Duden's stories the feminine economy is the economy of darkness, anguish, knowledge of suffering. It does not have any utopian function, for it is constituted precisely by those elements which society rejects. There is no simple synecdochic relationship between individual woman and feminine economy, no sense in which the protagonists are at ease with it just because they are female. On the contrary, the conflict between the symbolic and what it has excluded is ongoing, and far from depicting this conflict in terms of individual woman versus society, the stories show that the conflict is also internal to the narrators.

The themes of the symbolic and its Other, male violence against the female body and internal conflict within the narrator, interact with some complexity in 'Der Auftrag die Liebe', and undermine any attempt to limit the concept of a feminine economy to women themselves. In this story the narrator describes the feeling of being overwhelmed by love in terms of a physical attack on the body and as an occupying force. Love is personified as assaulting and invading the narrator, love describes herself as an illness and as such she infects the narrator's body: 'Die unheilbare Krankheit . . . saugte mich im Nu vollständig auf. Mörderisch war gar kein Ausdruck. Es ging kannibalisch zu' (Ü119). (The incurable disease . . . sucked me up totally in an instant. Murderous was not even the expression for it; it was cannibalistic.) Love's pain becomes the narrator's: 'Sie zitterte, sie knirschte in den Gelenken' (Ü119). (She trembled, her joints creaked.) However, love's attack, like the attack of an aggressor, does, by nature of the physical suffering it causes, ensure against forgetting: 'Sie läßt Vergessen nicht zu' (Ü117). (She does not permit you to forget.) Consequently, the narrator is distanced from normal social intercourse, '[die] Kunst des Lebens' (the art of living), by a transparent wall; she can neither work nor pursue other activities.

The narrator's experience of love, associated though it is with the positive attribute of not forgetting, is not regarded by her as revelatory or redemptive. The attack is precisely that, an incursion, a burden which she attempts to resist. She is determined not to surrender to the collapse into disorder which it signifies: 'Ich achtete in diesem Zustand vor allem auf eines: nicht aus der Form zu gehen. Das war meine einzige Chance bis zum Eintreten des Endes: Würde' (Ü119). (In this condition I was careful about one thing in particular; to keep my composure. That was my only chance until the end set in: dignity.) She is ashamed of the impropriety of love and wishes she could be without her. The narrator's resistance to love's invasion of

her body follows the conventional head–body divide. It is at this point in the story, however, immediately after the narrator's wish to rid herself of love, that she presents the figure of Piero della Francesca's St Michael. He is the incarnation of victory over the body: 'Immer wieder wird er schnellen Schnitts beweisen, das jeder Körper zu ersetzen ist. Michael hat es gerade getan: die Schlange durch das Schwert ersetzt' (Ü128). (With a quick incision he will prove again and again that everybody is replaceable. Michael has just done it: replaced the snake with the sword.) He himself betrays no physical signs of exertion or of a fight; his is the perfect form and his murder is clean. His victory is over the body, not of the body. The narrator emphasizes neither St Michael's maleness, nor that the snake is culturally associated with the feminine, for this is implicit in her description. The saint is awaiting his next task, and wishes to be seen by 'der Instanz, die die Aufträge austeilt' (Ü124) (the authority that shares out the tasks). This element is male, 'Gott Vater Herrscher' (Ü124) (God Father Ruler), and has weapons at its disposal. The victims will always be analogous to the female, 'das Tier . . . die Natur, Potentia, das Geschlecht . . .' (Ü128) (the animal . . . nature, *potentia*, sex . . .), which, in contrast to the hard sword which in victory divides above from below, are like a dead body, 'weich, nachgiebig, gewunden und gekrümmt' (Ü124) (soft, pliable, winding and crooked).

It is clear in this section that the sympathy of the narrator is with the dead body of the snake as a symbol of that which is slaughtered by the male 'Instanz'. Quite unlike the gallery scenes in *Das Judasschaf* , where the narrator 'enters' the paintings through her identification with the figures, here she cannot tell St Michael her view of him, but leaves, 'Worte und Gedanken ungebraucht' (Ü125) (words and ideas unused). This is a relationship of alienation, not identification. The narrator's attitude to St Michael echoes that of Duden in her essay on the theme of dragon-slaying paintings in general.[7] Duden refers to the victims in the paintings, arguing that their victimhood resides in their difference to humans, and consequently they must be eliminated. As victims they do not belong to any species but are always isolated, distinct, unassimilable, qualities which artists depicted in the form of repulsive bodies. Nothing can alter the difference of the dragon: 'Er bleibt Widersacher, ganz und gar. Aus Prinzip und für immer.'[8] (He remains the adversary, absolutely. On principle and for ever.) Duden's empathy is with the dragon rather than the slayers, who appear insipid in comparison. St George is devoid of heart and of emotion, dried out, whereas the Princess seems to want to retain the contact with the dragon. In keeping with the general tenet of her stories, Duden aligns the difference of the dragon to

femininity: 'beide befinden sich an derselben Leine'[9] (both are on the same lead).

To return to the story 'Der Auftrag die Liebe', the two sections seem to contradict each other in their expressions of sympathy. In the first section the narrator describes her fight against love and its bodily manifestation, her desire to resist it and the debilitating effect it is having on her social behaviour and ability to work. In the second section the narrator's sympathy lies with the defeated body against the triumph of a male order and its clean, aesthetically pure, emotionless form. The narrator's apparent identification with the victim continues in the final section of the story, in the way she describes being kissed by her lover: 'Der Krieger versiegelt sein Schlachtfeld' (Ü128). (The warrior seals his battleground.) This contradiction is, however, no more than the expression of the narrator's own internal conflict. Although in the abstract her sympathy lies with the victim, the reality of this adversary in the body is that it is just that, 'Widersacher, ganz und gar'[10] (adversary, absolutely). Sympathetic overtures towards the repulsive bodies must remain distanced, like the futile gazing at paintings, for the reality is that this Other remains Other:

Aus Prinzip und für immer glaubt er dem Menschen kein Wort, läßt er sich von ihm nicht ins Vertrauen ziehen, erwidert er seine Annäherungsversuche mit keiner Silbe, sondern, wenn überhaupt, nur mit Brüllen, Brummen, Heulen und Schreien, aufgesperrtem Maul und drohenden Pranken.[11]

(He does not believe a word that man says, on principle and for ever. He does not let himself be drawn into man's confidence and does not answer his overtures with a single syllable. But if he does so at all he responds with roaring, growling, crying and screaming, with gaping jaws and threatening claws.)

In 'Der Auftrag die Liebe' the narrator depicts the conflict between the symbolic and its excluded Other as gendered, and in contemplation she empathizes with the dead snake. But it is evident that this gendering is not simply a gesture based on biological essentialism, with the female narrator representing the slaughtered body, even if she in part identifies with it. The story opens with four brief sentences in the first person: 'Es ist alles in Ordnung. Ich habe ihr soeben den Kopf abgeschlagen. Sie blutete kaum. Was soll ich als nächstes erledigen?' (Ü117). (Everything is fine. I have just cut off her head. She barely bled. What shall I deal with next?) The reader can only later contextualize this opening as a reference to the deed of St Michael, indeed as the saint's own voice. But in a story in which the female protagonist narrates in the first person, a deliberate and unresolved ambiguity is established as to whether this is the narrator

speaking or St Michael. It is both; the narrator is as much St Michael as the snake.

The image of the fight pervades many of the stories, reinforcing the point that the narrators are themselves torn between resisting the anguish which is articulated through the body, yet knowing that they cannot comply with the perpetual denial or ignoring of violence and pain upon which normal existence depends. In 'Das Landhaus' the narrator tries to lock herself into her room, hang curtains, and distract herself with mundane chores to fend off the encroaching terror; in 'Chemische Reaktion' she does battle with the 'army' directly: '[ich] mußte also insgeheim zurückschlagen, mich wehren, ausweichen, mich verbergen, ducken' (Ü50) (so I had to hit back secretly, defend myself, dodge, hide myself, duck). In 'Fleischlaß' she speaks of the battle as though between two selves: 'Ständig mußte ich Streit schlichten, denn ich vertrug mich nicht . . . Nur noch sekundenweise hatte ich mich in der Gewalt' (W15). (I constantly had to settle quarrels, for I did not get on with myself . . . I only had myself under control for a matter of seconds.) In 'Wimpertier' the body has been drained of substance because the narrator needs 'allen Gallert . . . für den einen entscheidenden Kampf' (W27) (all the jelly . . . for the one decisive fight), and in 'Good Friday' the Truth creeping across her body brings with it a danger which she must escape, a confrontation which she calls '[eine] Schlacht' (W36) (a battle).

BUT WHERE DOES THIS GET US?

Hitherto I have discussed the ways in which the texts depict a polarity between the suffering body, woman, exclusion, awareness and darkness on the one hand, and society, order, man, light and excluding force on the other. They represent the feminine economy as the Other of the male social order, repressed, slaughtered and victimized by the male symbolic. The female body becomes the place where the violence and suffering upon which society is founded is inscribed and articulated, a violence which that society then denies to secure its own order. Yet at the same time, the stories do not establish a simple equivalence between this feminine economy and the individual woman; the repeated theme of the narrator's internal fight points to the fact that while rejecting the inhabitable yet repressive symbolic, its uninhabitable and terrifying Other threatens the narrator with dissolution.

But there is a problem here, the impasse of the double bind which the narrators construct for themselves. For by polarizing the masculine and feminine economies in this way, the individual narrator must either align

herself to the unbearable, incapacitating suffering and victimhood of the female position, or must attempt to fight the incursions of the Other and so become complicit with a social order of repression and exclusion. This she cannot do, for it is impossible to ignore something of which she has knowledge. Ultimately, therefore, each narrator seems to have no choice in her victimhood; whatever she does, she is either at the mercy of society's violence or exists in passive anguish in her recognition of the Other. But, as we have seen from the narrators' tendency to identify themselves with the feminine economy, the economy constructed out of darkness, suffering and exclusion, the texts seem to be making an ethical claim for this position, ascribing to it a value which justifies suffering *in and for itself*, and which offers a vindication of passive victimhood.

The relationship of the body and suffering to ethics is a complex one. Ethics has traditionally been conceptualized in terms of a neutral or male subject, who is then treated as a universal category in order to develop general principles. More recently, psychoanalytic theories, many strands of feminist theory, and philosophers, among them Emmanuel Levinas, have in different and often antagonistic ways pointed to the necessity of an ethics which is founded on the centrality of corporeality and gender. The interesting question then becomes what an ethics might look like which is founded upon a rupture with conventional ontology and which demands the acknowledgement of sexual difference. Will the insistence on the female body result in new generalizations and norms being established for women, or can the body be represented theoretically without reflecting restraints imposed by biology? To return to Duden's stories, these questions become crucial because of the narrators' double bind. If the suffering body is identified as feminine, then the stories would appear to do no more than develop the familiar cultural figure of the suffering woman in more physical, mucousy form. On the other hand it may be possible to see the stories as a literary complement to the demand for an ethics based on corporeality, even if some of the issues thrown up by that demand are not resolved. In order to explore this question, I shall reflect on the stories in the light of three thinkers, briefly comparing the interpretative possibilities suggested by their ideas. My purpose in doing this is to make explicit the process whereby I appraise their relative merits for the critical analysis of Duden's work. I wish thereby to emphasize that the adoption of a methodological framework in literary criticism does not spring from unreflected allegiance to a system of thought as is frequently assumed, but from the critical and politically creative potential that framework offers in its specific interaction with a particular text.

Duden's emphasis on the body is the most striking feature of these stories, and makes Judith Butler's work a stimulating point of reference in a discussion of corporeality and ethics. Butler argues that the body is a site of conflict and gender inscription. Fundamental to Butler's argument is her insistence that there is no outside of discourse, no pre-discursive space which guarantees the truth or certainty of a concept. Everything is constructed in the Symbolic and all terms are therefore subject to challenge. This applies also to the body, which is a site of conflict and gender inscription. Gender is constructed in the Symbolic through performative repetition, and dominant gender discourses are safeguarded through systems of prohibition and figures of abjection. The body itself belongs to this discourse of exclusion and abjection, is itself subject to the social regulatory definitions of 'inner' and 'outer'. Thus challenges to the construction of the stable body image which sustains the hegemonic projection of the symbolic must also undermine that claim to hegemony: 'If the body is synecdochal for the social system *per se* or a site in which open systems converge, then any kind of unregulated permeability constitutes a site of pollution and endangerment.'¹² Butler's ethical demand is thus not based upon a beyond, an archimedian point from which the Symbolic can be criticized, but rests upon her insistence that all terms are contestable and can be subverted from within the Symbolic. No discourse or concept is free from the process of violent exclusion and negation of an Other, and by exposing the polarity of 'inside' and 'outside' upon which it depends, the hegemony of any discourse can be challenged.

The attraction of drawing on Butler for many (feminist) critics is that she combines an awareness of the body and gendered discourses with a fundamental rejection of ontology, replacing what are arguably universalizing and ontologizing categories with historicist analysis. There are undoubtedly moments of congruence between Duden's short stories and aspects of Butler's work, most obviously in the emphasis both authors lay on the body. For both it is the site where the process of violent exclusion is performed and challenged, both point to the image of the stable body as one which sustains the dominant symbolic order, and both show that this order requires the abject Other. The image of the fight in these stories starkly conveys the fragility of the fiction of the stable body, while making tangible the pain and anguish of the abject figure. But if Butler's radicality lies in her insistence on the contestability of all terms and her advocacy of behaviour that denaturalizes the dominant discourses, then on the basis of her arguments the stories surely fail to be radical. Butler's ethical imperative to subvert may be matched by the text's unique representation of the suffering

body, but not in challenging the concept of sexual difference. The individual narrator witnesses, describes and suffers, but masculine and feminine economies remain polarized and there is little space for deviation. Her perspective is nowhere questioned or relativized, the intensely subjective narrative position dominates and even in those stories narrated in the third person, the perspective is almost exclusively from the point of view of the female protagonist. The reader's knowledge remains tied to the boundaries of the narrator's subjectivity, with no irony and no attempt by the narrator to create a distance to her experience. There is thus no textual invitation for the reader to contest the categories upon which the narrator depends; instead there hovers the implicit invitation to identify.

BACK TO LACAN

The depiction of the opposing economies seems to resist any reading which aims to question or undermine sexual difference, and in Butler's terms this can only function regulatively and does not move us beyond the criticism that the stories reinscribe gender norms. This suggests that an analysis based on psychoanalysis may indeed offer a more constructive reading, given that psychoanalytic thought sees sexual difference as primary and unalterable. There certainly seems to be a marked similarity between Julia Kristeva's model of the feminine economy and the repressed Other of Duden's stories. Kristeva understands by 'woman' 'that which cannot be represented, that which is not spoken, that which remains outside naming and ideologies',[13] but this definition of the feminine is one of relation: femininity is a patriarchal construct, that which is marginalized. She argues in 'About Chinese Women' that women are represented as the unconscious, outside the temporal symbolic order, that unless they totally identify with the symbolic order, they must then 'evolve[] into this "truth" in question', a 'truth' whose specificity resides in being 'a witch, a baccanalian, taking her *jouissance* in an anti-Apollonian, Dionysian orgy'.[14] Kristeva sees women faced with the extreme of either becoming 'the most passionate servants of the temporal order and its apparatus of consolidation',[15] or forever remaining 'in a sulk in the face of history, politics and social affairs: symptoms of their failure, but symptoms destined for marginality or for a new mysticism'.[16] Furthermore, Kristeva identifies feminism with this perpetual sulk, since 'a feminist practice can only be negative, at odds with what already exists'.[17] She calls instead for a refusal of these extremes, an ostensible paternal identification in order to have a voice in politics and

history, yet also for a rejection of existing roles so as to retain an echo of *jouissance*.

Following Kristeva's line of criticism, these short stories might appear to be little more than fresh attacks of sulking, perfectly justified given the marginality of women, but nevertheless a negative practice. The stories do not attempt the positive, albeit idealized and vague refusal of an extreme either/or identification which Kristeva encourages. Indeed, the experiences of Duden's narrators make it quite clear that compromise between the two economies, manifested in an external identification with the father, yet with echoes of *jouissance* to keep faith with the unconscious female, is not an option. The male–female polarity remains mutually exclusive, as the figure of the fight in the stories testifies; the 'echo of our *jouissance*, our mad words'[18] can be neither contained nor resisted. Thus Kristeva's uncompromising and negative assessment of feminism as a negative practice identifies and explains perfectly the impasse of the double bind the narrators are in, but seems to offer little scope for a more positive reading; from this point of view both the success and the failing of the stories is that they stand as symptoms of the failure of the symbolic.

However, despite the sometimes alienating response to feminism, there is no doubt that Kristeva's ideas are challenging and suggestive. Her definition of sexual difference as dynamic and relational is fundamental to a critical framework that works with sexual difference and the body, but which treats it structurally rather than biologically. Kristeva's approach to sexual difference is, of course, heavily dependent upon the psychoanalytical ideas articulated by Lacan, and it is to a more explicitly Lacanian analysis that I now turn in order to pursue further the potential offered by such an understanding of sexual difference.

In Lacanian theory, sexual difference is fundamental. It does not, however, have a bearing upon the biological sex of the subject; a male or female can take up either a masculine or feminine subject position. This is because sexual difference is defined in terms of the relation to the symbolic order. Neither the masculine nor the feminine positions are in themselves a positive sexual identity, but stand in a different relation to language. Man is wholly identified with language, with the symbolic, and is therefore said to exist. He is the limit to the symbolic. Woman, although a product of the symbolic, is defined as not-all, is a failure of the limit and is therefore in some sense outside language, beyond definition. As relational terms the two categories cannot be deconstructed, nor, since they are asymmetrically defined in relation to the signifier, can they be seen as complementary: the

sexual relation is one of failure. Unlike Butler's grounding of ethics in the
denial of any pre-discursive space and in the assertion that the subject is
the product of discourse, the central role in Lacanian theory of the concept
of desire forbids total identification of subject and historical discourse; for
Lacan, causality is not limited to discourse.

Lacan's formulation of the concept of desire is central to his understanding of subjectivity. Separation of the child from its mother is what leads
to existence within the symbolic order, for it is through the lack which
is caused by separation that the subject is formed. A subject is always a
desiring subject, seeking to regain a supposed lost unity. Lack and desire
are coextensive, the subject desires to fill the lack in the Other; 'It must
be posited that, produced as it is by an animal at the mercy of language,
man's desire is the desire of the Other.'[19] This desire for the Other's desire,
the desire fully to satiate the Other's lack, is structurally unfulfillable. This
is because the Other's desire will always elude the control of the subject,
just as the mother's desire eludes the control of the infant. 'For the fact is
that, try as it might, a child can rarely and is rarely allowed (or forced) to
completely monopolize the space of its mother's desire. The child is rarely
her only interest and the two lacks can thus never entirely overlap.'[20] Yet
it is the desire of the mother which functions as the cause of the infant's
desire, for the child wishes to be her only focus, her only interest. It is this
rift, the impossibility of the subject's desire and the desire of the Other to
coincide, a rift intrinsic to the nature of desire, that leads to the formation
of the object *a*.

The object *a* is the object-cause of desire; it can be seen as a trace of
the hypothetical unity of mother–child once that unity has collapsed, both
as a remainder and reminder of it, as Bruce Fink succinctly puts it.[21] It
is by clinging to the object *a* that the split subject is able to deceive itself
as to his or her wholeness, ignoring divisions and sustaining the illusion
of completeness. It is in fantasy that the subject relates to the object *a*:
'Object *a* as it enters into [subjects'] fantasies, is an instrument or plaything
with which subjects do as they like, manipulating it as it pleases them,
orchestrating things in the fantasy scenario in such a way as to derive a
maximum of excitement.'[22]

However, although it is through fantasy that the subject achieves an
illusion of fulfilment, it is by no means a relationship which is always
pleasurable. For desire is characterized by a twofold movement, the presence
of both pleasure and enjoyment. With the 'pleasurable' aspect of desire the
subject takes into account what is good or bad for him or herself; the pursuit
of pleasure, of wholeness, is guided by a moral self-regulation. It is a form

of desire which is identifiable with the 'good', understood as justice or well-being. This aspect of desire belongs to the realm of the signifiable, be it in the imaginary or the symbolic. The parallel movement of desire, enjoyment or *jouissance*, takes no account of what is satisfying for the individual; it is a transgressive desire, a desire which remains beyond signification. To quote Bruce Fink:

Given . . . that the subject casts the Other's desire in the role most exciting to the subject, that pleasure may turn to disgust and even to horror, there being no guarantee that what is most exciting to the subject is also most pleasurable. That excitement, whether correlated with a conscious feeling of pleasure or pain, is . . . *jouissance* . . . This pleasure – this excitation due to sex, seeing, and/or violence, whether positively or negatively viewed by conscience, whether considered innocently pleasurable or disgustingly repulsive – is termed *jouissance*, and that is what the subject orchestrates for him or herself in fantasy.[23]

An ethics based on Lacanian theory can therefore not strive towards an ideal future; it cannot offer concrete codes of behaviour or moral injunctions, since it accepts the impossibility of a harmonized system of the 'good'. Not only can the subject not attain that which he or she desires since there can be no harmony of the subject with him or herself, but furthermore desire is not dependent on what is good for the subject in any moral sense. Similarly, there can be no reconciliation of sexual difference, no ethics rooted in the hope of wholeness or unity, or even compatibility. It is an ethics 'founded on . . . the insistence that the subject's essential conflict with itself cannot be reduced by any social arrangement'.[24] This appears a rather bleak outlook perhaps, but on the other hand, as Copjec points out, it is in the service of harmony or complementarity that some of the worst injustices have been committed.

The question now is how the Lacanian conceptualization of sexual difference and desire can help in an understanding of Duden's stories. I would suggest that it closely reflects the way in which conflict is staged in the stories; fundamentally related to sexual difference but not dictated by sex. In addition, that conflict is staged as an internal conflict which social discourses cannot resolve. However, a Lacanian framework does not provide the basis for a feminist interpretation that seeks a positive (utopian) reading of the narrators' anguish. On the contrary, if in Lacanian thought ethics is no longer a question of resolution or harmony but of conflict and ambivalence, then such a framework invites feminist critical practice that does not seek to resolve conflict; instead it enables us to see Duden's imaginative labour as a dialectical encounter with negativity that continues to

challenge notions of femininity. This is not dissimilar to Butler's demand for contestation rather than agreement, yet it does, crucially, insist that the role of desire must be scrutinized as part of that dialectical exchange. For a critical response to the narrators in Duden's work, this means that it is not only crucial to examine the implications underlying the constellation of suffering and femininity, but also to explore the relationship of femininity, suffering and both aspects of desire.

With reference to Lacanian thought I would thus argue that each narrator's emphasis on suffering, her absorption in her pain to the exclusion of the social world, the way in which the text lingers on moments of violence or repulsive descriptions of the body suggests an indulgence in, if not a dependence on, the role of anguished victim. This is not an argument designed to deny suffering, or to relabel it as a derogatory 'sulk'. It is, though, to suggest that central to an individual narrator's double bind, her inability *not* to be victim, lurks her own unacknowledged fantasy of violence. She does not or cannot recognize a fascination, a desire, for that which she consciously abhors. It is this underlying desire which renders her unable to function, makes her refrain from intervention and focus on her own anguish.

There is a telling episode in the story 'Chemische Reaktion' in which the discrepancy between the narrator's ethical standards and her desire is revealed. Sitting on a bus, she is suddenly appalled to see a dying figure, 'eine Blutblase vor dem Mund, die fast so groß war wie ihr Kopf' (Ü57) (a bubble of blood in front of the mouth, that was almost as big as her head). Whereas some onlookers are standing around, some continue to do their shopping, and even the bus driver is unsure 'ob auch Sterbende in die Arche gehörten' (Ü57) (whether dying beasts also belonged in the ark). The narrator, on the other hand, immediately suffers too in response, as she identifies with the dying cat: 'Mein bitteres Unglück streckte sich ihr entgegen, zuckend, schluchzend' (Ü57). (My bitter unhappiness stretched out to her, twitching, sobbing.) Her pain, which has been accumulating since the previous day (in the form of the army attack), is overwhelming: 'Da traf mich endlich das ganze Ausmaß der Niederlage, ich brach zusammen und sah mir dabei auch noch zu' (Ü57). (There the full extent of the defeat confronted me at last, I collapsed and even observed myself collapsing.) What is important here is not just the narrator's response to the cat's dying, but that her pain is also an object of interest to her, which she observes like a film: 'Vor meinen Augen spulte sich noch einmal der Film der letzten Stunden ab: Anmarsch, Attacke, Kampf, Niederlage, Zusammenbruch, Sterben, der Tod und das Leben' (Ü57). (The film of the last few hours played again before my

eyes: advance, attack, fight, defeat, collapse, dying, death and life.) In the event, she does nothing except despair at the lack of response of those around her (and this is not merely because she is on a bus), and look at her own sorrow. It is the bus driver who acts, by telling a policeman of what has occurred, which transforms the narrator's mood. So the narrator awaits a response to suffering, but cannot herself respond other than to turn a fascinated and self-absorbed gaze upon her own pain.

This episode is a neat illustration of the relationship of suffering to desire; the narrator's very real suffering is nevertheless at one level something she is fascinated by, desires, even depends upon. It is this relationship that now needs further exploration. In this chapter I have examined different theoretical frameworks for understanding Duden's short stories and argued that a Lacanian reading offers greatest scope for a productive response to her specific representation of internal conflict and sexual difference. In the next chapter I shall continue to draw on Lacanian theory in order to develop the theme of female desire and analyze its relationship to suffering and identification in greater detail, but in relation to *Das Judasschaf*. This is a text in which female suffering is again central, but, as in Bachmann's texts, is now explicitly linked with the Holocaust and its survivors. *Das Judasschaf* raises difficult questions about female complicity with violence and the German past, and my analysis explores the possibilities for a feminist response and develops some of the ethical issues also central to Bachmann's *Malina*.

CHAPTER 5

Desire and complicity in Das Judasschaf

Anne Duden's *Das Judasschaf* is, like Bachmann's *Malina*, a book of central importance to feminism.[1] For in its exploration of subjectivity it forces a confrontation with complex issues of female identification and desire and raises the challenging problem of female complicity with oppression. It thus questions an understanding of feminism which defines the female subject in relation to an external oppressive order that denies woman her own voice, a feminism which places woman in the position of victim and thus cleanses her from responsibility for her subjectivity within the existing male economy. *Das Judasschaf* reveals that woman's desire situates her in a more difficult relationship to the society which oppresses her, and that acknowledgement of her own involvement in, indeed dependence upon the structures which she rejects, is crucial for understanding female subjectivity.

This interpretation of the text might be criticized as reading against the grain of the novel. Many feminist critics have implicitly accepted the narrator's perspective on her suffering and victimhood. What has been inadequately recognized is that the text manifests a fascination with violence and horror, an interest pursued to the point of indulgence. Violence is at once fantasized and suffered, and it is this relationship which must be explored before feminist interpretations of Duden can become convincing. The value of *Das Judasschaf* lies not only in the fact that it addresses disturbing aspects of female desire and fantasy, but that these fundamental constituents of identity are revealed as historically specific. Desire and the past are shown to be irrevocably linked; female identity and national identity are not separable concepts, but are constituted in relation to one another. Female identity is not treated as an ahistorical ideal, inviting an analysis in which the individual is subsumed into ontological generalizations. Nor is national identity conceived of as an ideology holding sway over a mass of undifferentiated individuals, where issues of gender have no place. Rather, through the figure of this narrator, who is preoccupied

with her own suffering and with Germany's past, Duden offers a study of identity which refuses to simplify critical issues.

THE NARRATOR

Das Judasschaf is a vivid and often lyrical account of the narrator's intense anguish and suffering as a normal condition of her existence. She remains nameless throughout, describing herself as 'eine schlanke weibliche Person mittleren Alters' (74) (a slim female person in middle age), and this anonymity aptly represents what is ostensibly an unremarkable and routine life. She is 'eine alltäglich Lebende' (72) (someone who lives a routine life); external events to which she refers are ordinary, including visits to museums and galleries, walks, and listening to music at a fair; two more unusual events are her trips to Venice and New York. It is not these outward facts of her life which are of interest to the narrator, however; there is little concession made to plot, and she does not seek to justify her perceptions by reference to a discrete outer reality. In this book reality and events are the narrator's perceptions themselves, her reactions to locations, her emotions, her dreams and her fantasies. The text's momentum is carried not by plot but by the narrator's emotional response to situations, her associations, recollections and unapologetic descriptions of what is significant to her.

The book is divided into four chapters: the first is set in Venice, the second and last are set in Berlin and the third takes place in New York. Geographical location offers the narrator no relief from her despair at the presence of cruelty. The beauty of Venice, the Hinterhof of Berlin and Central Park are backdrops against which different sorts of suffering are described or alluded to; her own, that of the Christian martyrs, the Holocaust victims, animals in the slaughterhouse. Her mundane daily existence is dominated by her awareness that violence, anguish and death are lurking behind the veneer of the 'Alltag' (everyday). So even when on a rare occasion she is able to admit that the world is beautiful, she herself remains barred from it: 'Aber die Welt war schön . . . ständig und überall . . . Machte sie jedoch schnell einen Schritt darauf zu, blieb es jedesmal unantastbar und gleich weit entfernt' (108). (But the world was beautiful . . . always and everywhere . . . Yet if she quickly tried to step towards it, it remained beyond her reach every time, and was immediately far away.)

The anguish of the narrator is ever present in terms of both mental anguish and fear, and in the physical manifestation of this anguish. There are constant references to pain and nausea, and she perceives her life as a life of surviving horror: 'Immer, wenn wieder ein Moment vergangen

war, hatte sie ihn mitüberlebt. Sie war ein Vehikel des Überdauerns' (12).
(Whenever another moment passed, she felt she had survived it. She was a
vehicle of survival.) Although at one point she writes that 'Schlafend ließ
[ihr Leben] sich am besten aushalten, aufwachend am schlechtesten' (17)
(her life was most easily endurable asleep, but least endurable awake), her
nights too are a constant torment to her. Every morning after a night of
nightmares and of confronting the dead, the narrator comments, 'Ich muß
nämlich eigenhändig meinen Körper aufsammeln, alle die Einzelteile, die
oft verstreut herumliegen' (68). (For I have to gather up my body single
handed, all the individual parts that often lie scattered around.) This image
of dismemberment conveys the narrator's perception of herself as disjointed,
or divided: 'Vom Hals an war sie ein aufgegebener und weggeschlossener
Körper. Der Kopf war etwas anderes . . . Oben tat er weh' (17). (From
the neck down she was an abandoned and imprisoned body. The head
was a different matter . . . It hurt.) Her inability to experience herself as a
whole woman is starkly manifested in her representation of herself through
the differently named narrative personae 'Ich' (I) and 'Die Person' (the
person). Just as the narrator in 'Übergang' feels that her shattered jaw is
the true representation of her subjectivity, that is, not whole or unified,[2]
in *Das Judasschaf* the narrator at one point exclaims 'Und sicher hülfe es
dem Schädel, gespalten, und dem Herzen, durchbohrt zu sein. Sicher wäre
es auch mir damit viel leichter möglich, wie die meisten anderen einfach
hinzuleben und fraglos kräftig dazusein' (37). (It would certainly help the
skull to be split and the heart to be bored through. It would also certainly
make it easier for me just simply to live like most other people and to exist
strongly and unquestioningly.)

The woman perceives her existence in relation to pain and illness:

Es war im Leben dieser Person immer ein und dasselbe gewesen, mehr als vierzig
Jahre lang bisher. Eine flache Süße wie von Süßstoff auf der Zunge . . . und
eine solche Bitternis im Herzen und darunter, daß das Blut und die anderen
durchziehenden Stoffe nie ausreichten, um sie abzutransportieren. Die flache Süße
war das Amlebensein, die Bitternis war alles andere, vor allem aber die Art der
Atemlosigkeit, die entsteht, wenn die Kranken, Halbkranken, Sterbenden und
Toten die Luft einzunehmen gezwungen sind . . . (33)

(The life of this person had always been the same, for more than forty years so
far. A shallow sweetness like sweetener on the tongue . . . and such bitterness in
her heart and below it that the blood and the other passing substances were never
sufficient to remove it. The shallow sweetness was being alive, the bitterness was
everything else, but especially the type of breathlessness that results when the ill,
half-ill, dying and dead are forced to take in air.)

Overall her despair is such that she identifies with those already dead, clearly distancing herself from other mortals, whom she feels unable to understand: 'Obwohl ich noch einmal im Monat blute, sind alle sonstigen Arrangements der Lebenden für mich aufgehoben. Wenn sie mir nur helfen könnten, diese Diesseitigen. Mich einmal ansprächen, aber so, daß ich es auch hörte und verstünde' (74–5). (Although I still bleed once a month, all other arrangements of the living have been done away with for me. If only they could help me, those of this world; could speak to me once, but in such a way that I could hear and understand.)

The cause of the narrator's personal suffering is made clear. It is related to the overwhelming knowledge and constant awareness of the violence and cruelty which underlie society. More specifically her anguish is caused by the atrocities of the Holocaust, but violence is by no means a German prerogative. When she is in Venice, St Mark's square becomes for her the square in Jacopo Tintoretto's painting, *Transfer of the Body of St Mark*, which depicts the dead body of St Mark, from which people are fleeing, 'irre, entleibt vor Angst und Panik' (25) (mad, dying of fear and panic). It is not from the raging storm that they are running, but from death itself, for 'der Tod muß so schnell wie möglich unsichtbar werden' (26) (death must be made invisible as quickly as possible) in order that society's veneer is sustained. But for the narrator death is not invisible, it is a constant debilitating awareness. Hers is the problem of how to live with the legacy of the atrocities, for whereas she sees others able to live normal lives, she, as a German woman, experiences memory as a perpetual torment. 'Schlimm waren nur die angehäuften Erinnerungen, die sich nie zersetzten und die ich Tag und Nacht allesamt aushalten mußte' (48). (Only the piled-up memories were bad; they never corroded and I had to endure them day and night.) And later she says 'Ihre Erinnerungen sind unheilbar krank. Wie immer schon' (67). (Her memories are incurably ill. As always.) The narrator is not referring to personal memories, but to a cultural memory, which encompasses awareness of Germany's past.

With strong parallels to the short stories, the narrator relates her torment to her strong identity as a woman, which she is concerned to emphasize: 'Ich bin eine Frau, ein Mädchen, ein weibliches Kind' (59). (I am a woman, a girl, a female child.) Her femininity is central to her suffering, and she asks herself the question 'Seit wann hatte ich mich bloß so verändert? Vielleicht waren es auch nur die Auswirkungen eines zu langen weiblichen Lebens' (54). (Since when had I changed so much? Perhaps it was just the effects of a female life that had gone on for too long.) Male and female economies do not overlap, and the narrator indicates her disillusionment with

constructive communication between the sexes in a reference to Carpaccio's *Birth of Mary*: 'Hingegen möchte ich . . . mein Leben noch einmal leben in einem der Bilder, die unverdrossen die Ruhe bewahren und in denen die Geschlechter gar nicht erst auf die Idee kommen, gemeinsame Sache zu machen oder Zusammengehörigkeit vorzugeben' (49). (However, I would like . . . to live my life again in one of the pictures that are unashamedly peaceful and in which it does not even occur to the sexes to act together or as though they belonged together.)

This clear setting-up of a male–female polarity in the text does not, however, rest upon the demonization of the individual male, or the ascribing of stereotypical traits to particular figures, as is so often the case in Bachmann's œuvre. On the contrary, in this book the narrator's unnamed male lovers are sympathetically represented; they seem to understand her suffering and to help her cope with it. So she writes of the support of her lover that 'das war ein unfaßbares Entgegenkommen gewesen, ein Liebesbeweis, der ihr gar nicht zustehen konnte' (115) (it had been an unbelievable kindness, a proof of love that she could not have deserved), and she says of a colleague, Eberhard, 'Daß er sie sofort verstand, war merkwürdig' (111). (It was strange that he understood her immediately.) Nevertheless, modes of perception are clearly depicted as gendered. Thus to ignore violence and atrocities, to repress the knowledge of death with which the narrator is confronted, is firmly defined by her as masculine: 'Männlichere Lebensaussichten konnte sie bei sich nicht anwenden. Denn es fehlte ihnen, was sie erst noch durch Zusammenstoß mit sich selbst und Versteinerung beseitigen mußte: Gedächtnis' (45). (She could not adopt a more masculine outlook on life for herself. Because it lacked that which she first had to eliminate through confrontation with herself and through petrification: memory.)

ARTICULATING SUFFERING

Das Judasschaf not only depicts the narrator's suffering, but thematizes the problem of articulating the knowledge which causes it, 'ihr nicht zu teilendes Wissen, auf das sie ununterbrochen zustürzte' (45) (her knowledge that could not be shared, that she was constantly rushing towards). Suzanne Greuner writes that 'Die Person [bewegt] sich selbst im ganzen Text immer wieder zwischen zwei "Zuständen" dieses Wissens, dem Schrei und dem Schweigen.'[3] (In the whole text the person repeatedly moves between the two 'conditions' of this knowledge, between the scream and silence.) The scream is repeatedly encountered in the book in different contexts as one possibility for expressing profound horror or despair, and is often coupled

with the alternative of silence: 'Entweder war sie ganz still und hörte nur das Rumoren und pausenlose Flügelschlagen dieses Ausrottungsvogels in ihr . . . Oder sie sagte selber Sätze . . . aber keinen einzigen ohne zu schreien' (52–3). (Either she was quite still and only heard the noise and endless beating of wings of this bird of destruction within her . . . Or she herself uttered sentences, . . . but not a single one without screaming.) The scream certainly precludes the possibility of spoken articulation: 'ihr fiel nichts ein außer wiederholtem Schreien ohne Worte' (46) (nothing occurred to her except repeated screaming without words), and is equated with the state of consciousness: the narrator describes the way animals are usually slaughtered not during the few seconds of unconsciousness, but when 'das Bewußtsein zurückkehrt mit einem Schrei' (55) (consciousness returns with a scream). That this description is transferable to the narrator's consciousness is apparent from chapter 3, which is entitled '*New York, mit einem Schrei*' (*New York, with a scream*), a chapter in which the narrator seems to yearn for death, since this is a state in which she can exist 'ohne Schrei und überhaupt lautlos' (62) (without screaming and generally in silence).

There are alternatives to the scream, however, the most important of which is stillness or quiet. It is not a silence based on repression or denial of knowledge and memory, but one in which memory is incorporated into the quiet. The narrator is able to enter into stillness through her contemplation of five Renaissance paintings. There are detailed descriptions of these paintings in the text as the narrator stands beholding them, her poetic prose conveying the images as though they are enacted before her. One of the paintings is by Jacopo Tintoretto (1518–94), the other four by Vittore Carpaccio (1455/65–1525/26). Four of the paintings depict Christian martyrs, individuals who have suffered torture as a direct result of their profound beliefs: St Mark, St Peter, St Jerome, Job and Christ. One depicts the birth of the Virgin Mary. From the narrator's point of view, these paintings are images of tranquillity, yet at the same time they do not deny suffering or death. Violence and pain have been frozen into images of calm, but have not been repressed. The images thus enable the narrator to detach herself from her immediate and personally debilitating perception of violence and suffering, while nevertheless being able to confront the reality of their presence. And by unfolding the theme of suffering, and of female suffering, through the motif of male painters painting male martyrs, the narrator faces both the structures of thought that have oppressed women, and that which has been repressed.[4]

The paintings are more than images. They are spaces which the narrator enters, places in which she gains a clarity of vision and understanding

which otherwise eludes her. She says of Carpaccio's *Preparation for Christ's Entombment*, 'Jetzt noch einmal, mitten in Deutschland . . . ließ das Bild mit dem liegenden Toten mich . . . ein . . . Vor innerer Schwärze konnte ich wirklich nichts mehr sehen, dafür sah ich in das Bild hinein wie in einen aufgeschlagenen Weltatlas, in dem man den Ozeanen bis auf den Grund schauen kann' (54). (Now again, in the middle of Germany . . . the picture with the dead man stretched out let me enter . . . I could really no longer see anything because of the inner blackness, but I could gaze into the picture as though into an open atlas in which one can see to the ocean floor.) Similarly, Carpaccio's *Meditation on Christ's Passion* 'läßt . . . mich ein' (95) (lets . . . me in), which has a profound effect: 'Ich bin mittlerweile in diese tiefe Stille so weit schon eingedrungen, daß ich mir nicht vorstellen kann, den Mund je wieder aufzumachen' (100). (In the meantime I have penetrated so far into this profound silence, that I cannot imagine ever opening my mouth again.)

It is in the *Meditation* that the narrator sees articulated the moment of interaction of knowledge and suffering, of silence and the scream. On either side of the dead Christ, St Jerome and Job, 'Wisser und Dulder' (100) (knowing and patient), sit 'an der Schwelle zwischen schrecklich Vergangenem und Nichts' (95) (on the threshold between terrible past and nothingness). They figure as 'Altgewordene Beweise . . . daß nahezu alle Erkenntnis sich noch lebend aushalten läßt' (95). (Proof grown old . . . that nearly all knowledge can be endured while yet still living.) Yet the point of this, the 'wozu?' (to what purpose?) remains unanswered, is directed by Job's pointing finger to the viewer herself. Important for the narrator, however, is not the lack of explanation, but the portrayal of a state of existence which is her own. 'Es herrscht uferloses Schweigen. Unvermittelbar und nicht mehr zu veräußern das Erfahrene, die Erkenntnis; das Wissen versiegelt in Körper, die es aushalten müssen, solange man sie leben läßt' (100). (Boundless silence reigns. Experience and insight are uncommunicable and can no longer be articulated. Knowledge is sealed away in bodies which must endure it as long as they are allowed to live.) The silence is a frozen scream, and on the crumbling throne are written the words 'MIT EINEM SCHREI' (101) (WITH A SCREAM). The painting also reflects the split identity that is her own; any assertion of identity in a simple 'I' is impossible with the awareness she carries, and this impossibility is pictorially manifested in the floating subclause written on the block of stone upon which Job is sitting: 'Daß mein Erlöser lebt' (103) (That my Redeemer lives). The 'Ich weiß' (I know) is missing, and the narrator searches for its presence in the painting, finding it only 'flüchtig im Hintergrund' (fleetingly in the

background) or in her own memory. But subject and object cannot be reconciled, just as the narrator remains divided between first and third person: 'Blindgeworden füreinander steht beides da oder geht aneinander vorbei. An ein Zusammentreffen ist nicht mehr zu denken' (103). (They have each become blind to the other or pass each other by. A meeting is no longer conceivable.)

The paintings dominate *Das Judasschaf*, both in terms of the detailed descriptions and commentary on them, and their effect on the narrator. However, they do not provide the only possibility for articulation of 'diese[m] kurze[n] Moment zwischen Leben und Totsein, Dasein und Beseitigtwerden' (104) (this short instant between life and death, existence and extinction). Music can also offer a momentary space within which the unspoken knowledge can be expressed. The presence of music is particularly evident in the first chapter, which is entitled '*E guerra e morte*', words taken from Claudio Monteverdi's *Combattimento di Tancredi e Clorinda*. The narrator has the final scene of the *Combattimento* before her eyes as she walks through Venice, a scene in which Tancredi's hatred and violence ends in the murder of Clorinda. But in his recognition of whom he has killed his victory is turned to anguish, a despair which he is condemned to live with: '*Ahi vista!* rief er, schrie er in seine eigene Bewegungs- und Sprachlosigkeit hinein, gegen sich selber an, gegen die Monotonie seiner langen und ewig andauernden besinnungslosen Unrast und Lebendigkeit' (30). (*Ahi vista!* he called, he screamed into his own inability to move or speak, he screamed at himself and at the monotony of his long and never-ending unconscious restlessness and liveliness.)

In her sensitive and detailed study of the role of music in Duden's work, Greuner shows how such interruptions into the narrative by quotations from both Monteverdi's *Combattimento* and *Pianto della Madonna* create gaps through which other layers of perception and expression can be glimpsed:

Der Weg der Person . . . führt hinein und hindurch durch Bildräume und Räume, die die Musik öffnet. Er läßt die Person hören, was nicht zu hören sein soll, sehen, was lange schon und immer von neuem ins Unsichtbare abgedrängt wird. Der Text schreibt dieses Sehen und Hören, indem er sich wie die Person ununterscheidbar an mehreren Orten zugleich aufhält, indem er diese vielen im Überall und Nirgends zusammenfließenden 'Stimmen' aufnimmt und beinahe gleichzeitig zur Sprache kommen läßt.[5]

(The person's path . . . leads in and through images and spaces opened up by music. This path enables the person to hear what should not be heard, to see what has always been forced out of view and is repeatedly forced out of view again. The text

writes this seeing and hearing by being in many places at once without distinction, just like the person herself. It does this by taking up the many 'voices' which are everywhere and nowhere, and almost letting them speak concurrently.)

Paintings and music fulfil similar functions for the narrator in that they both address violence, suffering, and their articulation. There are, though, a few brief occasions when the woman seems able to escape pain and experiences a pleasure which is fleeting, transitory and rooted in colour. Thus she recalls lying in hospital when she was younger, incapacitated with pain, when suddenly for a moment she was 'schmerzfrei' (without pain): 'Es war dieses kräftige Blau im Neonlicht, das für die Dauer des Moments selbständig und ganz und gar unangefochten neben ihr herlief. Eine Schönheit' (11). (It was this strong blue in the neon light that accompanied her independently and totally unchallenged for the length of the moment. A thing of beauty.) She buys a pullover because of its indigo blue colour: 'Plötzlich war eine Tiefendimension da in dieser Hitze . . . auf die man zugehen konnte, ohne gleich wieder mißmutig beim nächsten Morgen anzukommen' (59). (Suddenly there was a dimension of depth in this heat . . . which one could approach without immediately reaching the next morning all morose.) So although mentioned only in passing, colour adds an important dimension to the woman's ability to live with suffering. Following ten sides of description and contemplation of the *Meditation*, the narrator returns to the colours of the painting, for they carry the undefinable knowledge it expresses: 'Denn diese Art von Wissen verliert sich stets aufs neue. Nur in den Farben scheint es immerwährend auf . . . als nachglühende, weit entfernte Erinnerung, wie in einem Traum' (104). (For this type of knowledge is always lost again. It only shines forth perpetually in colours . . . It shines as an afterglow, a distant memory, as in a dream.)

OTHER SUBJECTIVITY

Painting, music, colour, the opening of spaces in which the narrator can confront and attempt to find expression for her suffering all place *Das Judasschaf* at the centre of feminist debates. The female subject appears as marginalized within the patriarchal symbolic, seeking to articulate her devastated and divided identity in ways that transcend the male *logos* and which are grounded in her bodily perceptions. The book has led to perceptive and interesting readings which accept the narrator's recourse to music and her 'entry' into the paintings as expressions of a female subjectivity. Such interpretations are all the more convincing in view of the book's

culmination and ending: the narrator's final entry into the *Entombment*. Quite unlike the narrator's 'murder' in *Malina* and her disappearance into the crack in the wall, in *Das Judasschaf* the entry is presented as a positive move, enabling a certain assertion of non-suffering subjectivity: 'Sie kann sich immer wieder nur dem Ausgestreckten zugesellen. Alles andere führt zu nichts, ist mühselig und immer das gleiche' (136). (She can only join the laid-out man again and again. Everything else leads nowhere, is arduous and always the same.) The narrator refers to 'sich selbst erkennen' (knowing oneself) and that 'die Welt ist vollständig hier' (129) (here the world is complete).

As Margaret Littler writes:

The woman's insistent gaze on the repressed history of Germany . . . motivates her recourse to art, where there is the possibility of non-linguistic articulation of the horror of the Holocaust. The mute horror is present throughout in the metaphor of the 'Schrei'. The paintings in *Das Judasschaf* do not offer a flight from reality, nor any hope of religious 'redemption', but the possibility of confronting 'forgotten' knowledge and of articulating protest at the senseless human suffering of our own time.[6]

Littler goes on to draw a distinction between the narrator's contemplation of the paintings and a 'masculine, modernist, contemplative gaze', arguing that 'There is no question of aesthetic edification through the detached contemplation of suffering in a world in which the subject/object distinction is radically redefined, and the distance between individually experienced and aesthetically represented suffering suspended.'[7] Littler thus implicitly accepts the male–female polarity set up by the narrator and views the temporary escape from suffering offered by contemplation as unproblematic:

The complete (and desirable) suspension of the subject/object boundary in contemplation of the painting is in keeping with a construction of subjectivity based on repression, and has clear resonances with post-Lacanian feminist theories of identity-acquisition. Equally, the recourse to painting or music as alternative signifying systems within the dominant symbolic order has become a recognizable strategy for women writers seeking to challenge the constraints of patriarchal discourse.[8]

Similarly Greuner identifies the 'Nicht-Ort' (non-place), to which access is gained through music, with the body of woman: 'Die Utopie der Musik . . . schließt in den Texten auch den Zugang zu all dem auf, was keinen Ort hat . . . Die Ungeheuer, Monstren, Drachen, Schlangen – "Verkörperungen", Zeichen, Chiffren auch für das, was seit je als das Andere bekämpft, besiegt und beseitigt worden ist, "wohnen" an diesen Unorten.

Sie bewohnen auch den Körper und allemal den der Frau.'⁹ (The utopia of music . . . also opens the way in the texts to everything that has no place . . . The ogres, monsters, dragons, serpents are 'embodiments', signs and symbols for that which has always been fought against, conquered and eradicated as Other. They 'live' in these 'non-places'. They also inhabit the body, especially the woman's body.) Sigrid Weigel also emphasizes the position of woman as marginalized in western culture, in terms which would apply equally to Duden's short stories. She too makes the distinction between the individual woman and a feminine economy: 'Nun wird dieses Gedächtnis von Anne Duden nicht als ein "weibliches Gedächtnis" dargestellt, wohl aber mit dem "Weiblichen" in Verbindung gebracht, weil der Ort des Weiblichen in der westlichen Kulturgeschichte mit dem Vergessenen, dem Verdrängten und dem Ausgeschlossenen im Zusammenhang steht.'¹⁰ (This memory in Anne Duden is not depicted as a 'female memory'; it is, however, bound up with the 'female', since in the history of western culture the 'female' is connected to what has been forgotten, repressed and excluded.) The paintings are so crucial to the narrator for they confront her with the structures that have oppressed woman, and with that which cannot be articulated: 'Es sind die Gemälde, in denen die Person die Gedächtnisstrukturen, denen sie selbst unterworfen ist, wiedererkennt und in denen sie auf eine Darstellbarkeit für ihr eigenes unartikulierbares Wissen stösst.'¹¹ (It is in the paintings that the person recognizes the structures of memory that she herself is subjected to and in the paintings that she encounters a way of representing her own unarticulable knowledge.)

These interpretations of *Das Judasschaf* are illuminating and offer an excellent understanding of a difficult book. However, Duden's emphasis on the female has provoked irritation in some quarters. Johanna Bossinade comments that 'The use of the female to represent "general" experience of suffering . . . has often been criticized . . . In principle I feel this criticism is justified, but doubt whether it is based on adequate analytical consideration of the text.'¹² This remark is unhelpful in two ways. First it seems odd to agree to something in principle that is based on inadequate consideration of Duden's work, in contrast to the three thorough analyses referred to above. But more important is Bossinade's passive agreement with the proposition that the female's suffering is general, and that the protagonist is merely a figure 'used' to represent this. On the contrary, I wish to argue that the complexity of *Das Judasschaf* resides in its insistence on the historical specificity of female identity and the suffering it involves.

This specificity is established through the narrator's emphasis on her Germanness and on recent German history. Whereas she feels that the

awareness of atrocities is usually repressed, it is made immediate and shocking in this book by the inclusion of historical documents testifying to the
cruelty and horror of the genocide. The documents include a quotation
from Kitty Hart, from the commander of Auschwitz and from Himmler,
and reports from Dachau concerning the use of victims' hair and the results
of experiments on humans. Just as the effect of these documents has not
diminished by being historical, so too the effect of Germany's past on the
narrator is not alleviated by virtue of their 'history'. With her stark assertion of nationality, 'Ich bin aus Deutschland' (59) (I am from Germany),
she recognizes that her identity is inseparably linked to the violent and
oppressive German past. German identity is here not equatable with political allegiance, which can be rationally argued over and changed when
appropriate. It is not acquired in response to political or economic circumstance, nor does it satisfy a prior need to belong. So although she asserts
at one point 'Ich wußte auf einmal, wohin ich gehörte. Obwohl mir das
veraltet und sentimental vorkam . . . Ich gehörte hierher, nach Berlin' (41).
(I suddenly knew where I belonged, even though it seemed to me to be out
of date and sentimental . . . I belonged here, in Berlin), Germany is a sti-
fling place: '[Es ging darum], daß sich Deutschland über einem ausatmete.
Unaufhörlich seit vielen Jahren. Auch über der Person. Und darum, daß
diese vollkommen verbrauchte Luft natürlich nichts mehr hielt' (47). (The
point was that Germany exhaled over people; it had done so, without pause,
for many years. And over the person. And of course that this completely
stale air no longer contained anything.)

The Nazi atrocities are central to the narrator's self-definition, and she
even measures out her life in relation to the Wannsee Conference – the conference of January 1942 which can be seen as the beginning of the planned
mass extermination: 'Neunzehn Tage nach ihrer Geburt war im selben
Wohnort während einer Konferenz der Beschluß gefaßt worden, elf
Millionen Menschen zu beseitigen' (43). (Nineteen days after her birth,
during a conference in the same place that she lived, the decision was
taken to exterminate eleven million people.) And then she goes on to say,
'Damit konnte man leben' (43). (You can live with that.) Yet she cannot live
with that: 'Der oberste Teil ihres Kopfes hatte aber merkwürdige Verhal-
tensweisen herausgebildet. Er konnte nicht zur Ruhe kommen, er pulsierte
gegenläufig bei allem, was die Person tat' (43). (The highest part of her
head had developed strange patterns of behaviour. It could not find rest, it
pulsated in the opposite direction to everything the person did.) Despite
the fact that she observes the success with which others repress the past,
she is unable to concur with the general forgetfulness.

I suggested earlier that the narrator's anguish centres upon the Holocaust, yet that her memory of atrocities is a cultural and not personal one, a memory which extends to the omnipresent threat of violence, terror and death. This notion of a cultural memory complements the feminist responses to the text that associate the narrator's memory with 'the female'. If, however, such awareness is presented as cultural and identified with an abstract idea of the feminine, if indeed the narrator finds her subjectivity best reflected in Renaissance Italian art and Italian music, then it seems fair to ask how far the novel actually addresses a specifically German concern. The narrator seems rather to be using the Holocaust as a symbol and symptom of the underside of western culture more generally and not responding to it as peculiar to German history.

Without denying that she does in part treat the Holocaust in this way, any attempt to conclude that this necessarily leads to a corresponding lessening of a concern with Germany would be too simple. The dual status of the Holocaust for the narrator, as an event that belongs to German history and that reflects on the thin veneer of western civilization, does not detract from the historically specific reference of the text. On the contrary, it gives literary expression to the conflicting responses to the Holocaust amongst historians, which in West German historiography culminated in the so-called *Historikerstreit* of the late 1980s. Mary Fulbrook traces the developments in the historiography of the Federal Republic in her chapter, which, with marked similarity to the concerns of 'Übergang' and *Das Judasschaf*, is called 'The Past Which Refuses to Become History'.[13] She analyzes the way in which, in the 1950s, historians' approaches generally reflected the prevailing conservative atmosphere of the Adenauer period by explaining Nazism as a European, totalitarian phenomenon, under which the normal Germans were repressed by a small group of heinous Nazis. 'This view both served to condemn Nazism and Hitler as evil, while at the same time asserting that Nazism neither arose from long-term trends in German history, nor had any intrinsic relationship with the German people, who appear simply to have bumped into it and been blown off their proper course.'[14] In the 1960s the impact of societal history resulted in a marked change of focus, with the causes of Nazism being sought in the specific developments of German society, politics and culture. Increasingly during the 1970s and 1980s a range of responses to the Nazi past became the norm and debates surrounding the causes of genocide advanced in complexity. However, crucially, the terms in which the debates were conducted were intensely political and impassioned: 'Responses to challenges were frequently highly emotional and vitriolic: the issue of whether an

interpretation was "left-wing" or "right-wing" appeared almost as (if not equally) important as any evaluation of fresh empirical evidence. There was an extraordinary emotional charge and contemporary political relevance to nearly all discussions.'[15]

This emotional intensity reached a climax in the historians' controversy of 1986–7, a very public debate between German historians that gave a high profile to the issue of the uniqueness or the comparability of the Third Reich, and whether the Final Solution could be compared with other atrocities in the history of Europe. Conservative historians argued for a 'normalization' of the German past and attempted to relativize German atrocity by seeing it as one of a number of crises marking modernity, for example the Gulag Archipelago, a view which solicited vehement and angry responses from the left. In many ways the historians' arguments are incidental for the purposes of this analysis.[16] What is vital is the fact that 'underlying all the debates, the specific arguments over points of detail, was the much wider issue: was it actually possible to treat the Third Reich "normally", like any other period of history?'[17] A crucial feature of the debate is precisely the emotional intensity and tension in which it is mired, which betray the importance and difficulty of the Final Solution as an event in relation to which German identity is negotiated. *Das Judasschaf* does not address a specifically German concern by reproducing the terms of the historians' debate. What it does is to give fictional representation to the centrality of the Final Solution for German identity, and the acute emotional response and anxiety it elicits. And it does so in the form of the narrator's emotional and undifferentiated response to it in the text.[18]

There is another way too in which the narrator's concern with the Holocaust and the way in which it permeates her consciousness is itself an important manifestation of post-war national identity. Connected to the Nazi period by nothing but her date of birth, the narrator is nevertheless afflicted by the burden of German history. The burden is unspecific and nebulous, for it does not originate in personal responsibility or involvement with the crimes that were perpetrated. But again, rather than detracting from specificity, the narrator's trauma, rooted in a past which remains unspoken and silenced, is historically specific. As Dan Bar-On makes clear in his work on the generational transmissibility of trauma, the children of both victims and perpetrators suffer guilt, fear and anger as a result of their parents' silence and the subsequent transformation of actual fact into 'putative' facts. Bar-On argues that these 'putative' facts cannot be discussed and that they remain untestable. As a result, their impact on behaviour and understanding may in the long term be stronger than the effect of actual facts that

can be talked about.[19] Bar-On is working within an individual, clinical context, but his work confirms the real traumatic effect of repressed events on individuals who have no 'objective' reason to be traumatized. The narrator is the daughter of the 'perpetrator' generation and her Germanness is a traumatic burden which she cannot escape. It is part of her, has always been with her, and the difficulty she has in defining it is indicative of the repression involved in the post-war 'normalization'. Thus she speaks of the 'etwas konstant Undurchlässiges . . . hinter welches nicht zu kommen war' (108) (something constant in its impermeability . . . that was impossible to get behind), which surrounds her and prevents her approach to what she sees as a beautiful world. The precise nature of it eludes her, it takes on different forms, and momentary comprehension of this impervious barrier is always quickly forgotten. But what is important is her association of it with Germany:

Es war auch von Anfang an dagewesen . . . Bisweilen nahm es auch mehrere unterschiedliche, immer jedoch äußerst vage Gestalten an. Einmal hätte es ein Gesenke sein können . . . oder auch ein offener Schlund mit dem unerschaubaren Engel des Abgrunds in der Tiefe; meistens aber schien es nur ein blendend helles Feld, eine Gefahrenzone, die nichts preisgab. Vielleicht war es Deutschland. (108–9)

(It had been there from the start . . . Now and then it took on various different, but always extremely vague, forms. Once it might have been a blind shaft . . . or even an open gullet, with the Angel of the Abyss in its depths, too terrible to behold. But mostly it seemed like a dazzling light field, a danger zone that revealed nothing. Perhaps it was Germany.)

Hitherto I have attempted to show that while suffering is bound up with female subjectivity in *Das Judasschaf*, it is also depicted as historically specific. This is a text which responds to a public discourse surrounding the legacy of the genocide while also pointing to the centrality of the symbolic and private legacy that still persists. But I wish to pursue the question of specificity further; it is crucial to interrogate exactly how in this book the female subject is constituted in relation to suffering and to history. The terms 'woman' or 'femininity' are not in themselves an adequate explanation or justification for suffering. It is necessary not to be drawn into the narrator's suffering. It is on this point that the interpretations of Littler, Weigel and Greuner can be seen as not going far enough, for they each approach the narrator too sympathetically, and accept her perspective on her own suffering too uncritically. There are issues which these critics do not address, but which need to be considered before an assessment of the narrator's female identity as 'Other' can be made.

The first of these is the textual fascination with violence. The knowledge of the Holocaust and of the threat of violence and death lying just below the surface of the 'everyday' at one level 'explains' the extraordinary levels of suffering and the concentration on the body. Yet there is an almost indulgent level of gruesome physicality in the text, a fascination with the very violence which causes such suffering, which does not fit easily with the narrator's position as victim. The second issue is the problem of the narrator's unreflected identification with victim figures; both the victims of the Holocaust and Christian martyrs. She presents herself as a victim of violence and terror, views herself as a survivor, while never having experienced what they did. The narrator's identification with victims, coupled with her concurrent fascination with violence, causes an unsettling tension in the text, and it is this which I shall now explore.

TRANSGRESSIVE DESIRE

The 'extraneous' material in the book, the paintings and the historical documents, signal the unexpected relationship between the suffering of victims and a fascination with violence. The images and the documents seem to illustrate opposites. On the one hand four of the paintings depict martyrs who have been victims of violence as a direct result of their profound beliefs. There is also a description of St Sebastian in the text, even though there is no visual reproduction to accompany it. On the other hand there is the material relating to the Holocaust, which, with the exception of the quoted sentence from Kitty Hart, are all from the perspective of the perpetrators. Victims and oppressors are juxtaposed in the text as opposites within a violent world; they are linked as the active and passive constituents of the dominant order. But through the manner of their presentation in *Das Judasschaf* such a link becomes both stronger and more problematic. For in terms of 'style', the representations of oppressor and victim are remarkably similar. They both convey a certain matter-of-factness, a calm despite the horrors they depict or which lie behind them. (Although the fifth of the paintings is of the birth of Mary and so is not part of the victim/oppressor theme in the text, it nevertheless transforms the agony and bloodiness of childbirth into a moment of stillness.) This similarity is most marked at the beginning of chapter 2, '*Panorama Berlin*'. Here, a document concerning the 'Verwertung der abgeschnittenen Haare' (uses for cut-off hair) of concentration camp inmates, including details as to the required length of hair to make its further use worthwhile, is almost immediately followed by an extract from the

Legenda aurea about St Peter, and then a description of Carpaccio's painting of him.

SS-Brigadeführer Glück could be reporting on the different sorts of bottles which can or cannot be recycled and sorted into the appropriate coloured glass: '*das Haar der männlichen Häftlinge (wird) erst dann abgeschnitten, wenn dieses nach dem Schnitt eine Länge von 20 mm besitzt . . . Die Mengen der monatlich gesammelten Haare, getrennt nach Frauen- und Männerhaaren, sind jeweils zum 5. eines jeden Monats . . . nach hier zu melden*' (34). (*The hair of male inmates is only cut when it has reached a length of 20 mm . . . The quantity of hair collected monthly, divided into women's and men's hair, must be reported on the 5th of each month.*) Soon afterwards the narrator introduces the painting of St Peter: 'Es ist ein Bild der abgebrühten Stille' (35). (It is a picture of hardened silence.) Here too is an image of violence presented as though nothing is going on: 'Das Krummschwert, das ihm seitlich in den hinteren Schädelteil gekeilt worden ist, steckt noch an derselben Stelle – wie nach getaner Arbeit die Axt im Baumstumpf. Es scheint ihm nichts weiter auszumachen, mit gespaltenem Schädel herumzulaufen' (35–6). (The scimitar that has been wedged sideways into the back of his skull is still lodged in the same place – like an axe in a tree stump at the end of the day's work. It does not seem to bother him, to walk around with a split skull.) The narrator's description of St Peter, while depicting him as 'der Überlebende' (the survivor), concurrently acts as a commentary on the tone of Glück's letter as routine, as 'one of those things': 'Es ist wieder Alltag geworden' (it has become routine again), 'Daß ein Dolch in seiner Herzgegend steckengeblieben ist, macht ihm nichts aus . . . Na und. Das bringen die Kriege so mit sich, alle Arten von Kriegen' (36). (It does not bother him that a dagger has become lodged in the region of his heart . . . So what? That's what happens in war, in all types of war.)

St Peter and Glück are undoubtedly subject to different moral evaluations here. There is no suggestion that the similarity of the distanced tone, of the 'normality' of violence rather than an emphasis on its horror, should somehow lessen the crime and evil of Glück's position. However, despite the opposite moral evaluation attached to St Peter as survivor and Glück as oppressor, a link is established through the tone of representation common to both historical text and paintings. The link is not one which dissolves the force of the moral judgement the narrator is making, but which suggests that they have something which connects them beyond the scope of moral authority; the link points towards the incursion of desire and fantasy into the conscious realm of which morality is part. It is with reference to Lacan's complex concept of desire and transgression that this link can be explored.

As was discussed in the previous chapter, the concept of desire is crucial to Lacan's understanding of subjectivity. Every subject is a desiring subject, unable to fulfil its desire; but through fantasy, the illusion of wholeness and fulfilment is achieved. The relationship of fantasy and desire is, however, by no means always for the 'good' of the subject in any moral sense, since one pole of desire is *jouissance*, a desire which may disgust or horrify, but which is most exciting to the subject. *Jouissance* is not regulated by any moral injunction and as such can be seen as transgressive desire. It is such desire which can be located in Duden's text. In Seminar VII, *The Ethics of Psychoanalysis*, Lacan describes two forms of transgressive desire in relation to Kant's example in the *Kritik der reinen Vernunft*. Here, a man can enter a room where the woman he lusts after is and can satisfy his desire or need, but next to the door is the gallows on which he will be hanged if he does so. 'As far as Kant is concerned, it goes without saying that the gallows will be a sufficient deterrent; there's no question of an individual going to screw a woman when he knows he's to be hanged on the way out.'[20] Lacan's point, however, is that Kant has missed something in assuming the man will resist temptation. He argues, 'It is not impossible for a man to sleep with a woman knowing full well that he is to be bumped off on his way out, by the gallows or anything else . . . it is not impossible that this man coolly accepts such an eventuality on his leaving – for the pleasure of cutting up the lady concerned in small pieces, for example.' He then goes on to say, 'I have outlined then two cases that Kant doesn't envisage, two forms of transgression . . . namely, excessive object sublimation and what is commonly known as perversion.'[21] In Lacan's example, perversion manifests itself as the murder of the woman. In contrast, object sublimation, the overevaluation of the object, conventionally the sublimation of the feminine object, means that the woman's value to the man exceeds that which he attributes to his own life.

To return to *Das Judasschaf* and the juxtaposition of St Peter and Glück, it is possible to see in each of them the signs of transgression. I would suggest that in St Peter we have a figure whose sublimation of the Christ figure has, so to speak, led to the gallows. His desire for Christ surpasses the value he puts on his own life. In the words quoted from the *Legenda aurea*: '*Er begehrte auch den Tod für ihn zu leiden*' (35). (*He desired to suffer for him even unto death*.) And whereas Lacan's pervert cuts up the woman, Glück is concerned with the cutting up of victims' hair; a bureaucrat doing his duty, to be sure, but if, as Kafka asserts, bureaucracy is closer to 'the origins of human nature . . . than any social institution',[22] then Glück represents the point 'at which desire itself becomes Law'.[23]

However, what makes this whole issue of transgressive desire particularly acute is that the narrator is herself implicated; not only does she bring object sublimation and perversion together in the form of 'extraneous' material, but she herself is caught up in these desires. The narrator portrays herself as suffering, and there is certainly no reason to be sceptical of this. But there is a dimension to this suffering which is enjoyment, *jouissance*; it is not pleasurable, but causes excitement even though it is consciously perceived as horrific and repulsive. The text's constant emphasis on dismembered bodies and on physical cruelty reveals not just horror, but an almost perverse fascination, a certain indulgence, which I also identified in many of Duden's short stories, not least in the descriptions of the wired-up jaw in 'Übergang'. The violent tone is already established on the first page of *Das Judasschaf* when the narrator is dreaming (or daydreaming) on the aeroplane to Venice: 'Drei Männer . . . sind sehr beschäftigt. Sie zersägen und zerlegen den toten Körper eines Schwarzen. Nein, nein, er war schon tot. Accidental death. Sie spalten und zerhacken ihn, bereiten die einzelnen Teile zu. Saubere Schnittflächen, geglättete Knochentrennungen, wie für das Schaufenster eines Fleischerladens' (7). (Three men . . . are very busy. They are sawing and carving up the dead body of a black man. No, no, he was already dead. Accidental death. They are chopping and hacking him, preparing the individual parts. Clean cuts, smooth separation of the joints, as if for the window of a butcher's shop.) As she wanders through Venice she has scenes of public executions before her eyes: 'Sie griffen ihn, warfen ein Seil um seinen Hals und schleppten ihn durch die Stadt. Da blieb das Fleisch seines Körpers an der Erde hängen und die Straße wurde rot von seinem Blut' (22). (They grabbed him, threw a rope around his neck and dragged him through the town. The flesh of his body stayed clinging to the ground and the street became red from his blood.) Or there is the ghastly description of animal slaughter:

. . . zwei bis drei Sekunden Schädelbeschuß [sind] die Regel. Danach wird eins der Hinterläufe an eine Oberleitung gekettet. Ein Stilett schlitzt die Kehle auf. Bisweilen geschieht das noch gerade während der zwei bis drei Sekunden andauernden Betäubung, meistens aber wird das Messer erst angesetzt, wenn die Betäubung wieder nachgelassen hat und das Bewußtsein zurückkehrt mit einem Schrei. Das meiste Fleisch blutet sich zu Tode, kopfüber durch den Schlund. (55)

(. . . a two- or three-second shot to the skull is the rule. Then one of the back legs is chained to an overhead cable. A thin blade slits open the throat. Occasionally this still occurs just within the two- or three-second period of unconsciousness, but usually the blade is applied when the stunning is wearing off and consciousness returns with a scream. Most of the meat bleeds to death, upside-down through the gullet.)

These scenes of violence provoke horror and repulsion on the part of the narrator and the reader, and thus undoubtedly function as effective critical pointers to the violence of society. However, this horror is not undermined by a reading of the narrator's focus on violence as one which goes beyond conscious suffering and condemnation. While repulsed by violence, she is also fascinated by it and, crucially, is even dependent on it for assertions of her own subjectivity, a point which is discussed shortly. First, though, to return to the other form of transgressive desire, that of object sublimation. The narrator's treatment of the Carpaccio paintings exemplifies the overinvestment of an object with significance. Her need to enter the paintings and to contemplate them at length offers her a release from suffering to such a degree that death becomes an enviable state; indeed the narrator herself relates the ability to enter the pictures to forms of death. Thus her ability to enter into the *Entombment* for the first time is presented as a consequence of her experiencing a sudden sense of belonging to the air above Berlin. Far from being described as a positive place, which the reader is led to anticipate, it is conveyed in the language of nuclear holocaust: 'Ob ich als Rauch aufstieg oder als Aschenregen niederschlug, ob ich als schwarzer Schnee fiel oder als kalter Lichtnebel mich in alle verbliebenen Luftschächte setzte; ich war weder zu erjagen noch zu vertreiben' (41). (Whether I ascended as smoke or poured down as showers of ash, whether I fell as black snow or entered all remaining ventilation shafts as a cold fog of light; I could neither be hunted nor chased away.) It is then that she writes, 'Und dem ausgestreckt daliegenden Toten konnte ich mich jetzt endlich entspannt und ruhig nähern. Zuvor war ich immer nur auf ihn zugegangen und hatte kurz vor ihm doch haltgemacht und mich dann auch wieder umgedreht' (42). (And now I could finally approach the stretched-out dead man lying there calmly and relaxed. Before, I had always only gone towards him and then stopped after all just in front of him, and then turned around again.) Similarly, at the end of the book she describes her only option as being able to join the spread-out Christ: 'Alles andere führt zu nichts, ist mühselig und immer das gleiche' (136). (Everything else leads nowhere, is onerous and always the same.) It is in the pictures that she is able to live by facing death; she invests them with greater value than she attributes to her own life.

SUFFERING AS COMPLICITY

Hitherto I have argued that while the narrator holds up an apparent juxtaposition of transgressor and victim, this opposition is not as simple as it initially seems. Furthermore, she is herself caught up in realms of desire

which make her position questionable. This tension is compounded by the fact that the narrator identifies herself fully with victims. She describes herself as a survivor: 'Immer, wenn wieder ein Moment vergangen war, hatte sie ihn mitüberlebt' (12). (Whenever another moment passed, she felt she had survived it.) Kitty Hart is also quoted using the word 'survive': 'Ich könnte Ihnen . . . auf den Kopf zusagen, wer von Ihnen überleben würde. Ich habe dafür in Auschwitz einen Blick bekommen' (26). (I could tell you . . . to a man which of them would survive. I got an eye for it in Auschwitz.) St Peter, too, is described as 'der Überlebende' (35) (the survivor), and the narrator compares his actual physical injury with her own feelings of injury, thus situating herself with St Peter as a victim: 'Mein Herz ist nicht durchbohrt, aber zerschlagen. Mein Schädel nicht gespalten, aber überdehnt' (36). (My heart is not bored through, but shattered. My skull is not split, but overstretched.) At one stage the narrator assumes the identity of St Sebastian when an image of him is described as though it were her, with the 'fünfzehn oder sechzehn Pfeile[n], die von den Füßen bis zu den Schulterrundungen aufwärts kreuz und quer in ihrer Körpermasse steckten' (125) (fifteen or sixteen arrows that were stuck into her body at all angles from her feet up to her shoulders).

Thus the narrator allies herself at once with the Holocaust victims and the Christian martyrs, a combination which, as Weigel points out, might cause irritation. She argues, though, that the use of Christian iconography for representing the impossibility of full knowledge of the Holocaust is valid, since the text 'das Bilderarchiv des kulturellen Gedächtnisses . . . gegen den Strich [liest], um darin die Spuren des Verdrängten und Vergessenen aufzusuchen'[24] (reads the picture archive of the cultural memory . . . against the grain in order to search for the traces of what has long been repressed and forgotten). This point, although it may dispel general doubts about the interweaving of the Holocaust with images of Christian suffering, does not address the problem that the narrator effectively establishes equivalences between victims. For her, the suffering seems to be alike, whatever its cause, whatever the choice involved. Yet the differences are fundamental. St Peter may, according to the *Legenda aurea*, pray to be able to suffer for his Lord, but this does not apply to Kitty Hart. Nor is the narrator's mental anguish and memory equivalent to that of the Holocaust victims. So however much it may stem from very real suffering, the narrator's self-alignment remains questionable. Furthermore, coupled with a lurking fascination with violence, it must lead to a consideration of the issue of complicity.

To speak of complicity in relation to a suffering first-person narrator is not to suggest that her suffering is not genuine, nor indeed that the narrator

is actively contributing to forms of oppression in such a way that she could then herself be described as a perpetrator. Complicity is in this context tied in with personal identity and how the subject takes responsibility for her or his identity. In relation to this narrator the question of complicity involves the reader looking critically at how she uses her suffering as a means to construct a certain identity. In any event, the reader is warned against privileging the narrator's perceptions because she is suffering.

It is interesting that the narrator is not unaware of this problematic area herself, and occasionally seems to address the question of whether and how far she should assume responsibility for her suffering. Thus she says of herself, 'Ich habe zu wenig gehandelt und zu viel gefühlt' (9). (I have done too little and felt too much.) And of others who, like herself, are distanced from reality, she comments that 'tödliches Schweigen herrscht in den Eingeweiden ALLER' (38) (deadly silence reigns in the innards of EVERYONE). At one point she admits, 'Es ging mir gar nicht so schlecht. Natürlich, ich hatte auch etwas davon. Ich war ja am Leben' (48). (I didn't feel too bad. Of course I got something out of it. I was alive at least.) And at one point she almost seems to be admitting to self-inflicted suffering. Directly after a letter reporting on 'Erwärmungsversuche' (warming experiments) in Dachau, the narrator appears to have a sudden moment of insight: 'Das hatte ich mir offenbar selber angetan mit meinem Leben' (52). (I had obviously inflicted it on myself with my life.) This last sentence does suggest an awareness of her own responsibility, but it is neither further explained nor expanded upon. It is as unexpected for the reader as it is for the narrator, and invites an alternative understanding of the narrator's suffering.

In order to explore the problem of complicity it is important to return to the notion of desire, central as it is to subject formation and identity. Implicit in what has been said about the importance of the Carpaccio paintings to the narrator is the textual emphasis on the eyes as a bodily organ and on the importance of looking. 'Sie war wie immer auf ihren Blick zurückgeworfen, obwohl doch der größte Teil des lebenden menschlichen Augapfels so flüssig ist, daß er schon bei relativ leichten Verletzungen schnell abfließt' (106). (She was as usual thrown back onto her gaze, despite the fact that a large part of a living human eyeball is so liquid that it will drain away with a relatively light injury.) In *Das Judasschaf*, looking at paintings is crucial to the narrator for satisfying desire; in front of them she is able to achieve calm and temporary release from suffering. This fits in closely with the role of fantasy as a means for the subject to achieve an illusion of completeness, and leads specifically to the problematic area of a subject's imaginary and symbolic identification and the notion of the

gaze. Imaginary identification is based on the subject's misrecognition of its mirror image as representing wholeness. The subject identifies with the mirror image, deriving narcissistic gratification from identification with an image which seems to guarantee completeness. Symbolic identification involves introjection from the field of the Other; in fantasy, the subject takes objects from outside (the symbolic) 'into' itself. Symbolic identification is therefore no longer limited to the one opposition of same/different, but involves language, morality, knowledge and authority. It is what the subject would 'like to be' in order to retain or regain that primary imaginary identification. As Rose puts it, it is 'necessary for the subject to be able to retain its narcissism while shifting its "perspective"'.[25] As was outlined earlier, part of the way in which the subject deceives itself as to her or his wholeness is by clinging to the object *a*. Lacan defines the gaze as object *a*, pointing to 'the presence or insistence of desire inside those very forms which are designed to reproduce or guarantee the specular illusion itself (image, screen, spectator)'.[26]

It is with these concepts in mind that the issue of the narrator's complicity can usefully be addressed. The narrator presents herself in the form of a split between 'Ich' (I) and 'Die Person' (the person), a split which does not simply represent her conscious sense of a lack of unity. For it seems to be closely related to the difference between imaginary and symbolic identification. The narrator identifies with the pictorial images, and importantly, all the descriptions of the pictures are presented from the perspective of the 'I'; the one exception is the last description of the *Entombment* where the narrator specifically comments, 'Ich komme an und werde wegen der herrschenden Lebensgefahr jetzt nicht mehr ich sagen' (128). (I am arriving and because of the general threat to life will now no longer say I.) After this she is 'die Frau' (the woman), and no longer 'die Person' (the person) until the very last line: 'Es ist schön und ich habe Angst' (138). (It is beautiful and I am afraid.) The assertion of the 'I' in front of the paintings is suggestive of the reassuring imaginary identification of the subject with the specular image. It fulfils the desire of the subject to find a guarantor of subjectivity in a specular image, as Lacan describes it in Seminar XI: '(The painter) gives something for the eye to feed on, but he invites the person to whom this picture is presented to lay down his gaze there as one lays down one's weapons. This is the pacifying, Apollonian effect of painting. Something is given not so much to the gaze as to the eye, something that involves the abandonment, the *laying down*, of the gaze.'[27] It is such a pacifying effect which the narrator experiences when she contemplates the paintings.

By identifying with the victims which they depict she derives narcissistic gratification, a guarantee of her subjectivity.

In contrast, her reference to herself as 'Die Person' conveys a sense of distance, of how she is watching herself, how she sees herself when viewed from a different perspective. Overall, her position is surely not unlike that of Hegel's 'schöne Seele' (beautiful soul), which he criticizes in *Phänomenologie des Geistes*.[28] Michael Inwood offers a succinct summary: 'He [the "beautiful soul"] is too conscientious to dirty his hands by acting decisively, but self-righteously condemns the actions of others as wrong and hypocritical. All action, Hegel argues, entails the loss of innocence. But it is a greater sin to abstain from action and to impute base motives to others, especially to world-Historical individuals.'[29] Lacan saw in the beautiful soul an appropriate image for the human ego, commenting that 'the ego of modern man . . . has taken on its form in the dialectical impasse of the *belle âme* who does not recognise his very own *raison d'être* in the disorder that he denounces in the world'.[30] Slavoj Zizek discusses Lacan's use of the term in relation to political examples, and sees certain sorts of dissidents in socialism fitting this definition. He also gives as an example the mother who sacrifices everything to be the pillar of the family. He writes:

The mother's fault is therefore not simply in her 'inactivity' in silently enduring the role of exploited victim, but in actively sustaining the social–symbolic network in which she is reduced to playing such a role . . . On the level of the ideal–imaginary ego, the 'beautiful soul' sees herself as a fragile, passive victim; she identifies with this role; in it she 'likes herself', she appears to herself likeable; this role gives her a narcissistic pleasure; but her real identification is with the formal structure of the intersubjective field which enables her to assume this role. In other words, this structuring of the intersubjective space (the family network) is the point of her symbolic identification, the point from which she observes herself so that she appears to herself likeable in her imaginary role.[31]

In *Das Judasschaf*, the narrator's symbolic identification is with a point from which society is perceived only in terms of atrocities. The genocide of the Jews in particular enables her to adopt and sustain her role as victim, a position which is further justified by her reference to other instances of destruction and pain. Furthermore, her assertion that others' lack of 'Gedächtnis' (memory) is male acts to bolster her role as victim in relation to her identity as a woman. It is in terms of this symbolic identification that the narrator's relationship to atrocities can be viewed as one of complicity. Her complicity does not reside in aiding and abetting the oppressors, or feeling sympathy for what they do; it resides in her dependence on the

horror that violence provokes and a dependence on others' and her own suffering for structuring her identity.

The question arises at this point whether the end of the book represents the narrator breaking through her dependence on the atrocities of the past and present in order to attain a positive assumption of female identity. In her lengthy final contemplation of the *Entombment* there is a switch from the first person 'I' to the assertion of 'die Frau' (the woman). Here the final sublimation of the picture is directly related to female subjectivity, and the narrator describes a reversal as equivalent to losing her Self: 'Es wird sie nicht mehr verlassen. Eher müßte sie sich selber zu entweichen suchen' (138). (It will no longer leave her. She would have to try to escape from herself first.) Hitherto object sublimation has been spoken of in terms of transgressive desire or *jouissance*. And it is as a form of *jouissance* that Lacan in his Seminar xx identifies sublimation as one of the paths to subjectification, not a healing process in the sense of attaining wholeness, for this can never be achieved. Rather, subjectification involves a recognition that our being is structured around a void at its centre, and it is through *jouissance* that this void can be encountered. This is important in relation to Duden's text, for Lacan views sublimation as the path which is particular to those characterized by feminine structure, be they biologically female or male. They have access to an 'Other *jouissance*', and the examples Lacan gives are those of the mystics, male and female. Although imaginary satisfaction is certainly present in religious ecstasy, or in the contemplation of art or music, there is also satisfaction which exceeds the narcissism associated with imaginary identification.

Das Judasschaf seems to fit well with this. The concluding pages apparently convey a movement through contemplation of the painting to the narrator's attainment of a different level of perception involving the acceptance of her fear: 'Es ist schön und ich habe Angst' (138). (It is beautiful and I am afraid.) This could be read as a utopian ending, where the narrator assumes a subjectivity which asserts itself as female, and with it the acceptance that beauty and fear co-exist, rather than being dominated by fear. Such a reading would make the text more approachable as a feminist text, in keeping with arguments outlined by Littler and Weigel. Yet I cannot reconcile myself to such a utopian reading of the end of this book. This stems in part from a certain unease in relation to Lacan's Other *jouissance*, 'a *jouissance* which goes beyond' as he terms it.[32] It remains unclear at what point the rapture associated with religious ecstasy or the contemplation of art or music moves beyond the realm of imaginary satisfaction and narcissistic gratification. And it is worth noting that in his earlier *Ethics* seminar,

Lacan is more sceptical about the 'excesses of the mystics'. He remarks that 'Unfortunately, many of their most notable qualities always strike me as somewhat puerile.'[33] The end of the novel does little more than depict another moment of *méconnaissance*: there is no evidence that the narrator confronts the problem of her own fascination with violence other than through narcissistic escape. She does not break through her bond of complicity with atrocities, past and present, and to accept her final release as utopian is to accept, if not to condone, her own problematic identification.

LOVE

The theme of love in *Das Judasschaf* has hitherto received little critical attention, which is surprising in view of the fact that the narrator emphasizes its importance to her. Love does not obviously dominate the text, but it deserves close scrutiny since it is intricately bound up with the complexity of the narrator's suffering and identification. Her ambiguous relationship to love and her ultimate rejection of it cast further doubt upon the nature of her utopia.

At one level love is shown as a positive alternative to suffering through the narrator's relationship with her lover. He supports her in her suffering and she describes him as one pole where she can momentarily find rest. In New York she lies down next to him and sleeps, untormented by nightmares. This image of lying down next to him initially suggests a comparison with the peace she finds when she lies down next to Christ in the *Entombment*. However, any desire to carry this analogy further and to make a claim for love as a redemptive moment in the text is thrown into question by other references to love which clearly link it to her suffering.

Love is coterminous with the pain of the narrator's existence as a woman. Like her memory, it is part of her female identity and causes the suffering which makes her life intolerable:

Ich bin eine Frau, ein Mädchen, ein weibliches Kind. Ich bin aus Deutschland. Von klein auf habe ich mich nicht davon ablenken lassen, ruhig erregt und ohne den Blick abzuwenden auf die Katastrophen zu starren und sie als solche zu erkennen ... Zu drei oder vier Menschen unterhielt ich Gefühle, die sich kein Lebender leisten kann; ich nannte sie Liebe und Mitleid. (59)

(I am a woman, a girl, a female child. I am from Germany. From a young age I have been unable to stop myself staring at the catastrophes and recognizing them as such, with calm agitation and without averting my gaze ... Towards three or four people I harboured feelings that no mortal can afford to have: I called them love and pity.)

Love confronts her at the point where life verges on death, at the moment of despair, when other options have failed, and even music and paintings are not sufficient: 'Sie mußte mit vielen Tabletten so tun, als sterbe sie nicht, als sei alles ganz normal. Bis hin zu der Liebe, die ganz ohne Daseinsberechtigung danebenstand und nicht von ihrer Seite weichen wollte' (47). (With the help of tablets she had to pretend that she was not dying, that everything was normal, including love, which with no justification for its existence stood next to her and did not want to leave her side.)

Far from being part of the moment of yearned-for peace, love is incompatible with the stillness and distance which the paintings and music offer. Indeed, in terms of causing suffering, love has a certain affinity with violence, reminiscent of its portrayal in 'Der Auftrag die Liebe'. Violence is depicted in the historical extracts and the paintings as matter-of-fact and distanced. Similarly, the effects of love are debilitating for the narrator and are described using the vocabulary of a massacre, but love itself remains aloof and cold. She describes an episode when she is desperate for a man to continue loving her, yet is ironically appalled at her own behaviour as inappropriate for a woman of her age. This tension develops into the familiar motif of the internal battle, culminating in the despair of a silent scream: 'Sie müßte jetzt endlich mal . . . die Schlacht einleiten . . . Aber ihr fiel nichts ein außer wiederholtem Schreien ohne Worte . . . Und bis zur Zimmerdecke stieg etwas völlig Unverletztes, nicht einmal leicht Angesengtes hoch. Die Liebe. Sehr unpersönlich und unantastbar' (46). (She now finally . . . had to start the battle . . . But nothing occurred to her except repeated screams without words . . . And something totally uninjured, not even slightly singed, rose to the ceiling. Love. Very impersonal and untouchable.)

Thus there appear to be two manifestations of love. One that works for the good of the narrator in the form of loving relationships, and one that is structurally akin to violence in the suffering it causes. What is particularly interesting about these manifestations is that they seem so opposed. The form of love which offers assurance and support is depicted in terms of a relationship to her lover; it has a human object, is individualized even if the lover remains nameless. In contrast, the love which causes suffering is personified as a being which will not leave her side, which is not attached to any one object: 'unpersönlich und unantastbar' (46) (impersonal and untouchable). It behaves as though independent, and 'ohne Daseinsberechtigung' (47) (without justification for its existence) it exists anyhow.

The disparity between the two faces of love points again to the question of identification and complicity. The unthreatening side of love always functions as a palliative to the narrator's suffering. The lover is there for

her, he comes to her when she is lying in bed in the knowledge 'daß sich so nicht leben ließ' (111) (that one could not live like this); his is the 'Entgegenkommen' (sympathy), the 'Liebesbeweis' (115) (proof of love), which she feels is undeserved. There is no evidence in the text of reciprocity, of support for the beloved. He is depicted only in terms of his ability to pacify despair. In this respect his position is similar to that of the image of Christ; both are there to save her. Standing in front of the *Entombment* she admits, 'Unglaublich, ein einziger Kuß konnte mich manchmal einen ganzen Tag lang retten' (132). (Unbelievable that a single kiss could sometimes save me for a whole day.) This love, which occurs in the text only in relation to the narrator's preoccupation with herself, is thus strongly associated with the narcissistic gratification provided by her identification with the martyrs.

In contrast, the love which is so central to her suffering is spoken of in terms of a movement outward, her own movement towards another. The momentum expressed in the language comes from her: 'Zu drei oder vier Menschen unterhielt ich Gefühle, die sich kein Lebender leisten kann' (59). (Towards two or three people I harboured feelings that no mortal can afford to have.) This is the love which is coupled with compassion, 'Liebe und Mitleid' (59) (love and pity), and which, in the enormity of its demand to love despite, if not because of, the sins of the world, drives the narrator to escape it, to cut it out of her life. The movement towards another, with the corresponding assumption of responsibility for the burden which love and compassion carry with them, is rejected in favour of a 'beyond love': 'Über die Liebe hinaus. Und mit allen Gemordeten als Wegzehrung, streetwise, hin zu dem einen Moment, wo die Töne, Geräusche, Mißlaute, das Gelächter und die Schreie in Musik übergehen . . . Ich werde kalt werden und nichts mehr brauchen' (62). (Beyond love. And with all the murdered people as journey provision, street-wise, towards the one moment when tones, noises, discord, laughter and screams turn into music . . . I will become cold and no longer need anything.)

Escape from life is equated with undoing her experiences in close relationships:

Ich möchte bis ins kleinste Detail und in die winzigste Nebensächlichkeit alles ungeschehen machen . . . Mein erster Geliebter soll nicht durch mich, nein, er soll überhaupt nicht gelitten haben . . . Meinen Brüdern wünsche ich eine Kindheit und Jugend ohne mich. Ich will nie erfahren haben, wie es ihnen erging . . . Selbst meinem Vater wünsche ich etwas. Nur erleben möchte ich es nicht. (47–8)

(I want to reverse everything that has happened, even the smallest details and tiniest irrelevance . . . My first lover should not have suffered because of me, no, he should

not have suffered at all . . . My brothers should have a childhood without me. I want never to know how they got on . . . I even wish something for my father. I just don't want to experience it.)

Once again the issue of the narrator's complicity with suffering becomes relevant. For by placing love and compassion at the centre of her suffering subjectivity, the narrator is able to justify her empathy for victims and her close identification with Christ. At an imaginary level her entry into the *Entombment* becomes nothing less than her own re-enactment of Christ's taking on the sins of the world. However, her symbolic identification, that which sustains her in the role of victim, is with a world in which horror and violence prevail. Thus the side of love which entails reciprocity and with it responsibility for and participation in that violent world, must be cut out. The apparently redemptive moment, her approach to the dead Christ, is in fact loveless, dependent as it is on the refusal of a love which insists on involvement in the world despite the fact that 'alles so war' (112) (that's how things were).

Nowhere is the narrator's underlying dependence on violence for sustaining her position as a victim, and the concomitant need to cut out love, more vividly expressed than when she gazes at the *Meditation*. She observes that the faces of those tortured and killed are as relaxed and without accusation as Christ's is, now that the relief of death is eternal. She then writes the following: 'Ich allerdings muß es an mir selbst erledigen. Keiner tut es mir an. Zuerst schneide ich mir die Lieben aus meinen Eingeweiden. Da sie auch draußen weitermachen, muß ich sie erwürgen, ausmerzen, die Reste begraben und dann täglich kalt über sie hinweggehen' (73). (I must, though, do it to myself. No one will do it to me. First I will cut out my loves from my insides. Since they will carry on outside, I have to strangle them, eradicate them, bury the remains and then coldly disregard them every day.) The narrator is willing to commit atrocities to herself (metaphorically speaking) in order then to attain the level of eternal 'Entspanntheit' (being at rest) that she sees in the face of Christ. Particularly revealing is the little 'Keiner tut es mir an' (No one will do it to me), for this exposes the extent to which it is she herself who seeks a position of suffering in order to find fulfilment in her identification with the martyrs. The love which binds her to the base world has no place here.

THE *JUDASSCHAF* AND FEMINISM

A reading of *Das Judasschaf* such as this, which is so critical of the narrator, might well be seen as denying women once again the voice to express and

denounce their own suffering. Is it not thus a deeply anti-feminist interpretation? Does it not belittle the woman's anguish and disregard her assertion that this anguish is rooted in her femininity? On the contrary. It is only by approaching the narrator critically that Duden's book can be taken seriously as a complex study of identity. Her exploration of female identity and desire is an analysis which refuses to simplify problems because they concern a female protagonist. The woman's suffering is shown to be caught up with fantasy, and her identification is shown to implicate her in the very system of which she believes herself a victim.

It would, however, be a serious and ultimately reductive flaw to equate such a discussion of complicity with a denial of suffering and hence see it as contrary to feminism. Jacqueline Rose discusses the inadequacies of a feminism which claims that there 'must be no internal conflict, no desire and no dialogue', and which insists that 'conflict must be external, the event must be wholly outside, if women are to have a legitimate voice'.[34] She is adamant that 'there can be no analysis for women which sees violence solely as accident, imposition or external event. Only a rigid dualism pits fantasy against the real',[35] and she makes the following appeal:

I would argue that the importance of psychoanalysis is precisely the way that it throws into crisis the dichotomy on which the appeal to the reality of the event (amongst others) clearly rests. Perhaps for women it is of particular importance that we find a language which allows us to recognize our part in intolerable structures – but in a way which renders us neither the pure victims nor the sole agents of our distress.[36]

Where many books depict female identity as problematic, Duden's book confronts the issue of women's own responsibility for that problematic identity. It forces the reader to ask questions about how women situate themselves in relation to their desires, and this may well be an unpleasant exercise. *Das Judasschaf* does not exonerate women by purifying suffering so it cannot be challenged, and it is precisely this which makes it valuable for a feminist critique. The questions it asks about identification, fantasy and complicity may be disquieting, but they make the book all the more indispensable. Furthermore, and herein too lies the strength of Duden's book, female identity and desire are not approached in the abstract as ahistorical, essential characteristics which transcend the contingencies of birth, nationality and the implications of history, but are firmly rooted in the historical moment. Conversely, national identity is shown to be invested with the complex and contradictory dynamics of an individual's desire, and to function as part of the fundamental processes of fantasy and narcissism. The German context of atrocity and forgetfulness both leads to

the narrator's heightened awareness of violence and suffering and perversely also enables her to assume the role of victim. Nazi atrocities become a crucial point of reference, consciously and 'positively' as something which must not be forgotten, but also for sustaining the narrator's image of who she would 'like to be'. Thus facing the past, while necessary to overcome the trauma that continues to be transmitted through the generations, can also serve to consolidate the centrality of violence to identity.[37] In its complex critique, which undermines any naive understanding of what coming to terms with the past involves, the text offers a timely invitation to consider the ongoing and growing fascination with the Holocaust.

It is important finally to comment on the title of the book. The *Judasschaf* is referred to only once, when it is described at the end of chapter 2, following the description of animal slaughter which was quoted earlier. It is the sheep, or sometimes the goat, which meets the shipment of animals to be killed, and which leads them into the slaughterhouse. It does not itself get slaughtered, but returns to meet the next batch of condemned beasts. A powerful and unpalatable image, this treacherous beast is not explicitly related to a human equivalent. But there can be no stronger signal of the text's preoccupation with the problems of identification and the identity which it sustains than giving the book the name of this animal. For this image is about identification; the sheep comply with the smooth functioning of the slaughter because the *Judasschaf* appears to be like them. It vividly represents the danger of unreflected identification.

The image functions as a figure of reading, whereby the narrator fixates her readers into identifying with her because she appears to be like one of them, with fatal consequences if we abandon our critical gaze. Feminist criticism must not itself be captivated by representations of the suffering female. Captivation can too easily lead to disablement, whereby the image of suffering or of victimhood is the endpoint of criticism rather than the point from which exploration of identity can start. Suffering is real; it is also complex. Identification is not always what it seems.

PART III

Emine Özdamar: performance and metaphor

CHAPTER 6

Tradition out of context

Emine Sevgi Özdamar has become one of the most cited authors in German multi-cultural studies. Born in Malatya, Kurdistan in 1946, she went to Berlin for two years when she was nineteen to work in a factory. Here, she was introduced to the work of Brecht, and on her return to Turkey in 1967 she began her studies at drama school in Istanbul. In 1976 she left Turkey again to work at the Volksbühne in East Berlin as an actor and assistant director with Benno Besson, a pupil of Brecht's. From 1979 to 1984 she worked at the Schauspielhaus in Bochum, and it was here that she began to write. She wrote her first commissioned play, *Karagöz in Alamania*, in 1982 (first performed in Frankfurt in 1986), her book of short stories *Mutterzunge* was published in 1990, and her second play, *Keloglan in Alamania*, in 1991. It was with her novel *Das Leben ist eine Karawanserei hat zwei Türen aus einer kam ich rein aus der anderen ging ich raus*, (1992) (*Life is a caravanserai; it has two doors, I came in through one and went out of the other*), that she had her breakthrough, and an excerpt won her the Ingeborg Bachmann prize in 1991. A second novel, *Die Brücke vom Goldenen Horn* (*The Bridge of Golden Horn*), a sequel to the first, was published in 1998 and a second collection of stories, *Der Hof im Spiegel* (*The Courtyard in the Mirror*), was published in 2001.

As the interest in minority writing has grown amongst critics, so too have the discussions surrounding how it should best be approached. Margaret Littler sums up the debate:

While the practitioners of *Interkulturelle Germanistik* seek intercultural dialogue from within the tradition of German hermeneutics, cultural studies approaches draw on insights from post-structuralist and post-colonial theory to interrogate the ontological assumptions on which this tradition is based. There are those who caution against the application of inappropriate western theoretical frameworks to interpret the products of emphatically non-western cultures, and those who object to the ghettoisation of minority writing which can result from such scruples.[1]

Littler herself, in her study of the stories 'Mutterzunge' and 'Groß-vaterzunge' opts for 'a cultural studies approach', drawing on postcolonial theory to argue that the stories represent identity as performative, and that they undermine any notion of an 'original' Turkish identity. Leslie Adelson describes the juxtaposition of cultural studies and intercultural hermeneu-tics as a 'staged encounter',[2] yet even if it is staged, we can sense in this encounter a tension between what is perceived to be a more traditional methodology and an apparently radical new epistemology. The 'answer' as to how best to approach Özdamar's texts seems to me to be suggested by the stories themselves in their explicit concern with tradition and its decontextualization. If Gadamer insists on the importance of tradition in order to achieve 'Ein mit methodischem Bewußtsein geführtes Verstehen' (methodologically conscious understanding),[3] Özdamar's stories too point to the centrality of a critical understanding of tradition to identity.[4] And if cultural studies interrogates the assumptions upon which tradition is based, the stories insist upon the radical reappraisal of tradition through its decontextualization. Thus the texts themselves resist any simple oppo-sition and concurrently celebrate and question the role that tradition plays in identity formation.

'MUTTERZUNGE', 'GROSSVATERZUNGE'

Özdamar's exploration of the identity of a Turkish woman living in Germany is inextricably linked to language. The two stories 'Mutterzunge' and 'Großvaterzunge' depict the narrator's search for her identity now that she has 'lost' her mother tongue, Turkish, and speaks fluent, but flawed, German. She does not know when she lost her mother tongue, but the loss has profound implications, affecting communication with her family. The narrator recollects an occasion when she and her mother were conversing in Turkish, but the apprehension of not being able to understand each other accompanies the mother while they speak: 'Meine Mutter sagte mir: "Weißt du, du sprichst so, du denkst, daß du alles erzählst, aber plötzlich springst du über nichtgesagte Wörter, dann erzählst du wieder ruhig, ich springe mit dir mit, dann atme ich ruhig" ' (7). (My mother said to me: 'You know, you talk as though you think you're telling me everything, but you suddenly jump over unsaid words, then you carry on speaking calmly. I jump with you, then I breathe calmly.') However, just as important is the fact that she is alienated from her own memories of her Turkish youth, since she now either remembers in German, or it is Turkish which seems to her as though it is 'eine von mir gut gelernte Fremdsprache' (7) (a foreign language I've

learned well). So she remembers the words of a Turkish mother whose son was executed on the spurious charge of being an anarchist 'als ob sie diese Wörter in Deutsch gesagt hätte' (9) (as though she had spoken in German), and the text of a Turkish newspaper report 'kamen auch in meine Augen wie eine von mir gut gelernte Fremdschrift' (9) (also looked to me like a foreign script I'd learned well).

The narrator's problems regarding identity are not, however, limited to her relationship to German and Turkish. Her attitude to her mother tongue is complicated by its violent dislocation from its traditional Arabic roots by the reforms of Atatürk in 1927. Her objection to these reforms is not purely theoretical; they are felt by her as a disruption of her family identity. For as she points out, her grandfather knows only the Arabic alphabet, she knows only the Latin alphabet, so 'Wenn mein Großvater und ich stumm wären, und uns nur mit Schrift was erzählen könnten, könnten wir uns keine Geschichten erzählen' (12). (If my grandfather and I were dumb and could only speak through writing, we couldn't tell each other stories.) It is from her need to re-establish her link with her mother tongue and the tradition in which Turkish is rooted that she decides to learn Arabic, the language she associates with her grandfather: 'Vielleicht erst zu Großvater zurück, dann kann ich den Weg zu meiner Mutter und Mutterzunge finden' (12). (Perhaps if I find my way back to my grandfather, I'll find the way to my mother and my mother tongue.)

The narrator's need to negotiate three languages in order to understand her identity is not simply narrated by her, but is directly apparent in the textual practice. The story is told in fluent, often lyrical German, but mistakes are common. Furthermore, the narrator not only describes the process of learning Arabic, but on occasion also proffers lists of Turkish words which have an Arabic root, thus self-consciously confronting the reader with the experience of learning. This textual practice, emphasizing as it does both the process of learning a new language and the excellent but flawed mastery of German, reflects Özdamar's view that migrants' identity resides in the mistakes they make. In an interview with Annette Wierschke she describes sitting in a train with *Gastarbeiter* of different nationalities, whose only common language is German, and who, in the process of translating from their own language, make mistakes:

Und diese Fehler habe ich sehr gemocht, weil ich gemerkt habe, daß das eigentlich eine neue Sprache ist, die von ca. fünf Millionen Gastarbeitern gesprochen wird und daß diese Fehler, die wir in dieser Sprache machen, in der deutschen Sprache, unsere Identität ist. Und ich habe deswegen Fehler auch als Kunstform benutzt und damit gespielt, z.B. in 'Karagöz' oder auch in 'Mutterzunge' . . . Daß die

Fehler dann natürlich auftauchen sollen und es dem Leser ein bißchen schwierig machen sollen, damit man den Schwierigkeiten dieser Figur auch ein bißchen näherkommt.⁵

(And I liked these mistakes very much, because I noticed that it's really a new language that is spoken by about five million *Gastarbeiter* and that these mistakes we make in German are our identity. And so I used just these mistakes as an art form and played with them, for example in 'Karagöz' or in 'Mutterzunge'. . . . That these mistakes should pop up and make life a bit difficult for the reader means you can relate more closely to the difficulties of the character.)

As Wierschke comments, for Özdamar 'Sprache *ist* Identität'⁶ (language *is* identity).

Just as the image of tripping over the mistakes in the text is a physical one, and just as such mistakes can jar almost physically upon the reader, so too the relationship of identity and language is not a theoretical one, but one that is located in the body. So identity is language, but it is also physical. The narrator tells her Arabic teacher, Ibni Abdullah, '[Atatürk] hätte die arabische Schrift nicht verbieten müssen. Dieses Verbot ist so, wie wenn die Hälfte von meinem Kopf abgeschnitten ist' (27). (Atatürk shouldn't have forbidden Arabic script. This ban is like having half of my head cut off.) Similarly, the fact that the narrator has lost part of her Turkish is directly related by her mother to another, physical loss: 'Sie sagte dann: "Du hast die Hälfte deiner Haare in Alamania gelassen"' (7). (Then she said 'you've left half of your hair in Germany.') When the narrator attempts to work out when it was that she lost her mother tongue, she describes the way in which she initially refused to look at Cologne cathedral. Symbol of the still-alien German culture, when she does finally look at it, the 'letting in' of this other culture is fundamentally physical: 'Einmal aber machte ich ein Auge auf, in dem Moment sah ich ihn, der Dom schaute auf mich, da kam eine Rasierklinge in meinen Körper' (10–11). (Once, though, I opened one eye and that moment I saw it: the cathedral looked at me and a razor blade entered my body.) Here, confronting German culture in the form of turning her gaze upon it involves the recognition of the reciprocity of the gaze; she too is observed, and cannot remain aloof and untouched by what she sees.

The physicality of language is emphasized by Özdamar, and related by her to her involvement in theatre and performance: 'It's also a physical thing. You must remember that my first encounter with German was via the the-atre. I experienced the language as it were bodily, either by speaking lines myself or hearing them from the bodies of fellow actors. You could almost say that words themselves have bodies.'⁷ Indeed, in 'Großvaterzunge' the words often do have bodies, they take on live forms: 'Es kamen aus meinem

Mund die Buchstaben raus. Manche sahen aus wie ein Vogel, manche wie ein Herz . . . manche wie laufende Schlangen' (16). (The letters came out of my mouth. Some looked like a bird, some like a heart . . . some like slithering snakes.) The Arabic words which the narrator is trying to learn are often personified as her companions in the room: 'Die Schriften sprachen miteinander ohne Pause mit verschiedenen Stimmen, weckten die eingeschlafenen Tiere in meinem Körper' (24). (The texts spoke together in different voices without a break and woke the sleeping animals in my body.) The narrator says, 'Ich saß da, schaue in die Augen von Schriften, die Schriften schauen in meine Augen' (38) (I sat there looking into the eyes of the texts, the texts looked into my eyes), and towards the end of the story Ibni Abdullah's words are 'Seine Wächter, seine Wörter standen im Zimmer' (42). (His guards, his words stood in the room.)

The proximity of language and the body is not only manifested in the fact that words are given bodies, but also in the description of human expression as letters from the Arabic alphabet. Twice the narrator compares Ibni Abdullah's face to a letter. On one occasion his face 'sah wie ein zorniger Buchstabe aus' (17) (looked like an angry letter); on another it 'hat etwas von einem bettelnden Buchstaben, der auf Knien läuft' (21) (was a bit like a letter begging on its knees). In a moment of inarticulacy, just prior to their admission of love, the narrator is unable to touch him when he trembles: 'Meine Hände lagen wie Buchstaben ohne Zunge auf meinen Knien' (22). (My hands lay on my knees like letters without a tongue.) The narrator's exploration of her identity involves the learning of a new language, but again the experience is not merely mental or spiritual, but profoundly physical. She submerges herself in Arabic, and does not physically leave Ibni Abdullah's room for forty days. And her desire to understand her identity by understanding the roots of her mother tongue translates into her desire for the man who teaches her those roots. As she herself admits upon leaving his room and him, 'Ich habe mich in meinen Großvater verliebt' (44). (I've fallen in love with my grandfather.)

There is general agreement among critics that the relationship established between identity and language in these stories is such that neither Turkish nor German identity is privileged. Horrocks and Kolinsky describe Özdamar as '[refusing] to take sides'[8]; but this argument, although understandable, nevertheless detracts from Özdamar's active exploration of specific subject positions. When they comment that 'Neither an interested nor a disinterested party, Özdamar is involved and detached, insider and outsider, non-believer and believer', although attempting to point to the complexity of her approach to identity, they effectively reduce identity

to further polarities which are somehow opted in and out of at will. Far from being neither interested nor disinterested, Özdamar's writing, in my view, reveals a committed interest in subverting any attempt to understand identity in terms of opposition, a commitment which is undermined if the critical vocabulary itself draws upon a string of oppositions.

In contrast, Wierschke's argument for the importance of Özdamar's writing is compelling:

Aus dem Mangel an Polaritäten in Özdamars Texten ergibt sich Raum für wandelbare Mehrfachidentifikationen, die unserer komplexen, dynamischen Welt eher gerecht werden als ein System fixer Identitäten, das in Dichotomien verharrt . . . 'Fehler' . . . sind Ausdruck einer Identität, die sich im Wandlungsprozeß befindet.[9]

(The lack of polarities in Özdamar's texts allows room for changing multiple identifications, which do more justice to our complex, dynamic world than a system of fixed identities that adhere to dichotomies. 'Mistakes' . . . are the expression of an identity in flux.)

Wierschke points to the importance of Özdamar's style in producing a subversive effect. For it is not only the occasionally faulty German that might alienate the reader, but also the unusual, even strange metaphors, of which there are two in the opening paragraph: 'Ich saß mit meiner gedrehten Zunge in dieser Stadt Berlin . . . Ein altes Croissant sitzt müde im Teller' (7). (I sat in the city Berlin with my twisted tongue . . . An old croissant sits tired in the plate.) The reasons why this style might be described as 'subversive' can perhaps usefully be explained with reference to a debate within postcolonial studies concerning the significance of writing in one's mother tongue or in the language of the colonizer, be that English, French, Spanish or any other. Although the historical relationship between Germany and Turkey has not been one of colonizer to colonized, the marginal position of Turks in Germany seeking to articulate their identity in the face of prejudice and the pressure to assimilate to German cultural norms creates parallels with the situation of, for example, indigenous African or Asian writers faced with the dilemma of whether to write in their own tongue or that imposed by the nation which colonized them.

The root of this controversy lies in the question of whether indigenous identity and resistance to the colonizer can be articulated in the colonizer's language. So where in the African context Chinua Achebe argued that despite the appearance of betrayal and the guilt it produced, he would continue to write in English, Ngugi Wa Thiong'o argues that the English imposed on him was 'the most important vehicle through which that power

fascinated and held the soul prisoner'.[10] Consequently, resistance must be in his native Kenyan Gikuyu. This debate cannot find easy resolution, but Chantal Zabus examines the work of those writers who, like Achebe, write in the European language, to argue for the importance of 'relexification'. It is this term which in many respects also describes Özdamar's German. Relexification is when a 'new' language is produced as a result of the particular contact between languages and the artist's imaginative use of that situation. This definition differs from Özdamar's own in its stress on the artist's imaginative use of the language rather than simply the German spoken by the *Gastarbeiter* on the train. The important point is that 'When relexified, it is not "metropolitan" English or French [or German] that appears on the page but an unfamiliar European language that constantly suggests another tongue.'[11] These texts become like palimpsests, for 'behind the scriptural authority of the target European language, the earlier, imperfectly erased remnants of the source language are still visible'.[12] Zabus argues that it is as a sort of palimpsest that such texts become open for a wide variety of readings and reach a broad audience in different sociolinguistic contexts.

Özdamar's 'palimpsest' involves the authority of German, the echo of Turkish, and the further incorporation of Arabic and the Koran.[13] Thus the subversive effect which Wierschke identifies in the writing, the fact that identity is shown to be a dynamic and often incoherent process, is not subversive purely in relation to Turkish identity, with the disruption of fixed expectations of what that might be. For if the German language too is part of this palimpsest, lending authority, yet both flawed and enhanced through the process of relexification, then it is shown to be an integral part of the narrator's ethnicity. German is not something against which ethnicity is measured; it is in these stories itself a constituent of a particular ethnicity, that of the Turkish narrator. And if German is a constituent of this ethnic identity, the unavoidable implication is that German identity itself is unstable, incoherent and *ethnic*.

Ethnicity is, of course, a term which is much debated, not least because historically it has been deployed in the service of racist discourses in order to support narrow and exclusive definitions of national identity. 'Ethnic' becomes that which does not belong, as defined by the dominant social group, and such a demarcation of difference in terms of Same/Other has also resulted in ethnicity becoming a term of resistance for anti-racist discourses. My use of the term 'ethnic' here follows Stuart Hall's reconsideration of the term in the context of what he describes as 'the end of the innocent notion of the essential black subject',[14] and the analysis of the politics of representation. He writes:

If the black subject and black experience are not stabilized by Nature or by some other essential guarantee, then it must be the case that they are constructed historically, culturally, politically – and the concept which refers to this is 'ethnicity'. The term ethnicity acknowledges the place of history, language and culture in the construction of subjectivity and identity, as well as the fact that all discourse is placed, positioned, situated, and all knowledge is contextual.[15]

What Hall advocates is not a notion of the ethnic which is connected to the dominant discourses of nation and 'race', but a recognition that everyone is '*ethnically* located'.[16] His is a definition of ethnicity which includes within it the dominant groups of society, which, because of their hegemony, do not represent themselves as ethnic at all. As he points out, the conception of 'Englishness' under Thatcher was not one which was conceived of as 'ethnic'.[17]

If Özdamar's stories point towards German identity being as ethnic as any other identity, she is implicitly denying the possibility of defining national identity in any way other than as historically, politically and culturally contingent. This is why she appears not to 'take sides'. Not because she is adhering to notions of fair play where each nationality has something to offer, but because she is questioning the very notion that identity is immutable, defined and constrained by national borders. There are no 'sides' to take, but there are specific explorations to be made.

Hitherto the discussion has revolved around the issues of ethnic identity and the centrality of language for that identity, but these issues also have important implications for questions of female identity. In 'Großvaterzunge' the independent and articulate female narrator subordinates herself to Ibni Abdullah, and remains in his room for forty days before throwing the key to someone in the courtyard to unlock the door. If the narrator has the key to the room her sojourn is clearly a voluntary one, but it has the appearance of a woman locked away, kept from the gaze of strangers. Even within the room, Ibni Abdullah hangs a curtain behind which the narrator remains while his pupils attend. This aspect of the story has provoked criticism for its apparent endorsement of repressive motifs, although Özdamar's delphic response to such criticism is to quote Hamlet: 'There are more things in heaven and earth, Horatio, than are dreamt of in your philosophy.'[18] What Özdamar seems to be suggesting here is that her narrator's exploration of subjectivity need not comply with expectations of emancipation rooted in the western feminist tradition. It is this aspect of the stories which I shall now explore; whether it is possible to argue that the narrator's female identity is being subordinated to the greater ideological concern with ethnicity.

The relationship of feminism to ethnicity is no easy one. Debates rage among feminists and post-colonial writers and theorists about how to articulate racially inflected feminism, and about which category should be privileged: race or gender. Conflicts arise when contemporary feminist theory, with its roots in western thought, is perceived to be applying its analytic categories and assumptions as though they were universal and above cultural and racial differences. On the other hand, an emphasis on race is frequently suspected of a dependence either on essentializing categories or on the intrinsic value of experience. This debate is further inflected by the disagreement over the value of certain theoretical directions; thus complex theory is held by some to be only a further assertion of the domination of the western academy over the female voice at the margins, articulating her lived experience of race.[19] The question of how race and gender relate also influences the expression and perception of a woman's allegiance. So in the case of a Turkish woman in Germany, a desire for greater autonomy or self-expression, or criticism of certain practices, might be interpreted as a concomitant rejection of her culture and all its values. Equally, an affirmation of other family structures or the refusal to accept the emphasis on individual autonomy as a priority for all women, can appear to German feminists as a denial of oppressive practices or an internalization of discourses which empower men.

In 'Mutterzunge' and 'Großvaterzunge' the narrator indicates that she was confronted with specific expectations of women's behaviour both when she was politically active in Turkey and in relation to Turks in Germany, yet during the course of the stories she gives the impression that her exploration of ethnicity and language involves entering a world in which men dominate and patriarchal structures persist and are not challenged. When still in Turkey, she works in a communist commune as the only woman, and when one day the police raid it, her involvement there is seen as proof of sexual licence and as an affront to her father: 'Der Kommissar fragte mich: "Diese Kerle hier, laufen die alle über dich?" . . . Kommissar sagte: "Hast du kein Herz für deinen Vater, ich hab auch eine Tochter in deinem Alter, Allah soll euch alle verfluchen Inschallah"' (11). (The inspector asked me: 'Are these men here all over you?' . . . The inspector said: 'Haven't you a heart for your father? I've got a daughter your age too. Allah should curse you all, Inshallah.') The narrator loses her virginity to a Turkish communist activist, who, despite his political allegiances, is still bothered by the lack of blood on the sheets: 'Er sagte mir am nächsten Tag, ich bin keine Jungfrau, im Bus kam Blut, ich lachte im Bus, er dachte vielleicht, ich mache ihm seine politische Karriere kaputt' (33). (The next day he said to me I wasn't

a virgin. Blood came in the bus and I laughed. Perhaps he thought I would ruin his political career.)

It is perhaps indicative that the narrator articulates her desire to learn Arabic in terms of family structure and gender, referring to her grandfather and mother as she does. The grandfather represents not only a tradition and language that is being lost, and a path through which she may learn about her own language, but he is also cast in the role of mediator between the narrator and her mother. The search for identity is from the outset associated with the figure of a family patriarch in the narrator's mind, an association which is then realized in her love for Ibni Abdullah. Even as she introduces herself to him, she seems willing to enter into the language of obedience to the authoritative male, legitimizing her desire to learn by reference to her father's partial surrender of ownership of her to the new teacher:

Wenn mein Vater mich in Ihre Hände als Lehrling gebracht hätte, hätte er mich in Ihre Hände gegeben und gesagt, 'Ja, Meister, ihr Fleisch gehört Ihnen, ihre Knochen mir, lehre sie, wenn sie ihre Augen und Gehör und ihr Herz nicht aufmacht zu dem, was Sie sagen, schlagen Sie . . . ' (13)

(If my father had put me into your hands as your pupil, he would have said, 'Yes master, her flesh belongs to you, her bones to me. Teach her. If she does not open her eyes and her heart to what you tell her, then beat her . . . ')

As has been said, the narrator later remains within Ibni Abdullah's room for forty days, kept from the eyes of his pupils by a curtain. She becomes the temptation that he must resist; where he wants only pure love, she initiates sex with him and loves him 'wie eine gebärende Frau' (37) (like a woman giving birth), threatening the equilibrium he must maintain in order to continue teaching successfully. She is both the beautiful object upon which he gazes 'als ob ich eine seltene Blume wäre' (23) (as though I was a rare flower), and the sensual temptress whose gesture of reconciliation and apology is to admit to and show shame: 'Ich schämte mich vor meinen offenen Haaren, vor meiner nackten Haut, ich dachte, alle Farben vom Schriftzimmer schreien auch aus Scham' (40). (I was ashamed of my uncovered hair and my naked skin. I thought all the colours of the writing room were crying out for shame.)

The narrator is often unconcentrated on her work, speaking with the figure of Ibni Abdullah in her head, and the words she uses employ the image of willing sacrifice: 'Ich opfere mich für deine Schritte' (29). (I sacrifice myself for your steps.) He looks at her as a beautiful object, and she is happy to cast herself in the role of the object: 'Ich gebe mich zum Opfer

deinem Blicke . . . Ich bin die Sklavin deinen Antlitzes. Zerbrich nicht diese
Kette, lehne mich nicht ab, Geliebter, ich bin die Sklavin deines Gesichts
geworden' (29–30). (I give myself in sacrifice to your gaze . . . I am the
slave of your countenance. Do not sever the chains, do not reject me,
beloved, I have become the slave of your face.) Her voluntary subjugation
is emphatically conveyed in 'Großvaterzunge' in the ongoing theme of the
importance for a woman of showing patience. She herself relates the story
which her grandmother told her about the girl who is told to wait forty
days for a dead and very beautiful man. She does this, but is deceived at
the last minute by another woman, who claims for herself the honour of
having waited, and is rewarded by marriage to the now awakened man. All
is finally resolved when the man overhears the girl telling her 'Geduldstein'
(patience stone) of what has occurred, and in response to the question of
whether it could have endured this, it shatters. The man punishes his wife
by having her torn apart by forty horses, and he then marries the girl.
Patience is rewarded, calculated action revenged. Ibni Abdullah also relates
a story about a woman's patience; this time it is the story of Zeliha and
Yusuf, a version of the tale of Joseph and Potiphar's wife. The beautiful but
pious Yusuf resists Zeliha's attempt to seduce him and spends years in jail;
it is only when, years later, Zeliha's husband dies that she is finally able
to have the honour of becoming Yusuf's wife. It is the women who are to
be tested by trying their patience, and the narrator recalls her grandfather
telling her that a woman must show patience in the suffering caused by
love. The narrator views herself as the lover put to the test, identifying with
the waiting girl by asking Allah to give her a 'Geduldstein' (patience stone)
while Ibni Abdullah sleeps. She too waits for forty days, but she is not
rewarded; rather than showing patience, she finally seduces Ibni Abdullah,
threatening his autonomous position and his carefully regulated life. She is
not prepared to accept a relationship which is 'pure'.

It is this failure to conform to the figure of the patiently waiting and
suffering woman which functions as an important counter-argument to the
suggestion that the narrator is condoning the assumption of a subjugated
role as part of her search for identity. The mythical forty days are not only
days of temptation for Ibni Abdullah, but also for her. She is tempted
by the fantasy of a simple, homogeneous and prescribed identity, and she
is clearly tempted by the fascination of Arabia. During the period of her
involvement with her Arabic teacher the contrast between her mundane
experiences out on the streets of Berlin and the exciting allure of the carpeted
room is marked. When Ibni Abdullah returns to Arabia for one month, the
narrator too wishes to go. Her desire for such an exotic crossing of borders

is in stark contrast to the two women crossing from East to West Berlin: 'Die Nichtblinde sagte zu der Blinden "Jetzt gehen wir zu ALDI zu ALDI"' (18). (The non-blind woman said to the blind woman 'Now we're going to ALDI to ALDI.') On another occasion she overhears two old East Berlin men talking at the border. One of them decides not to cross to the West on that day: '"Heute habe ich frei, heute habe ich Geburtstag"' (19). ('Today I'm having a day off, it's my birthday.') Crossing borders is an effort, is work, and the narrator entertains the Oskar Matzerath-like fantasy of returning to a place that is secure and enclosed, under the skirt: 'Ich ging den arabischen Frauen mit Kopftüchern hinterher, ihre schwangeren Töchter neben ihnen, ich will unter ihre Röcke gehen, ganz klein sein' (19–20). (I followed the Arabic women wearing headscarves, their pregnant daughters next to them. I want to go under their skirts and be very small.)

The narrator's sojourn in her teacher's room is the realization of this escapist fantasy, the fantasy of entering into a discrete and self-contained cultural world, without the effort of crossing borders. But that it is a fantasy is constantly signalled by the repeated reference to the forty days as a magical figure, taken from the context of stories in which magic plays a central part. The narrator does not, however, submit to the temptation of simplification; she cannot ignore the identity which she brings with her into the room, cannot ignore the demands of her own body in the face of Ibni Abdullah's wish for 'heilige Liebe' (41) (holy love). The narrator is experimenting with the adoption of a role which she ultimately casts off. This does not, however, imply that the role is invalid or futile. For, as she points out, when she entered the room she had only three words of her grandfather's language. Through her relationship with Ibni Abdullah she has many more, all of which have now acquired a childhood, a memory, a cultural history: 'Ich habe mich in meinen Großvater verliebt. Die Wörter, die ich die Liebe zu fassen gesucht habe, hatten alle ihre Kindheit' (44). (I have fallen in love with my grandfather. The words I tried to find to express love all had their childhood.) The narrator explores a particular form of identity which becomes available to her through learning Arabic, and finally abandons that role and the expectations which attach to it. She enjoys the role, tests its parameters, and learns from it. What she does not do is deny the importance of the role to her cultural heritage and therefore to her own understanding of her identity as a woman.

For forty days the narrator assumes a role of voluntary purdah, which she then critically discards without, however, negating the positive contribution it has made to her search. She has learned more words, they all have 'a childhood', so she has learned more about her identity. However, the

criticism that the narrator is conforming to male discourses of submissive femininity in order to further her comprehension of her ethnic identity is refuted not only by pointing to the fact that the forty days are a fantastic temptation which she leaves behind her. To leave the argument at this juncture would be to miss a much more radical statement about the interaction of ethnic and female identity which emerges from the narrator's interest in the relationship between written and spoken language. For although initially it seems to be spoken language which is at stake, with the emphasis on the mother tongue, the narrator repeatedly points to the importance of the written word. Thus it is the effect of Atatürk's reforms to the alphabet, and not any interference with the spoken idiom, which would impede communication with her grandfather in the unlikely event that they were both struck dumb. Whereas the story 'Mutterzunge' opens by stressing the tongue's flexibility, it closes with an altered emphasis; Ibni Abdullah is introduced as a great teacher 'der arabischen Schrift' (12) (of Arabic script). It is the relationship of the spoken and written word in 'Großvaterzunge' that I shall now pursue.

Ibni Abdullah's room is repeatedly described as the 'Schriftzimmer' (15) (writing room), and at one point the narrator uses the word 'Schrift' (writing/text) five times in two sentences:

Ich konnte aus diesem Schriftzimmer nicht mehr raus. Ibni Abdullah ging nach seinen Schriftunterrichten abends weg, ich zog den Vorhang zur Seite, saß mit Schriften in dieser Moschee, die Schriften lagen auf dem Teppich, ich legte mich neben sie, die Schriften sprachen miteinander ohne Pause mit verschiedenen Stimmen. (24)

(I could no longer leave this writing room. Ibni Abdullah went out in the evening when he had finished teaching Arabic script, then I opened the curtain and sat with the texts in this mosque. The texts lay on the carpet, I lay down next to them. The texts spoke to each other in different voices without pause.)

As I commented above, letters and words are personified, taking on a life and an impetus of their own. The meaning that the narrator sees in them is not related to their Arabic meaning; they are freed from this original signifying system and assigned a new role determined by the narrator's fantasy. Letters and words are not limited in their meaning, not defined by or limited to one context. This also becomes apparent in the way in which the Koran is quoted. Students of Arabic learn by quoting this sacred written text at length; the narrator demonstrates the infinite flexibility of the quoted word by juxtaposing what she is reciting with the words that the German students are reciting. The narrator recites verses about the creation; the students

recite verses about the meanness and greed of the non-believers. The result is a sequence of sentences in which the positive vision of creation seems suddenly almost to incorporate the negative images of greed and meanness. Almost, because grammatically the whole sequence does not make sense, but nevertheless the impression made by the intermingling remains:

ICH: '. . . hervor bringt er das Lebendige aus dem Toten und hervor . . .'
DIE ANDEREN: '. . . rollenden Augen wie einer, der vom Tod . . .'
ICH: '. . . das Tote aus dem Lebendigen, das ist Allah und wie . . .'
DIE ANDEREN: '. . . überkommen wird, ist aber die Furcht vergangen, dann . . .'
ICH: 'Seid ihr abgewendet.' (23–4)
(I: '. . . he brings forth the living from the dead and brings forth . . .'
THE OTHERS: '. . . with rolling eyes like one whom death . . .'
I: '. . . death from the living, that is Allah and like . . .'
THE OTHERS: '. . . will overcome, but if fear has left, then . . .'
I: 'You have turned away.')

Here the Koran is mixed with itself, but on another occasion the narrator mixes it with a Turkish song. The Koran's firm lesson about the fate of the wretched who must languish in fire for all eternity unless Allah wills otherwise is interspersed with extracts from a love song, in which a lover declares lifelong love, which will remain pure even if he must fling himself into fire. Again, no specific sense is created by such juxtaposition, but what is important is that the passionate voice of the Turkish lover is heard through the scriptural authority of the Koran, offering the hope of human passion in the face of eternal punishment:

TÜRKISCHES LIED: 'Ich werde sie nie beschmutzen, wenn ich mich auch ins Feuer werfe.'
KORAN: 'Was die Elenden anlangt, so sollen sie ins Feuer kommen.'
TÜRKISCHES LIED: 'Ich werde nie satt werden, wenn ich auch tausend Jahre an diesem Busen läge.'
KORAN: 'Ewig sollen sie darinnen verbleiben, solange Himmel und Erde dauern.' (31)
(TURKISH SONG: 'I will never tarnish her, even if I must throw myself into the fire.'
KORAN: 'As for the wicked, they will be thrown to the flames.'
TURKISH SONG: 'I will never be satisfied, even if I lie on this breast for one thousand years.'
KORAN: 'They shall remain there for eternity, as long as heaven and earth continue.')

Just as letters and words are shown to take on new meaning when freed from their original context, so too the generation of new meanings through the limitless possibilities offered by quotation is here demonstrated.

In this context it is worth turning briefly to Derrida's discussion of the written sign, and his emphasis on writing's ability to break with its context. He argues that a

written sign carries with it a force that breaks with its context, that is, with the collectivity of presences organizing the moment of its inscription. This breaking force [*force de rupture*] is not an accidental predicate but the very structure of the written text . . . But the sign possesses the characteristic of being readable even if the moment of its production is irrevocably lost and even if I do not know what its alleged author–scriptor consciously intended to say at the moment he wrote it, i.e. abandoned it to its essential drift.[20]

Derrida takes his argument further by arguing that spoken language falls within his definition of 'writing' since it, too, fulfils the criteria of iterability (repeatability). Hence any sign, whether spoken or written, can be cited, and 'in so doing it can break with every given context, engendering an infinity of new contexts in a manner which is absolutely illimitable. This does not imply that the mark is valid outside of a context, but on the contrary that there are only contexts without any center [*sic*] or absolute anchoring [*ancrage*].'[21] The narrator's interweaving of a sacred text with itself and with a song, her personification of Arabic letters, all have the effect of decentring any 'original' or 'authentic' context. Her exploration of her identity through Arabic script, which initially seems to involve submission to a prescribed system, is in fact revealed as empowering. It is in the very nature of language that the narrator cannot be required to conform to the purported 'intention' of the text. Indeed, she shows how it can be quoted, enjoyed and transformed in new contexts, contexts which are defined by her. Thus, when Ibni Abdullah insists on pure love and locks her into the room, after initially feeling intimidated by his words she then sees in the Arabic text the narrative of her own love for him, and then her escape in the figure of the bird:

In der Schrift: Ein Pfeil ging aus einem Bogen raus. Da steht ein Herz, der Pfeil ging, blieb stehen im Herz, ein Frauenauge schlug mit den Wimpern. Jetzt hat sie ein Auge von einer Blinden, ein Vogel fliegt und verliert seine Federn über dem Weg, wo der Pfeil gegangen ist. (42)

(In the text: an arrow left a bow. There stood a heart and the arrow struck the heart, a woman's eye batted its lashes. Now she has the eyes of a blind person, a bird flies and loses its feathers above the path that the arrow took.)

In the stories 'Mutterzunge' and 'Großvaterzunge' identity is shown to be inseparable from language. Furthermore, identity is not linked only to spoken language, but to the written text, text which is then spoken and lifted out of its context. Because it is impossible for language to be anchored

in one authentic context, the narrator can positively incorporate the Arabic of the Koranic verses, acquiring the cultural depth to her language and her identity which she set out to find, without accepting the female role which both she and her teacher associate with the scriptures. She certainly lives the role for the magic forty days and is enriched by what she learns. Thus her identity is enhanced not by rejecting traditional roles, but by exploring them in her own context. Far from calling for a new language, she repeatedly speaks the already written or previously told, but adapts it to her situation. In this text, identity depends not on a rupture with language and the traditional discourses which it perpetuates, but on looking at the significance and potential of those discourses out of that traditional context.

This nexus of identity, speaking the already written and decontextualizing traditional roles, is the focus of the story 'Karriere einer Putzfrau' (Career of a Cleaning Woman), in which *Hamlet* becomes the canonical text used to comment on contemporary Turkish and German identity.

'KARRIERE EINER PUTZFRAU. *ERINNERUNGEN AN DEUTSCHLAND*'

The narrator of this story is the cleaning woman of the title, but she has not always been a cleaner. 'In meinem Land war ich Ophelia' (102). (In my country I was Ophelia.) In Turkey, she married a rich son 'mit einem Einzel-Kind-Drama' (102) (with an only-child neurosis), who rejected her with encouragement from a friend, and left her in order to contemplate the re-establishment of democracy. After the narrator's metaphorical drowning 'in dem schwarzen Bach meiner Bettwäsche' (103) (in the black stream of my bed linen), black because, according to her mother-in-law, she has not been a good wife by keeping the linen clean, she leaves for Germany. She relates, in an often bizarre and playful style, how she does the dirty work for the Germans, first cleaning up dog shit, then working in a block of flats. On a chance compliment by a female junk-dealer, who thinks she is beautiful enough to have been an actress and not a cleaner, the narrator starts fantasizing about the theatre. Over six sides of italicized text the grotesque actions of important historical and mythological figures, most of whom have been either characters in plays or dramatists, are described as they deport themselves on stage. Admitting that 'Ich habe soviel Blödsinn wie alle Toten' (118) (I have as much nonsense as all dead people), the narrator goes to the nearest theatre for a job. She immediately succeeds in getting a job, not as an actress, however, but as the woman who polishes the stage. There the story ends: 'Das war es' (118). (That was it.)

Obviously, the main intertext for this story is Shakespeare's *Hamlet*. In the opening episode, set in Turkey, the narrator recalls her final dismissal by her husband, which is an exchange constructed from *Hamlet* quotations. Her husband, portrayed as a self-absorbed only child, exhorts her to leave with Hamlet's words to Ophelia in Act III, Scene i: 'Geh in ein Kloster! Geh! Leb wohl. Oder wenn du durchaus heiraten willst, heirate einen Narren, denn kluge Männer wissen ganz gut, was für Monster ihr aus ihnen macht!' (102). (Get thee to a nunnery. Go. Farewell. Or if thou wilt needs marry, marry a fool. For wise men know well enough what monsters you make of them.) Her husband's friend, a medical student, encourages the separation for political reasons, stressing that it is easier to keep silent if alone. Using Horatio's words from Act I, Scene v he comments, 'Mylord, es muß kein Geist vom Grabe aufstehen, uns das zu sagen' (103). (There needs no ghost, my lord, come from the grave to tell us this), to which the husband offers Hamlet's response: 'Ha, richtig, das ist richtig. Und darum, ohne weiteren Umstand, denk ich, wir schütteln uns die Hände und gehen ab' (103). (Why, right, you are in the right, And so, without more circumstance at all, I hold it fit that we shake hands and part.) The narrator's comment is Ophelia's from Act III, Scene i, despairing of the change she witnesses in Hamlet: 'Oh welch ein edler Geist ist hier zerstört' (103). (Oh what a noble mind is here o'erthrown.) There are more verbatim quotations incorporated into the italicized section, which depicts the narrator's stage fantasies, but the echoes of Shakespeare's text do not depend only on such quotations. Thus, for example, when Ophelia returns to the stage mad in Act IV, Scene v, her lewd songs are in stark contrast to her previous modest demeanour. In Özdamar's story, the narrator's fantasies appear similarly irrational and brazen: '*[Cäsar] läßt Kleopatra die Pißbecken saubermachen. Sie tut es, und als Rache fickt sie mit mehreren Männern, die dorthin pissen kommen und alle kriegen Trichomonaden – wie Limonaden*' (112). (*Caesar makes Cleopatra clean the pissoirs. She does it and for revenge fucks a number of men who come for a piss, and they all catch chlamydia – like pepsi-cola.*)

Shakespeare's *Hamlet* is not the only intertext. The presence of Heiner Müller also looms large in the story as a dramatist who took central characters from the canon of high drama in order to question its traditions, such as using Hamlet and Ophelia as protagonists in *Die Hamletmaschine*. Although this radical reworking of the text is the most obvious manifestation of Müller's interest in *Hamlet*, he was also fascinated by the possibilities of performance offered by the Shakespeare play, and directed a seven-and-a-half-hour version during the period of the *Wende*. As he commented to Alexander Kluge at the time, 'Gerade in Zeiten von nachlassender

Inspiration ist es eine Bluttransfusion, sich mit Shakespeare zu beschäftigen.'[22] (Especially in times of ebbing inspiration, it's like a blood transfusion to work with Shakespeare.) Certainly Müller's influence is visually identifiable in the italicized section, as this is a technique typical of his own work.

It is not only the presence of Shakespeare's play and Müller's work in Özdamar's story which is of interest, but the way in which they are incorporated into the structure of the story. Although Shakespeare's *Hamlet* is quoted in the italicized section, the play is most markedly in evidence at the beginning, when the narrator is still in Turkey. In contrast, the influence of Müller is felt in the section of the story set in Germany. Thus a contrast is established: the canonical early-modern play is related to and used to elucidate a contemporary Turkish situation, whereas Müller's challenge of traditional drama is a point of reference in the narrator's perceptions of Germany. It is this contrast which I shall now look at in detail, examining first the implications of *Hamlet* for understanding the narrator's brief references to the Turkish political situation and her identification with Ophelia. Subsequently I shall consider how far the narrator's critical position is informed by Müller's appropriation of Ophelia as a symbolic figure of revolutionary anger.

Özdamar's satiric humour is at its best in her incorporation of *Hamlet* into her story about a Turkish cleaning woman. For what could be more German than Hamlet? 'Deutschland ist Hamlet!' (Germany is Hamlet!) In 1844, seeing in Shakespeare's character the perfect expression of Germany's own indecisiveness, Ferdinand Freiligrath wrote:

> Er spann zuviel gelehrten Werg,
> Sein bestes Tun ist eben Denken;
> Er stak zu lang in Wittenberg,
> Im Hörsaal oder in den Schenken.
>
> Drum fehlt ihm die Entschlossenheit[23]
> (His best action is thinking;
> He stayed too long in Wittenberg,
> In lecture halls or in the inns.
>
> Thus he lacks decisiveness)

The preoccupation with *Hamlet* in German literature is not, of course, new in Freiligrath, for it is also a source of fascination for Wilhelm in Goethe's *Wilhelm Meisters Lehrjahre*; the protagonist is eager to stage the play and perform the role of Hamlet himself. Although he does not make any explicit association of Hamlet with Germany, he is very aware of the Danish

location for influencing how the character should be played: 'Als Däne, als Nordländer ist er blond von Hause aus und hat blaue Augen.'[24] (As a Dane, as a Northerner, he's blond and has blue eyes.) Aurelie's response is suitably sceptical and exposes the hero's naive assumptions: 'Sollte Shakespeare daran gedacht haben?' (Is Shakespeare meant to have thought of that?) Nevertheless, *Hamlet* is a critical reference point for Wilhelm in books four and five of the novel, and is central to that novel's exploration both of how one might live in eighteenth-century Germany, caught between the claustrophobic bourgeoisie and the shallow aristocracy, and of what might constitute German theatre.[25] In a contemporary setting, similar questions find resonance in the work of Heiner Müller, again reflecting the continued importance of Shakespeare's tragedy to German writers, as a text with and through which they seek to comment on Germany. As Müller said to Kluge of his decision to stage *Hamlet* in 1989, at this critical moment of political and social change in Germany, *Hamlet* seemed to him to be the most fitting choice of play: 'Da fiel mir eigentlich nur *Hamlet* ein, weil ich das Gefühl hatte, daß dies das aktuellste Stück zu der Zeit in der DDR wäre.'[26] (Really only *Hamlet* occurred to me, because I had the feeling that this was the most relevant play for that time in the GDR.)

Özdamar's Hamlet is Turkish, both as an individual and as a symbol of his country's procrastination under the newly imposed military rule. As a person the narrator's husband does not act against the injustices of the new regime (knowing, for example, that his friend's wife died in police custody), but he uses his opposition as an excuse to indulge his own concerns, his 'Einzel-Kind-Drama' (102) (only-child neurosis). So, according to him, whereas in the previous democracy it was acceptable for him, a wealthy man, to marry a woman from a lower class, now the class difference is a threat: ' "Zwischen uns ist Klassenunterschied, und als Frau hast du mich nicht geschützt" ' (102). ('There's a class difference between us, and as a woman you haven't protected me.') The change in government is both offered as a reason for the failure of personal relationships and as a call for action, action which is contemplated but not realized: ' "Sieh doch, es ist die Zeit zum Schweigen und die Demokratie wiederaufzubauen", sagte mein Mann . . . er [ging] mit seinem Einzel-Kind-Drama und seinem Medizinstudenten-Freund zum Wiederaufbau der Demokratie ins Restaurant' (103). ('Look, it's time to keep silent and to rebuild democracy,' said my husband . . . and he went off with his only-child neurosis and his medical student friend to a restaurant to rebuild democracy.)

As a symbol of the country as a whole, in the Freiligrath sense of 'Deutschland ist Hamlet!', Turkey can evidently assume that role of tragic hero too

if desired, caught between Europe and Asia, democracy and military rule, secularism and Islam. Attaching individual or national narratives to the tragic figure of Hamlet is not Germany's prerogative alone. But nor is it without ambiguity. For although any reference to *Hamlet* initially seems to offer a certain explanation of national identity, with all the immediate associations of 'thought versus action' that the play carries with it, at the same time the dependence on a literary text signals the fictionality and role-play involved in interpretation. Identity, individual and national, is likened to a role in a play; a scripted part, the performance of which is at once constrained and open to changing interpretations influenced by altering values and expectations.

But if, as the narrator says of her husband, he was a man 'der Hamlet spielen wollte und sollte' (105) (who wanted to play Hamlet and did so), what of the narrator's own identification with the role of Ophelia? This is itself a significant gesture, since Ophelia has become an important popular icon. As Elaine Showalter points out:

> Though she is neglected in criticism, Ophelia is probably the most frequently illustrated and cited of Shakespeare's heroines. Her visibility as a subject in literature, popular culture, and painting, from Redon, who paints her drowning, to Bob Dylan, who places her on Desolation Row, to Cannon Mills, which has named a flowery sheet pattern after her, is in inverse relation to her invisibility in Shakespearean critical texts.[27]

It is by assuming the role of Ophelia that the narrator actively introduces into the story her concern with female identity, for if Hamlet is associated with high politics, issues of national identity and existentialist worries about the value of existence, Ophelia becomes that which is lost or marginalized as a consequence. Hamlet labels her as 'frailty' and 'woman', and, like him, the characteristics associated with her exist both at the individual level and the level of representation.

The question of what Ophelia represents has increasingly become of interest to feminist critics, whose conclusions are influenced according to ideological persuasion. Showalter outlines three general approaches to Ophelia, the first of which is the attempt to reconstruct the identity and story of the 'real' Ophelia, to fill in the gaps which Shakespeare left. Given the paucity of information supplied by the play, this seems a futile venture. Next, Showalter discusses the 'French feminist' line, whereby woman can only be represented as lack or absence within the patriarchal symbolic. So when Hamlet twists Ophelia's words 'I think nothing, my lord' to meaning that 'nothing' lies 'between maids' legs', this exemplifies the male association

of the 'lack' of the female genitalia with the absence of valid speech. Finally, Showalter identifies a trend to 'read Ophelia's story as the female subtext of the tragedy, the repressed story of Hamlet'.[28] Hamlet projects onto Ophelia his disgust at his own 'feminine' weakness; she represents to him everything that a 'reasonable' man should not be. Showalter herself, never keen on theory which has been emptied of 'Yankee knowhow',[29] opts for an interpretation based on an analysis of how Ophelia has been represented on stage in order to understand the changing historical discourses surrounding women and madness. She concludes:

The representation of Ophelia changes independently of theories of the meaning of the play or the Prince, for it depends on attitudes towards women and madness. The decorous and pious Ophelia of the Augustan age and the post-modern schizophrenic heroine who might have stepped from the pages of Laing can be derived from the same figure . . . There is no 'true' Ophelia for whom feminist criticism must unambiguously speak, but perhaps only a Cubist Ophelia of multiple perspectives, more than the sum of all her parts.[30]

Showalter's emphasis on the changing contexts within which Ophelia has been performed, rather than on the primacy of her role as representative of woman, fits well with the narrator's decontextualizing of written texts in 'Großvaterzunge'. For in 'Karriere einer Putzfrau' Ophelia is not only a woman of a lower class, but is specifically a Turkish woman of lower class, subject to the expectations of her culture, most obviously manifested in the controlling interference of her mother-in-law. The narrator's identification with Ophelia undeniably makes female identity a theme of the story, but she also makes use of the familiar icon to point to the invisibility of the Turkish woman working in Germany. She drowns as Ophelia in Turkey and comes into the world again as a cleaner, but the theme of invisibility has been established. She need display no other characteristics than 'Schwarze Haare und weiße Plastiktüte, das reichte' (105) (black hair and white rubbish bags, that was enough), for these are colour-coded emblems of invisibility. The physical attribute is black and is the sign of invisibility accorded to her by virtue of ethnicity; the accessory is white, and represents the invisibility of her femininity: 'For the French poets . . . whiteness was part of Ophelia's essential feminine symbolism . . . Yet whiteness also made her a transparency, an absence that took on the colors of Hamlet's moods, and that, for the symbolists like Mallarmé, made her a blank page to be written over or on by the male imagination.'[31]

By seeing herself cast in the role of Ophelia the narrator could perhaps be seen as acquiescing in a role as victim, and accepting madness and death as

her response to marginalization. But the narrator is not concerned with the 'authenticity' of her performance in terms of a scripted text, but with the relevance of the symbolic meaning which the character of Ophelia carries with it. Certainly the narrator is a victim in terms of being marginalized and derided both in Turkey and in Germany, and her grandmother is pessimistic about this ever changing, saying ' "am Ende gewinnen immer die Bösen" ' (105) ('the baddies always win in the end'). But whereas in Shakespeare's text madness and death seem to be the only hopeless options for Ophelia, which, even if madness is read as a form of resistance, is a resistance rendered futile by her impending death, in 'Karriere einer Putzfrau' death and madness sharpen the narrator's critical voice. Her death as Turkish Ophelia precedes the period of madness, rather than being a sequel to it, and the narrator twists the theme of madness to show that it is not she who is mad, but the society which defines her as invisible. The cleaner has become a contemporary incarnation of the figure of the fool, making deflating observations and comments on the splendours and pretentions of the great.

In her two-coloured black and white appearance she finds employment cleaning up the faeces of a new German prince, a dog whose owner wants the faeces as 'ein Andenken von ihm' (106) (to remember him by). Working in a block of flats, she observes people's idiosyncrasies: the man taken to hospital for 'cracking' his penis, claiming that such 'Knackerei, das ist ein Volkstanz' (110) (cracking is a folk dance); the man who rings the doorbell, calling for widow Köhler, and who, when she denies being a widow, informs her that her husband has just fallen from the eighth floor. The final straw for the narrator is when she finds the corpse of a woman in a bin, the legs reaching to the sky. Two *Gastarbeiter* assess the lost sexual potential: ' "Guck mal: Standard. Die hätten wir noch 30 Jahre gebraucht" ' (110). ('Hey look: standard. She'd have been good for another thirty years.') If in Shakespeare Ophelia's madness is associated with singing, in Özdamar's story singing is largely, although not exclusively identified with those around the narrator. Prinz's owner sings weeping down the telephone, and in the block of flats the narrator hears the residents singing from behind their closed doors. She does not hear their stories, but their songs, and when she has heard all there is to hear, she moves on: 'Ich kenne alle Lieder dieses Hochhauses, es ist Zeit, wegzugehen' (110). (I know all the songs that are sung in this tower block, it's time to go.) If singing is an indication of the madness of individual isolation, then the narrator too is touched by the madness, singing 'Eine Leiche fliegt im Himmel tralala Himmel Leiche Wasser Leiche tralala' (107). (A corpse flies in the sky, tralala, sky, corpse, water, corpse, tralala.) But unlike those she hears, she is able to listen to the songs, stand back from

them and move on, and she points to her prior death as that which has enabled her to assume her critical perspective: 'Wenn man in seinem eigenen Land einmal getötet ist, kann man überall schlafen, egal wo' (110–11). (Once you've been killed in your own country, you can sleep anywhere.)

It is worth turning now to a discussion of what possibilities are offered for interpretation by the evident presence of Heiner Müller's work in the story. Wierschke suggests that Müller's influence is at work in Özdamar's adoption of his figures of literary and political history,[32] and feels that they add a layer of interpretative uncertainty: 'Knüpft sie an die Müller-Tradition affirmativ an, oder stellt sie diese in Frage?'[33] (Does she work positively within the Müller tradition, or is she questioning it?) Without offering a convincing response to her own question, she concludes truthfully, if a trifle obviously, that 'Özdamar [macht] Müllers Reinskriptionen westlich-monumentaler Theatertradition in das zeitgenössische Theater für sich nutzbar.'[34] (Özdamar uses Müller's reinscriptions of the western monumental theatre tradition within contemporary theatre for her own purpose.) In order to take the question a step further, it is useful to look at what the role of Ophelia represents for Müller in order to assess whether his avant-garde approach is being ironized or upheld.

Georg Weighaus argues that Müller is constantly concerned to explore the contradiction between two aspects of revolutionary commitment, exemplified in the figures of Debuisson and Sasportas in *Der Auftrag*: Debuisson is the bourgeois lover of revolution from a privileged background; Sasportas the representative of the oppressed masses, filled with hate which is transformed into fanatical enthusiasm and a hardness which is directed also against the masses themselves. Ophelia is associated with the latter, filled with untrammelled hatred, and the desire for an avenging revolution which takes no account of the cost. She represents the masses for whom history has always meant labour, the victims of suppression and exploitation who have had no voice with which to protest, articulating their anger and hatred. In the fifth section of *Die Hamletmaschine* Ophelia delivers her hate monologue as Elektra, while sitting in a wheelchair being turned into a mummy, determined to speak the anger and revenge of being silenced:

Ophelia: Hier spricht Elektra . . . Im Namen der Opfer . . . Nieder mit dem Glück der Unterwerfung. Ich stoße allen Samen aus, den ich empfangen habe. Ich verwandle die Milch meiner Brüste in tödliches Gift . . . Es lebe der Haß, die Verachtung, der Aufstand, der Tod.[35]

(Ophelia: Here speaks Elektra . . . In the name of the victims . . . Down with the joy of submissiveness. I expel all the seed that I have received. I transform the milk of my breasts into deadly poison . . . Long live hatred, scorn, revolt and death.)

There is, in fact, a remarkable lack of hatred and resentment in Özdamar's narrator's account of her invisibility. Even in the italicized section which most closely resembles Müller's work there is not talk of hatred, but instead the narrator describes her whole stage fantasy as 'Blödsinn' (112) (nonsense). Her nonsense is not without certain critical effect, with sexual and racial discrimination and intellectual colonialism portrayed in bizarre form. The stage is *'ein einziges Männerpissoir'* (*one single men's pissoir*), dominated by men for whom the women continue to perform sexual favours even if, like Medea, they are fighting for equality: *'Medea kämpft dafür, daß die Frauen auch ins Männerpissoir reinkommen dürfen und streichelt dabei die Eier von Brutus'* (112). (*Medea fights for the right of women to enter the men's pissoir, while at the same time stroking Brutus' balls.*) Hitler, Eva Braun and their dog Prinz appear, bringing with them the spectre of anti-Semitism and demonstrating the arbitrary imposition of racist identity: *'Der Dicke Hund sagt: "Lacht nicht, ich entscheide hier, wer der Jude ist" und beißt den Hamlet'* (113). (*The fat dog says, 'Don't laugh, I decide here who's the Jew,' and bites Hamlet.*) Western cultural imperialism is economically ridiculed in Caesar's order to Hamlet: ' *"Du bist nicht mal richtig politisch, Hamlet, du gehst ab sofort in die Dritte-Welt-Länder-Pissoirs und bringst den Leuten bei, was Humanismus it"* ' (116). (*'You're not even properly political, Hamlet. Go immediately to the third-world pissoirs and teach the people what humanism is.'*)

However, these critical moments are certainly not informed by the hate-fuelled will to revenge that is characteristic of Müller's Ophelia. Indeed, if anything, these critical elements are submerged by the endless nonsense of the fantasy, and the constant introduction of important historical characters who are promptly caricatured and thoroughly demystified. The impression that this is precisely what the narrator says it is – 'Blödsinn' (nonsense) – is dominating. This would suggest, then, that Özdamar is ironizing the theatrical avant-garde, with the implication that Müller himself belongs to the company of the men's pissoir. Caesar's self-importance becomes a parody of the self-importance of radical theatrical experimentation, where the participants and public need to be forced into an appreciation of its importance. After all, the stage fantasy ends with Caesar's threat ' *"Findet mich gut – sonst töte ich euch!"* ' (118). (*'You'd better think I'm good, or I'll kill you!'*) Perhaps too, the inadequacy of avant-garde experimentation, where radical social comment is in part felt to reside in the inaccessibility or non-sense of the performance, is indicated in the fact that for the narrator, her fantasy changes nothing. She remains a cleaner, and life remains separate from the stage. In a statement which seems to confirm the futility of striving

for change the narrator concurs with her grandmother's opinion: 'Die Bösen gewinnen im Leben, aber die Toten dürfen auf der Bühne ihren Blödsinn machen' (111). (The baddies win in life, but the dead are allowed their nonsense on the stage.) The stage fantasy becomes a parallel to the narrator's husband disappearing off into the restaurant to discuss democracy; neither will alter the reality of the woman's continued marginality.

If cumulatively towards the end of the story the mood is one of disillusionment, since it is impossible for the narrator to be seen as anything other than a cleaner, it is interesting that there should be such an absence of anger. Müller's Ophelia draws a certain strength from her fury, whereas this narrator concludes with a verbal shrug, 'Das war es' (118). (That was it.) But far from being seen as a gesture of pessimistic resignation, it may, in my view, be read as the narrator's 'That's all folks!' flourish at the end of a bizarre, mad or confounding performance, not unlike Looney Tunes or Janis Joplin's cackle which concludes 'Mercedes Benz'. With it, the narrator invites us to recognize her awareness of and pleasure in her own performance, thereby pointing to the importance she ascribes to performance even while ironizing certain forms. For, despite the end, despite her rejection as an actress and the apparent perpetuation of the status quo, the narrator affirms the interlinking of life and performance. The avant-garde is ironized because it does not go far enough and restricts performances to the stage, whereas she is pointing to the centrality of role-play in the life of an ordinary woman. Although, as her story makes clear, she is restricted to certain roles by the limited vision of others, who are all too willing to typecast, performativity also carries within it emancipatory potential, offering as it does the possibility of alternative roles and the limitless scope of alternative interpretations.

Thus the narrator's radicalism lies not in a demand to demystify the great characters of the western canon, although this might serve a certain satiric function, but to insist that these roles gain contemporary validity through their iterability away from the stage and away from the context of the self-consciously oppositional male avant-garde. As in 'Großvaterzunge' it is not the rejection or belittling of tradition that is important in the quest for understanding identity, but rather a utilization of the texts it provides quoted 'out of context'. Tradition carries with it the social discourses that perpetuate racist and phallocentric definitions of national and personal identity, but the search for a redefinition of identity cannot rest upon a rupture with those discourses. Indeed, although certain assumptions need to be challenged, Özdamar points in her stories to the importance of traditional discourses in subject formation; words need a childhood, identity

needs its cultural experience. Which is not to say that words or cultural experience should not be challenged, but that they cannot be rejected or ignored, for they constitute identity; they are, in Judith Butler's words, 'enabling constraints'.[36]

The decontextualization of established discourses, which offers new opportunities for negotiating identity, does not exist in a vacuum. Thus, although nothing has immediately altered in the narrator's marginalized position, she uses the role of Ophelia to articulate and criticize her position, and she forces the reader to consider the subversive possibilities of performance off the stage. Yet there is good reason for not reflecting this subversive quality in the conclusion of the story. Performativity, when removed from the context of the stage and seen as central to identity formation, is not a simple matter of learning lines and reciting them. As the narrator writes, 'Ich bin die Putzfrau . . . in meinem Land war ich Ophelia' (102). (I am the cleaning woman . . . in my country I was Ophelia.) She *is* the cleaner, she *was* Ophelia. These are not roles she can assume and discard at will, but she is constrained within them. She cannot escape those constraints by deciding to take the law into her own hands and become a Portia. As Butler writes, 'Performativity is . . . not a singular "act," for it is always a reiteration of a norm or set of norms',[37] which means that 'it is only *within* the practices of repetitive signifying that a subversion of identity becomes possible'.[38] The narrator's awareness of her roles of Ophelia and cleaner does not mean she can step out of them at will, but it does mean she can subvert them and the dominant discourses which attempt to perpetuate them.

In 'Karriere einer Putzfrau', the narrator's 'performance' of Ophelia reveals her to be in the role of the silenced woman, easily cast aside by her husband; but it also enables her to voice her critique of that victim role without once again positioning herself as disempowered victim. She does this by exploiting the potential of her invisibility to assume the position of observer, revealing not herself to be mad, but the society which ignores her. Furthermore, by adopting a role from the canon of West European literature, and one which has, by certain German writers, been seen as exemplifying the problems of German national identity, her emphasis on performance extends to encompass definitions of national identity. That too is subject to the enabling constraints of tradition, and is an identity whose re-enactment must alter in response to new interpretation; so when the Turkish cleaner uses Ophelia to expose the madness and prejudice of those around her, then it is also time to reconsider the 'tragic' procrastination of Hamlet the German, or even Hamlet the Turk.

In Özdamar's short stories the complex nexus of female and national identity is central but not life-threatening. The self-conscious representation of the iterability of language and the proximity of identity to performance allows for a critique of stereotyping expectations while sustaining an optimistic vision of the adaptability of an identity enriched by tradition. Such optimism has strong political force in the general context of Western Europe's bigoted and undifferentiated fear of Islam and in specific responses to other recent stories about Turkish women in Germany. Saliha Scheinhardt writes of the horrifying and abusive relationships to which many Turkish women are subjected, of 'Frauen, die sterben, ohne daß sie gelebt hätten' (women who die without having lived), works in which women are cruelly exploited by their menfolk and repressed by their traditions.[39] Scheinhardt's stories act as a powerful protest against the degradation of the women, but unfortunately at the same time feed the prejudices and stereotypes of a reading public which eagerly made *Nicht ohne meine Tochter* into a bestseller.[40] It is these prejudices that *Mutterzunge* effectively confounds in its engagement with Turkish and German identity. In my next chapter I look at how far Özdamar's optimistic vision, transposed onto a childhood in Turkey, fulfils a similar political function, or whether optimism transforms into the politics of idealization.

CHAPTER 7

Metaphor's creative spark

In *Das Leben ist eine Karawanserei*, the unnamed first-person narrator traces her life from embryo to her departure to Germany as a young woman of approximately eighteen or nineteen years old. Although the story is governed by a conventional chronological framework, specific references to the narrator's age are extremely rare, and dates are entirely withheld. Time and age are not in themselves of importance to this narrator, whose impressions and responses to her experience of family, neighbours, neighbourhoods and customs provide the text's momentum. The narrator tells the story of her family's many moves from one town in Turkey to another, following her father, Mustafa, in his constant pursuit of employment as a building contractor. Born in Anatolia, the narrator lives first in Istanbul, then in the small religious town of Yenisehir, then for a long and largely happy time in Bursa, until the increasing pressures of unemployment and poverty force the family to move to Ankara. After a period of near destitution, Mustafa succeeds in finding a job through an old acquaintance in Istanbul, and they return to this city, from where the narrator departs for Germany.

This text is intensely impressionistic; the narrator recalls events, people and places, does so evocatively and with sensual immediacy, but makes no attempt to link episodes, explain them or subordinate them to a unifying scheme or plot development. People and experiences are described because of their value and interest at that point; the people go, the experience passes and either the narrator moves on, or change is imposed. Indeed, the leaps from one episode to the next are often startling. When the narrator is left in an empty grave either to overcome apparent illness or to die, she is rescued by the sudden appearance of a stranger: 'In diesem Moment klatschte jemand in die Hände, klack, klack und sagte: "Huuuuuuuh"' (14). (At that moment someone clapped their hands, clack, clack, and said 'Hoooooh.') Thus Ayse, her paternal grandmother, is introduced, and suddenly the family is in Istanbul: 'Dem Tod gestohlen in Anatolien ... saß ich vor einem Photographen ... am Meer in Istanbul' (15). (Snatched from

death in Anatolia . . . I sat in front of a photographer . . . by the sea in Istanbul.) Transition does not present a problem to this narrator, for she merely elides it, moving on often with only the thinnest of narrative devices, such as the sudden awakening out of sleep. This is the move to Yenisehir: 'Ich fiel mit Benzingeruch in den Schlaf und wachte in einem anderen Holzhaus in der Kleinstadt auf' (65). (I fell asleep surrounded by the smell of petrol and woke up in another wooden house in a small town); this the move to a new house: 'Ich bin wach geworden in unserer halbfertigen Villa im Bürokratenviertel' (102). (I woke up in our half-finished villa in the bureaucrats' quarter); this the awakening in Bursa: 'Ich weiß nicht, wann ich gestorben bin. Ich wachte auf in einem Bett, in einem Hotelzimmer' (113). (I don't know when I died. I woke up in a bed in a hotel room.) Fantasy, too, is useful for whisking characters from one place to another. The family are blown by a powerful wind from their communal picnic outing at a graveyard in Bursa to their isolated new home on the desolate plain on the edge of Ankara.

The methods by which the transitions are effected do, of course, themselves contribute to the emphasis on impression. The abruptness of the moves, the sudden disruption they cause, the newness of the different house and street as perceived by the child are strongly conveyed without the need for explicit statement. Similarly, the turmoil of the powerful wind blowing the family across Turkey, a flight in which the narrator glimpses generals in their military aircraft while being fearful of losing her grasp on her grandmother's headscarf, condenses both the family's confusion and loss of control, and the broader upheaval in the immediate aftermath of a military coup, into one compact image. Similarly, when the birth of the narrator's little sister, Schwarze Rose (Black Rose), is presented with the statement 'Sie war plötzlich da' (141) (She was suddenly there), the suddenness is tangible for the reader, as is the shock, although again, this is not explicitly articulated. And when as a teenager the narrator abruptly turns from one of her grandmother's stories to inform us that 'Bald zog ich eine Treppe tiefer in ein kleines Zimmer um. Mein Busen war gekommen' (243). (Soon I moved into a small room one floor lower. My breasts had come), what she conveys is not the fact that breasts appear overnight, but that awareness of change and its implications can be sudden, even if the change itself is gradual or cumulative.

The immediacy of the text is enhanced by a framework structure of rapid and constant switching of scenes, reminiscent of the theatre. More important, however, is the narrator's focus solely on what she sees and perceives around her, which she succeeds in conveying with astounding

vividness. This is achieved not through detailed, precise visual descriptions, but it is the emphasis on other senses, the centrality of smell and sound, that makes her impressions so rich. Smells permeate the text, are more important than appearance in conveying the characteristics of people and objects. So when Grandfather Ahmet arrives in Ankara, the narrator, who has not seen him for ten years, does not describe his appearance, other than to remark that his clothes are the same, but smells him in order to establish familiarity: 'Ich roch an seiner Jacke und Weste, auch sie rochen nach Pflaumen, Pfirsichen und Getreide, ich roch heimlich an seinem Kopf, er roch auch nach Pfirsichen und staubiger Hirse' (305). (I smelled his jacket and waistcoat; they also smelled of plums, peaches and grain. I secretly smelled his head, which also smelled of peaches and dusty millet.) It is with his smell that he becomes approachable: 'Da dachte ich, daß auch er mal einen Vater und eine Mutter gehabt hatte' (305) (That's when I thought that he must have had a mother and father once too), and it is with his smell that his presence and memory linger with the narrator after his departure. Indeed, the lingering influence of his visit passes only when a new smell of burned cabbage and mincemeat forces itself into the new basement flat, associated with the violent death of a boy, whose flesh, after being dragged along by a crashing military aeroplane, became mixed with the mincemeat he had just bought.

Many characters are presented through the essence of their smell: the soldiers who accompany her mother in the train possess coats 'die . . . nach 90.000 toten und noch nicht toten Soldaten [stanken]' (9) (that . . . stank of 90,000 dead and not yet dead soldiers), and a teacher at school smells of tobacco. Houses and their atmospheres too have their smells, and as with Grandfather Ahmet, smell represents familiarity and the presence of life. Thus during the day in Yenisehir, the absence of the working men and the extreme quiet that dominates the little town is summed up as 'es kam tagsüber nur Frauengeruch aus diesen Häusern' (74) (during the day only the smell of women came out of these houses), and in Bursa the wealthy but pale and listless women live in stone houses, 'aber es kam kein Oliven-, kein Aprikosen- und kein Paprikageruch aus ihren Häusern' (119) (but no smell of olives, apricots or paprika came from their houses). In contrast, the smell of poverty is intense, a smell 'der wie ein anderer Himmel über [den Männern] stand' (144) (which stood over the men like a second sky), and which in the slums must be drawn aside like a curtain before entering the house (338). It is, though, a smell, and is therefore representative of people and of life, and able to trigger positive associations; it is the rich with their absence of smells who are pitied.

If smell is central to the narrator's evocation of people, sound plays a similar role in relation to action, as the physical reality is stressed by the attempt to reproduce its noise. Thus the representation of sound in this text is often onomatopoeic: the fly buzzing at the moment of an old woman's death (34); the men sitting still outside the shops, waiting and turning their rosaries, 'cikcikcikcikcikcikcikcikcikcikcikcik' (85); her father's long yawn, 'Hehehehehehehehe Hehehehehehehehe' (97), and the man with a tracheotomy, 'hih hih hih hih hih hih hih' (277). In one example onomatopoeia is juxtaposed to silence in order to convey an atmosphere of waiting, an atmosphere in which the constant sound of cracking sunflower seeds becomes magnified until it literally dominates all else, including the written page. In this example, in the already quiet town of Yenisehir, Mustafa goes to borrow money after a disagreement with Fatma. The three women, Fatma, Baumwolltante and Ayse, sit waiting: 'Der Steinberg schweigt, der Kalkbrunnen schweigt, die Felder schweigen . . . Ich höre nur das reife Sonnenblumenkerngeräusche in den Mündern meiner Brüder. cit cit cit cit cit . . .' (107). (The stony hill was silent, the chalk spring was silent, the fields were silent. I only heard the sound of the ripe sunflower seeds in my brothers' mouths cit cit cit cit cit . . .) There are 254 of these 'cits', a sound which, like the drip in the opening scene of *Once Upon a Time in the West*, finally comes to represent heat, silence, waiting and monotony in one syllable.

Quite different from the onomatopoeic reproduction of individually recollected noises is the constant repetition of words. That the texture of the narrator's life is woven through with repeating patterns of word-sounds is reflected in their actual textual repetition, and it is precisely in the repetition of the words that the emphasis on sound rather than meaning lies. Furthermore, the narrator does not even know what the words mean; they are heard and used before they are comprehended. Thus the word 'Bismillâhirahmanirrahim' 'kam aus den Mündern von vielen Menschen' (55) (came out of the mouths of many people). The narrator goes on to list how it can be used in almost any situation except on the toilet, determined herself to utter it at every conceivable opportunity. In all, she repeats the word forty-four times over three pages, admitting that she did not know what the word meant until she looked it up as an adult, and only informing the reader of its meaning after the fortieth repetition. Its literal meaning, 'Im Namen Gottes, oder im Namen Allahs, der schützt und vergibt' (58) (In the name of God, or in the name of Allah, who protects and forgives), has not been important; its omnipresence has, a situation that is textually mirrored for many readers.[1]

In condensed form a similar process occurs with the word 'Bismillah', which is repeated eleven times in one paragraph (58–9), the word 'Masallah', repeated twenty times in close succession (93–4), and the words 'Vallahi Billahi', fourteen times (109–10). The narrator also emphasizes the beauty and constant presence of Arabic prayer. When the narrator first hears Ayse recite prayers in the graveyard, the beauty of the sound and the images they conjure up are what impress her: 'Die Buchstaben aus dem Mund meiner Großmutter [wurden] im Himmel des Friedhofs eine schöne Stimme und ein schönes Bild' (18). (The letters coming out of my grandmother's mouth became a beautiful voice and a lovely picture in the sky above the graveyard.) As the narrator comments later, 'Ich wußte nicht, was diese Wörter sagten' (55). (I didn't know what the words meant), and although she soon becomes aware of the status of the words as prayers, it is their recitation that remains paramount, rather than the conscious and self-aware statement of belief. Thus when Fatma is entertaining neighbours, the old women ask the narrator 'ob ich beten könnte. Ich sagte ja und sprach sofort einmal das Fâtiha-Gebet' (160) (whether I could pray. I said yes and immediately recited the Fatiha prayer). Her ability to recite affords them enormous pleasure. The ignorance of literal meaning does, of course, apply to most readers. But by the time the prayer has been repeated six times at intervals throughout the book, these sounds, which are so inextricably linked to the narrator's impressions of childhood, become gradually familiar even to readers unfamiliar with Turkish and Arabic.

I have argued that the repetition of words emphasizes the important background of sound rather than meaning, but it also points to the importance of repetition itself, including its more ritualized aspects. It is no accident that the words carry religious meanings, and the fact that they are central to common social discourse and function independently from a specific religious context says much about religion's role in the narrator's family and close community. It reflects its ambivalent function as an important structuring and enabling discourse, yet one which is made to fit with or run parallel to other prevailing interests or beliefs; it is social rather than explicitly theological. Thus on the one hand religion plays a central role; many in the family keep the fast of Ramadan, the children are sent to the mosque to learn the Koran, Ayse and the narrator pray to Allah together, the local Hodja is called in at critical points, and Fatma will not turn out pregnant or nursing cats because she 'hatte Allah-Angst' (181) (feared Allah). On the other hand, Islam is not experienced as restrictive, because the parents adapt it or reject it according to circumstance. The narrator sees her mother in a headscarf for the first time in Yenisehir,

wearing it not out of conviction but because theirs is 'eine religiöse Straße, man muß die Menschen nicht stören' (66) (a religious street, you shouldn't disturb people). As soon as they move to the area where the bureaucrats live, Fatma will discard it. Similarly, the raki-loving Mustafa does not fast at Ramadan: 'Er mußte jeden Abend trinken, sonst meinte er, würde er die Heiligen, die am Raki-Trinken gestorben sind, traurig machen' (60). (He had to drink every night because he said that otherwise he would make the saints who had died of raki-drinking sad.) Instead he sins further by buying fast-days from his daughter. At moments of transgression, like cavorting in a Chevrolet with two women, or spending every evening in nightclubs, turning to prayer, the Koran and Allah is for Mustafa a way of expressing his guilt and regret, even though he cannot read the Sacred Text.

More generally, Islamic custom can suit the purposes of Fatma and other women very well. The month of Ramadan is a time of sociability and exchange, and when it falls in winter, the doors are always open, as on summer evenings. 'Alle, ältere und jüngere Frauen blieben nicht mehr zu Hause' (231) (All women, young and old, didn't stay at home any longer), but they go visiting the graves of holy men. These visits offer the women marvellous opportunities in the spring, when they often call to one another to visit one of the many graves, enabling them to go off as they please. As Tante Sidika comments, ' "Allah sei Dank, daß es so viele heilige Männer gibt, so lüften alle Frauen im Frühling ihr in Mottenpulver gelegtes Leben und ihre Schachteln" ' (247). ('Allah be praised that there are so many holy men, so every spring all women can air their mothball-smelling lives and their fannies.') When the women then arrive home late, they pull serious faces and report on where they have been: 'Dann schwiegen die Männer' (247). (Then the men were silent.) What emerges clearly from the text is the extent to which the centrality of Islam depends upon its extreme flexibility as a reference point. Nowhere is this more apparent than in the confounding of Islam and superstition. When the narrator has tuberculosis, for example, Fatma, Ayse and Baumwolltante initially see it as Allah's punishment for their sins (such as smoking, drinking, farting during prayer, wearing lipstick), then seek out holy Hodjas who make special potions out of burnt and soaked Arabic texts for the narrator to drink. Much later, in Bursa, the local women believe that the narrator can dream their futures, a belief which fits easily with their approach to religion; so first the narrator is washed and recites her prayers, then the woman in question blows her wish on the narrator's face before she sleeps. Religion thus offers a pliable and extensive framework, called upon when convenient, which enables individuals to express their desires, hopes

and anxieties, and allows for the articulation of what is little known or understood.

If religion offers a pliable framework, it is, however, by no means the case that everyone has the same relationship to that framework, and it is clear that Fatma and Mustafa's pragmatic approach is also evidence of a generational difference and the effects of modernization and urbanization within Turkey. Whereas Fatma and Mustafa belong to the slowly expanding urban bourgeoisie, enjoy going to the cinema and imitating film stars, and value education above early marriage for their daughter, both Ayse and Fatma's father express their suspicion of industrial modernization and its implications for tradition. Ayse condemns the cinema as sinful for the escapism it offers, she describes electricity as a 'Ketzererfindung' (67) (heresy), and scorns the bureaucrats with whom Fatma wishes to socialize as 'Leute, die das Loch, aus dem sie auf die Welt gekommen waren, nicht mehr gut fanden, weil sie Schreiben und Lesen gelernt hatten' (66). (People who no longer thought the hole through which they entered the world was any good because they had learned to read and write.) When, many years later, the matchmakers pay a visit, Ayse views it as a missed opportunity when Fatma does not agree to marry her daughter. Fatma is appalled: ' "Greisin, heirate du, wen du willst, meine Tochter wird in die Schule gehen" ' (272). ('Old woman, marry who you want, but my daughter will go to school.') The lingering difference between rural tradition and urban aspiration is expressed in the different songs which are sung in the family circle: 'Großmutter konnte nur Dorflieder singen. Mutter sagte: "Wir singen klassische Musik" ' (128). (Grandmother could only sing village songs. Mother said, 'We sing classical music.')

Critical and wary of new technology and mores though Ayse may be, she nevertheless lives harmoniously within the family, has chosen to follow her son to the city, and definitely becomes aware of certain benefits that modernization has brought for her as a woman. She thus figures less as an active and hostile opponent of change than as a positive link with tradition, especially for the narrator, with whom she has a strong bond. Furthermore, certain of her objections are little more than the apparently inevitable pessimism of one generation about the waywardness of the next, so just as Ayse condemned her daughter's avid cinema-going, so too Fatma is later horrified by her children's comic-reading, expressing just the same fears and suspicion of heresy. But in contrast to the positive and generally tolerant figure of Ayse, Fatma's father is an uncompromising representative of patriarchal polygamy. At the time of the narrator's birth, he has five wives, but the narrator's grandmother, another of his wives, is no longer

alive. When he heard from one wife whose son had just died that Fatma's mother went to a wedding and hennaed her nails despite this child's death, he tied her hair to his horse's tail and dragged her over rocky ground. He disregarded her claim that she knew nothing of the baby's death, and she died soon afterwards. Ahmet's assumption of supreme authority, although he becomes milder with age, living to regret his wife's murder, continues to dominate his family when he is present. When he comes to help them at a time of extreme poverty in Ankara, the whole family sits on the floor with him, because he does not wish to sit in a chair, the family must pray five times a day, Fatma and Mustafa smoke secretly in the toilet, and Ahmet teaches his granddaughter the traditional and subservient role of women. Far from being resented, he is a charismatic figure who is much loved and respected by his daughter and granddaughter, although their relationship to him is facilitated by the fact that his strictures are only temporary. Furthermore, both Mustafa and Ayse are critical of his authoritarian manner, and consider him 'ein unbarmherziger Bandit' (307) (a merciless bandit). Thus through this figure the family, and the reader, are shown a glimpse of a way of life and attitudes that have only a temporary effect on the family, do not limit the narrator's opportunities and so provoke no anger in the narrative.

Indeed, Ahmet's concerns about female behaviour and the importance of modesty are comprehensively undermined by the narrator's evident enjoyment of the body and physicality throughout the book. Nor is this enjoyment exclusively hers, or the exuberant discovery of youth, but is a reflection of broader attitudes to corporeality in her family and among acquaintances. References to the body and its functions are ubiquitous in the text. Within the narrator's family, there is no false shame attached to urination, defecation, farting or awareness of genitals. The Baumwolltante refers to the narrator as 'eine kleine Scheiße im Bauch deiner Mutter' (9) (a small shit in your mother's tummy), and her grandmother reassures her that 'Scheißen ist ein Geschenk Allahs' (37) (shitting is a gift of Allah's). At one point neighbourliness is defined by being in earshot of each other's farts (159), and farting is also a useful expression of scorn: Mehmet Ali Bey farts on the history textbook and goes on to parade his backside to aid his satiric rendering of Turkish history (194–5); Grandfather Ahmet farts on Atatürk's mausoleum in protest at its alienating grandeur (316). It is certainly the case that sexuality has rules attached, as becomes clearer as the narrator enters puberty, and as will be analyzed in detail below, but to speak of it is no taboo. Ayse enjoys telling the children of her three husbands, including the fact that the third, Sükrü, taught her to go on top during lovemaking, and she goes on to let them scratch her back, pull her hanging

breasts and wobble her stomach. The narrator occasionally goes with three girlfriends to view the spectacle of an old man exposing his 'Ware' (176) (wares), and when her father's penis slips out of his pants, it is an object of general amusement, looking like 'ein aus dem Fenster schauendes, seltenes Tier' (177) (a strange animal looking out of the window). In order to help her daughter quench her adolescent desires, Fatma, the narrator's mother, recites number-verses, 'und nach jeder Zahl kam beim Reimen das Wort Ware oder Schachtel' (330) (and used 'willy' or 'fanny' as the rhyme after each number). The whole family enjoys the joke. The extent to which sexuality is accepted within the family as normal for men and women is perhaps most evident in Ayse's reassurance that mutual masturbation amongst little girls is fine: ' "Ich habe auch, als ich so klein war wie du, mit den Mädchen im Dorf Schap Schap gemacht" ' (76). ('When I was as small as you I played shap-shap with the girls in the village.')

As was hinted at above, the acceptance of physicality and sexuality, including expressions of child sexuality, does not mean that attitudes towards its expression and control by boys and girls is similar as they mature. On the contrary, expectations of male and female behaviour are distinct, and it is these differences and the narrator's response to them that I shall now explore.

GENDER

The narrator recounts an episode at school when the English teacher asks one of the girls to say 'I am sick.' The girl refuses to say it correctly, saying 'si' or 'sak', because the word 'sick' sounds exactly like the Turkish word for penis, 'sik' (178). The teacher awards her a zero and tells her not to be ashamed since 'es gibt kiloweise sik bei euern Vätern und Brüdern' (178) (your fathers and brothers have got loads of sik between them). Upon hearing this, Fatma says she would not have been given zero, whereas the girl's father is furious. This brief anecdote is important for revealing the differences in attitude between the narrator's family and others. Fatma is not alone in not being a prude, for nor is the teacher, but equally, the narrator's family and the narrator herself cannot be read as representative. Conversely, a lack of prudishness does not equate with the abandoning of gender stereotypes, stereotypes which are reinforced by her own family as well as by generally held expectations.

Grandfather Ahmet is, not surprisingly, strict in his views concerning men's and women's roles. Women are to be modest, obey their husbands and be patient. To demonstrate and teach the virtue of patience to his

granddaughter, he takes her fruit from her sometimes at mealtimes and eats it himself, informing her 'Mädchen sein, heißt Geduld haben' (311). (Being a girl means being patient.) Her brothers are given a detailed explanation of how to behave towards a wife who refuses to obey or refuses to come to their bed, a process of exerting authority culminating in beating, preferably on the hips. These views are the most extreme articulation of role division in the book, but milder forms persist. Although the narrator's parents do not generally impose their authority through restrictions enforced by violence, Ayse and Fatma are nevertheless quick to justify Mustafa on the one occasion when he does hit the narrator for staring at a boy for a long time. They refer to the general relationship between fathers and daughters: 'Großmutter sagte: "Weine nicht, dort auf dem Gesicht, wohin der Vater schlägt, wird eine Rose blühen." Meine Mutter sagte: "Wer seine Tochter nicht schlägt, schlägt später seine eigenen Knie"' (82). (Grandmother said: 'Don't cry. A rose will bloom on your face where your father hit you.' My mother said: 'The man who doesn't hit his daughter will later be slapping his own knees.') Just as in 'Großvaterzunge' Ibni Abdullah presents patience as a female virtue,[2] the view that it is girls who should be patient is also accepted in the narrator's family, even if it is not enforced. Thus, although Ayse tells her of the importance of patience for people in general (54), and Fatma describes it as a virtue in Allah's eyes, in practice it is girls and women who do their chores and prepare their dowries while sitting quietly for hours. Fatma tells her daughter, ' "Ein Mädchen muß über ihrer Schachtel sitzen und arbeiten" ' ('A girl must sit on her fanny and work'), whereas ' "Die Jungs können ihre Waren spazieren führen" ' (220) ('The boys can take their wares for a walk').

Whereas boys are permitted to wander as they please, girls and women are not. As was mentioned above, they must excuse their outings with suitably pious and therefore uncontroversial visits to the saints. Women belong in the domestic sphere, confirming and consolidating neighbourhood bonds through extensive rituals of asking after each family member in order of importance (166). Work and money are the prerogatives of the men, as Mustafa makes clear to Ayse and Fatma when they urge him not to borrow more money: ' "Ihr sollt euch mit eurer teigverschmierten Hand nicht in Männersachen einmischen" ' (233). ('You shouldn't stick your dough-covered hands in men's business.') The clear hierarchy of male authority over female is reflected in people's bearing, and for a man to express respect to another in a position of greater authority involves the temporary assumption of the female role: 'Mein Vater saß nicht wie er selbst vor ihm, er saß wie eine Frau vor einem Mann, mit leiser Stimme, die Hände über

seine Beine gelegt' (327). (My father didn't sit in front of him as himself, but like a woman in front of a man, speaking with a quiet voice, hands laid across his lap.) The safeguarding of male authority is, of course, closely linked to respecting male potency, which can take on greater importance than religious custom; Ali does not have to fast for Ramadan, since, as his protective mother puts it, ' "Er ist ein Junge, wenn er Lust kriegt auf Essen und nicht essen darf, wird sein Pipi runterfallen." ' ('He's a boy, and if he feels like eating and isn't allowed, his willy will fall off.') It is not difficult to see what the adult version of this myth will be. When girls reach puberty and start being sexually interested in boys, they need to be protected and controlled, and become a burden to their mothers. Fatma grumbles with a neighbour about girls: ' "Ein Mädchen ab sieben Jahren: Entweder zum Mann oder unter die Erde" . . . "Mädchen kann man nicht im Bazar verkaufen, Mädchen haben lange Haare, kurzes Gehirn" ' (217–8). ('A girl over seven: either give her to a man or bury her . . . You can't sell girls in the bazaar, girls have long hair but a little brain.')

In fact the mothers bemoan their fate of having daughters with great good humour, and Fatma, despite the numerous occasions upon which she appears to confirm the general assumptions regarding gender roles, does little, if anything, to ensure that the narrator conforms. She and Mustafa are remarkably tolerant of the narrator's independent and sometimes eccentric behaviour, and even when this is a tolerance born of despair, they show no inclination to control her through restrictive disciplinary measures, a tolerance that is also manifested in Mustafa's attitude to his wife. She, it seems, does not have to find excuses for a long walk with the narrator and Ayse: ' "Wir haben uns gelüftet" ' (140). ('We've been for an airing') is all she says. Both parents want their daughter to continue her education for as long as she can, and even Ayse encourages her to learn ' "damit du nicht die Füße des Mannes waschen mußt" ' (213) ('so that you won't have to wash a man's feet'), although Ayse is far from consistent in offering this advice. The parents do not forbid the narrator's roamings through Bursa with a group of boys whom she befriends, are happy for her to earn money through acting, resign themselves to her shaven head, and finally accept her decision to go and work in Germany.

If Fatma and Mustafa's tolerance is remarkable, this is not to say that it is rooted in any fundamental reassessment of gender, even though the effect is undoubtedly to allow the narrator freedoms that do not conform to the norm. Her behaviour is not normal, and is typically seen as that of a boy, as a sign of immaturity, or even as madness. Indeed, the narrator herself first sets off to wander through Bursa in the attempt to run through a rainbow

and so become a boy, feeling rejected as her mother's daughter by the birth of her sister Schwarze Rose. Although her desire to become a boy soon fades, her father asks her daily upon her return home whether she is a boy, and Fatma warns her ' "Bei dir wird ein Pipi wachsen" ' (147) ('you'll grow a willy'). They do not, however, forbid her adventures, and soon Ayse follows her lead. When the narrator is older, Fatma explains her behaviour as ' "sehr naiv . . . Ich glaube, ich habe sie ohne es zu wissen, als Jungen geboren" ' (218) ('very naive . . . I think she was born a boy without me noticing'). Typically, this is coupled with the anxiety about her eligibility for marriage. However, the narrator's repeated denials that she is a boy in response to Mustafa's question reflect the fact that for her, independence, the desire to explore, see more and meet new people is neither a rejection of femininity, nor of the female domestic sphere. She is just as eager to be involved here, is fully integrated into and loves the neighbourhood structures with the rituals of polite greeting and response, even if this means being late for school. She may be poor at the female skills of sewing, crochet and cooking, but is eager to please her father when demonstrating how well she can iron a crease into his trousers and make him coffee with foam, and nearly faints with joy at his praise (224). Her portrayal of two visits to the Turkish baths is of a positive haven, where women can steal a day for themselves; she is quick to comply with the expectations of the other women and lets her mother remove her pubic hairs so that she can visit the baths without feeling shame, a process that is common to all the girls and women in the street, which for her now becomes 'ein heiliger Mutter-Meryem-Maria-Mösenplanet' (264) (a holy Mother-Miriam-Mary-pussy-planet).

The fact that the narrator's unconventional behaviour does not form part of a simple rejection of femininity and desire to be a boy leads to tensions within her which manifest themselves in ever more idiosyncratic behaviour as she enters puberty. As has become clear, those around the narrator cannot think of her behaviour as extending or redefining what it might be to be a girl, but can only name it in relation to a rigid male–female polarity. Not surprisingly, the narrator herself is still caught up within this polarity even while experiencing its inadequacy herself. The clearest example of this is when her mother's cousin comes to visit, the respected man before whom Mustafa sits like a woman. He joins Fatma in the kitchen to help make the meal, and immediately becomes a woman in the narrator's eyes: 'Da wurde mein Onkel zu einer Frau, von ihm kam jetzt ein Tantengeruch . . . Dann fingen er und meine Mutter an, von ihren Toten zu reden, und beide seufzten wie zwei alte Frauen, da wurde er zu meiner Großmutter' (331). (Then my uncle became a woman, he smelled of Aunt . . . Then he and

my mother began to speak of their dead and they both sighed like two old women. Then my uncle became my grandmother.) Caught between her awareness of her own femininity, a fascination with new and varied experiences in all spheres of life, which undermines conventional definitions of femininity, and her own awareness of gender polarity, it is not surprising that the onset of menstruation results in a period of intense melancholic introversion. The narrator withdraws into the tiny dark room in which her washed towels dry out of sight of the menfolk, sings mournful songs to herself, keeps herself awake by wearing a wet shirt, and shaves her head. This is not the first time that she has responded to a growing awareness of her own sexuality with behaviour that has confounded her family. When her breasts grow, she becomes fascinated by men, including her father, and with sex, sucking her own arms to make lovebites, and drawing marks over her body, yet at the same time she clings to her mother every time they walk past a man, and pretends to be blind or lame if women pass by.

Such unusual behaviour results in her parents wondering whether their aberrant daughter is mad, let alone like a boy. Fatma sees in the narrator's eagerness to observe and participate actively in her surroundings similarities to the mad: ' "Meine Tochter ... warum öffnest du deine Augen wie die Verrückten. Die Männer werden vor dir Angst kriegen" ' (218). ('My daughter . . . why do you open your eyes like a madman. Men will get scared of you.') She confides to her cousin ' "Sie öffnet, wie die Verrückten, ihre Augen so weit" ' (328). (She opens her eyes so wide, like mad people do.) Here madness provides an easy framework for explaining a woman who does not confine herself to the norm, given the absence of other explanations, for with puberty even the excuse of the narrator's boyishness seems inappropriate. Yet this absence of explanation is in itself a feature of the narrator's situation; she does not attempt an explanation and does not reflect upon the reasons for or meaning of her reactions. Although fully in character with the narrator's constant urge to explore, it is not difficult to surmise that her decision to leave Turkey springs too from a desire to express herself as a woman without provoking the accusations of maleness or madness. It must be stressed, however, that the narrator does not herself suggest reasons for her decision to go to Germany, but again merely describes the process of informing her family. And this is an important absence. For central to any understanding of this text is the fact that the lack of analysis or explanation is also a fundamental feature of the narrator's narrative style; she offers no retrospective elucidation of her younger self, describing no more than she felt at the time, arguably even less. This crucial aspect of the text will be analyzed in detail below, and its implications considered. First, however, it

is necessary to turn to the broad theme of history, and its relationship to national identity and death.

NATIONAL IDENTITY, DEATH AND HISTORY

"Karagöz ist ein Zigeuner oder Bauer, Hacivat ist ein Stadtmann, Lehrer vielleicht, und sie sprechen und verstehen sich immer falsch. Dann lachen die Menschen. Im Schattenspiel gibt es Juden, Griechen, Armenier, Halbstarke, Nutten, jeder spricht einen anderen Dialekt, jeder ist ein anderes Musikinstrument, redet nach seiner eigenen Zunge und versteht die anderen nicht . . . Das ist unser Land . . . wir sind ein an Menschen reiches Land, aber ein armes Land." (157)

('Karagöz is a gypsy or a farmer, Hacivat is from the city, maybe a teacher, and they talk and always misunderstand each other. That makes people laugh. In a shadow play there are Jews, Greeks, Armenians, hooligans and prostitutes, everyone speaks a different dialect, everyone is a different musical instrument, speaks his own language and doesn't understand the others . . . This is our country . . . we are rich in people, but a poor country.')

It is telling that Fatma's description of Turkey depends upon the fiction of the shadow puppet characters, stories that render comic the deep rift between educated urban and traditional agricultural Turkey, between citizens of different faiths and origin who fail to understand each other, stories that are accessible to a general population through visual and oral effects. It forms part of a sustained juxtaposition in the text between an expression of identity dependent on oral tradition on the one hand, explaining the past through the medium of stories and character stereotype, with an emphasis on the fate of the common individual, and the official reality of the Turkish nation on the other hand, the remote and corrupt parties and politicians with their susceptibility to American manipulation and disregard of the common man.

The text makes it very clear that Turkey is a country in which differences of all sorts abound, differences which are not necessarily respected or tolerated. The contrast between urban and rural traditions is becoming ever more marked, as are generational differences, both of which become evident during Ahmet's stay with Fatma. Class and education are divisive, so that when the narrator is in hospital, her parents and the doctors speak to one another as though in a foreign tongue (353). The narrator suffers and benefits from strongly held regional prejudice. When at school in Istanbul, her teacher belittles her for being born in Malatya, Anatolia, taunting her ' "Kurdin, du hast einen Schwanz an deinem Arsch" ' (37). ('You Kurd, you've got a tail on your arse.') In contrast, at school in Yenisehir, she is the

'girl from Istanbul', and is praised daily for her cleverness. Fatma is appalled when her daughter returns from her holiday in Anatolia with an acquired regional accent, and fines her until she has learned to speak Istanbul-style again, a painful process for the narrator. However, these often profound differences do not contradict the notion of Turkish identity represented by Fatma's description, since that particular idea of Turkish consciousness allows for people doing their own thing, even if it is disliked. Indeed, it would initially appear that the narrator is eager to depict Turkish identity as premised upon a multiplicity that she refuses to idealize; for she not only exposes the antagonism it can cause, but concurrently seems to emphasize the proximity of identity to fictionality and performance through explicitly linking the theme of national identity with shadow puppetry.

Thus from the point of view of the narrator and her family, national consciousness is not felt to be represented in a particular set of people deemed to be more 'Turkish' than others. However, it becomes clear that there is nevertheless a more nebulous affirmation of certain qualities, which are consistently set in opposition to the influence of the United States. Neighbourliness, storytelling and the importance of community are presented as positive qualities which the increasing remoteness of the politicians, their corruption and the pandering of the ruling party to the United States threaten to undermine. These qualities are nowhere explicitly defined as Turkish, nor presented as exclusively Turkish characteristics. They are, though, qualities that, by being linked to the legacy of Atatürk and through their juxtaposition with an increasingly pervasive and corrupting American presence, are implicitly given the function of representing Turkishness, thereby in fact offering an essentializing countermovement in the text.

Throughout the book, politicians are depicted as remote and removed from the interests of the common people, as merciless men who have no understanding of the poverty and hardship being suffered. When the narrator asks, ' "Wer ist der Staat?" ' (62). ('Who is the state?'), Ayse responds: ' "Die da oben, Sie pinkeln von oben herunter auf unsere Köpfe." ' ('Those up there: they piss on our heads.') More specifically, these politicians belong to the ruling Democratic Party, whereas the allegiance of the narrator's family lies with the republican People's Party, the party of Atatürk. The Democrats are shown to resort to undemocratic measures to undermine political opposition: the 'furzende Onkel' (farting uncle), Democrat Mayor, attempts to tamper with the voting forms (211); '[Mehmet Ali Bey] war von den Demokratischen Partei-Leuten in dieses Dorf verbannt worden, weil er in der republikanischen Volkspartei war' (193). (Mehmet Ali Bey had been exiled to this village by the Democratic Party people because he was in the

Republican Party); and shopkeepers are forbidden to admit that there are shortages, instead telling customers ' "alles ist verkauft" ' (251) ('sold out'). The most profound resentment is provoked by the fact that this evident corruption is combined with what is perceived as selling out to the Americans. According to Tante Sidika, ' "Die Demokratische Partei hat das Land, ohne unsere Mütter zu fragen, Amerika in einer Nacht als Nutte serviert, auf dem Tablett . . . Kinder, eure Ärsche bereithalten, es wird alles von Amerika gefickt" ' (171). ('In one night the Democratic Party served our country to America as a prostitute on a platter without asking our mothers . . . Children, get your arses ready: everything is fucked by America.') The Democrats' turning away from the needs of the people in order to pander to the Americans seems to the narrator's family and friends to take on tangible shape in the form of American food aid that no one can eat. The powdered milk makes the narrator vomit (132), and is refused even by the alley dogs (164), and the meat is American meat, three years old and frozen. The resentment against the apparent Democrat – United States complicity in exploiting and victimizing large sections of the population is summed up in an extreme, but not unrepresentative manner by the student Arkadas, a particularly ardent People's Party supporter: ' "Hier, was der Demokraten-Bettler aus Amerika für uns gekriegt hat, vielleicht ist es Indianerfleisch. Sie haben ja nicht alle getöteten Indianer begraben" ' (255). ('Maybe what the Democrat-beggars have got for us from America is Indian meat. They never buried all the murdered Indians.')

This reference to the Native Americans is an interesting one, for with it Arkadas establishes an implicit identification between them and the People's Party which is suggestive of a claim to authenticity. If the Native Americans were the original Americans, later to be treated ruthlessly for the gain of the white settlers, so too the People's Party was the original democratic party, founded by Atatürk, whose supporters are now being ruthlessly excluded for the gain of the Democrats. I have no desire to labour this particular comparison, marginal as it is in the text. However, it does reflect a more pervasive tendency within the text to idealize the legacy of Atatürk and to associate him with the desires of the ordinary individual. Again, this is conveyed through the family's unwavering political allegiance to the party he founded and the esteem in which he is held, particularly by Fatma. As she explains to the narrator, ' "Wie kann man Atatürk nicht lieben. Wenn es ihn nicht gegeben hätte, wären jetzt nicht wir hier so schön gelaufen, sondern unsere Schatten" ' (138). ('How can you not love Atatürk? If he hadn't existed we wouldn't have gone on such a nice walk, our shadows would have done.') As a woman Fatma is particularly aware of the impact of

his policy of modernization and secularization, but she also emphasizes his normality as someone who visited her school in Anatolia and who died of raki-drinking. It is this perceived normality that the official state memorials ignore, sacrificing individuality to grandeur. Atatürk's mausoleum belittles its visitors through its imposing marble columns, marble stairs, marble walls and marble coffin, all of which are guarded by soldiers whose helmets nearly cover their eyes and whose expressions are no longer their own. The narrator concludes that 'Dieses Marmorzimmer war nicht für Atatürk gemacht. Das Zimmer war so gemacht, daß wir sahen, wie alt unsere Kleider und Schuhe waren' (314). (This marble room wasn't made for Atatürk. The room was made in such a way that we saw how old our clothes and shoes were.) The mausoleum is a betrayal of Atatürk; even the sultans never erected such buildings: 'Ihre Zimmer waren wie für Nomaden gemacht' (315). (Their rooms were made as though for nomads.)

Thus what the narrator emphasizes about Atatürk is not the grandeur of his status as head of state, represented in the anonymity of state monuments, but his role as Father-Turk, the title proffered him by the Assembly in 1934; in the eyes of her family, and of many, he was a man who did not become remote through high office, but remained one of his people. As 'Father-Turk' he remains identified with community, whereas the corrupt Democrat politicians have betrayed Turkey to the Americans for personal gain. It is in keeping with the impressionistic nature of the narrative technique and its emphasis on the narrator's immediate experience, that no broader analysis or comment on politics or Atatürk's legacy is offered to contextualize what is depicted. The family's affiliations and prejudices are presented without mediation or reflection, a crucial aspect of the text which will be discussed in detail below. The point here, however, is that it does not matter whether Atatürk actually died of raki-drinking or not, or remained in contact with ordinary people or not, but that the narrator, her family and acquaintances stress those qualities which, in their view, are sadly lacking in the contemporary political world. By showing how her family links community and concern for the ordinary individual with the figure of Atatürk, the narrator reveals implicit assumptions about those qualities that are felt to be typically Turkish.

The strong sense of community and the importance of neighbourliness mean that no one is regarded as being beyond the appeal to a common humanity. All people have family and the effect of this is to level out differences. So the Democrat leaders may have acquired power and status, but they still have mothers: ' "Wenn nur ihre Mütter sie einmal lange genug schlagen würden" ' (261). ('If only their mothers would beat them for long

enough.') But when two leading Democrat politicians are finally punished following the military coup, resulting in their death by hanging and the subsequent dragging away of the bodies by a rubbish-lorry, both Fatma and Ayse are horrified: 'Großmutter . . . fing an zu weinen und sagte: "Aboooo, was machen jetzt ihre Mütter? . . . Kann der Bruder den Bruder töten, wie Kabil und Habil? Ich scheiße auf diese Welt" ' (349). (Grandmother . . . started to cry and said, 'Abooo, what are their mothers doing now? . . . Can one brother murder the other like Cain and Abel? I shit on this world.') Ayse's linking of contemporary political debates with the story of Cain and Abel is significant, for it points to the close relationship of notions of community with storytelling, which adds a further dimension to the juxtaposition of the corrupt politicians, sacrificing Turkey to America, with the more humane qualities of the 'ordinary people'.

Storytelling has a central role in the life of the family. It is usually a shared experience, whether they are listening to one of Ayse's old stories or whether the narrator and Ali are reading *Madame Bovary* aloud to Ayse, Baumwolltante and Savki Dayi. Generally, Ayse's tales are moral stories with themes such as patience rewarded, adultery punished, or the dangers of not listening to one's wife. In the form of a *Märchen*, moral messages are couched in fantasy, giving rise to a dispute between Fatma and Ayse about how true a story is. For Fatma, a *Märchen* is not true because it did not really happen, whereas Ayse comments that ' "die Sterne können mit den Sternen sprechen, die Menschen können mit den Menschen nicht sprechen" ' (257) ('the stars can speak with the stars, but people can't speak with people'), suggesting that stories are a better form of communication than dialogue. Few would dispute Ayse's point if made in relation to evidently fictional forms. However, her assertion becomes more controversial if storytelling skills and the fictions they employ are directed to representing history, which is precisely what Grandfather Ahmet and Mehmet Ali Bey choose to do.

On the long train journey from Istanbul to Anatolia, when the seven-year-old narrator is travelling with her Grandfather Ahmet to spend the summer with him, he tells a long story: 'Sein unrasierter Bart wuchs auf seinem Gesicht, und der Bart fing an, einen Teppich zu weben' (38). (His unshaved beard grew on his face and the beard began to weave a carpet.) On this carpet are depicted the moving images of Ahmet's tale, thereby combining one symbol of the Orient, the (magic) carpet, with another, the tradition of oral storytelling. Ahmet's story is the story of his own lifetime, of his emigration from the Caucasus in the time of the Tsar; his success as a farmer in Anatolia, where he lived with five wives and children; of his fighting in the First World War; and of his time as a bandit

and smuggler after the war. His personal story is entwined with political history in fictionalized form; the decline of the Ottoman Empire under the sultans and the ruthless exploitation of architectural and mineral wealth by the Germans, British, French and Italians: 'Bismark [kam] wieder zum Teppich und brachte deutsche Eimer, mit denen er das Öl von Bagdad mit nach Hause schleppen wollte. Die Engländer und Franzosen und Italiener hörten es und kamen mit ihren eigenen Eimern in die Türkei' (39). (Bismark came back to the carpet and brought German buckets to carry home the oil from Baghdad. The English, French and Italians heard of it and came to Turkey with their own buckets.) History is shrunk into caricature; the foreign powers become buckets, all the sultans become one figure, Atatürk is the blue-eyed officer, and the new officials of the Republic of Turkey the men in tail-coats and bowler hats. Finally Ahmet describes the Americans as gum-chewing vampires, who forget their words of freedom and equality and suck Turkey dry.

Mehmet Ali Bey's rendering of history does not incorporate his own biography, but he too is eager to undermine 'official' versions of history, farting on his son's history book and replacing it with his own satirical story. With his trousers round his ankles and with a pomegranate tree as his main prop, he enacts a tale of European greed and Turkish vanity:

Dann kletterte Mehmet Ali Bey auf den Baum, seine heruntergelassene Hose hing jetzt den Baum herunter und flatterte im Wind . . . 'England und Rußland hatten 1907 abgemacht, das Osmanische Reich zu zerschneiden . . . Dann kamen die Deutschen, als Archäologen verkleidet, und suchten Petrol. Die Deutschen hatten es eilig. Sie hatten sich verspätet und wollten sich schnell nach Osten ausbreiten.' (196)

(Then Mehmet Ali Bey climbed up the tree and the trousers he had let down hung from the tree and flapped in the wind . . . 'England and Russia had agreed in 1907 to divide the Ottoman Empire . . . Then the Germans came disguised as archaeologists and looked for petrol. They were in a hurry. They'd arrived late and wanted to spread out quickly in the East.')

Both men, in their different styles, make political history personal and accessible through the art of storytelling. Ahmet reveals to the soldiers sharing his compartment their own grandmothers in his unfolding carpet, and Mehmet Ali Bey exposes the petty but damaging humanity of the leaders through his critical buffoonery. In their examples, history represented as oral story rather than official discourse allows for the affirmation of community, and emphasizes the importance of the individual in constructing their version of events. In this text, it is through the medium of storytelling

that a sense of Turkish identity is asserted in opposition to the Western European and American powers; it is done both explicitly in the content of the stories the men tell, and implicitly in the manner of the telling.

Overall, the narrator treads a wary path between on the one hand refusing to define any specific national identity by celebrating the diversity of people and classes in Turkey while not pretending that these different groups necessarily like or understand each other, and on the other hand juxtaposing qualities of community, neighbourliness and storytelling with Americanization and individualism in such a way that the former qualities clearly assume the status of a positive alternative to the latter. At best, such positive qualities are depicted as part of the wider context of the narrator's childhood and youth, and are thus shown to be part of the pragmatic and changing responses to tradition and modernization that her family make. In this reading, national identity is historically specific and cannot be isolated as an abstract concept separable from the individual's experience; so even the dominating figure of Atatürk, the 'father of Turkey', loved by Fatma for the emancipation and modernization he imposed, is not without ambiguity. As the narrator points out, repeating a point made in *Mutterzunge*,[3] he was responsible for the alphabet reform that would prevent the narrator communicating with her grandparents if they were deaf and dumb (69). National identity is the product of the individual's interaction with the community, and is therefore in flux and potentially ambivalent or contradictory.

But it is indeed a problematic path: a more sceptical reading of the contrast between the virtues associated with the community and the ills linked to the predominantly male public and political sphere exposes the tendency towards idealization and simplification. 'Turkishness' begins to assume almost stereotypical characteristics associated with the Orient: the extended family, the supportive female domestic sphere, the community with its rules of hospitality now lost to the West, the corrupt public servants and unstable government and so on. Furthermore, the narrator runs the risk of consolidating rather than challenging the gendered discourses surrounding the public/domestic dichotomy; hence the traditions of orality and the *Märchen*, exemplified in the figure of the old grandmother, become unquestionably feminine. I would not wish to argue that the narrator does this consistently, since in the figures of Grandfather Ahmet and Mehmet Ali Bey orality is shown not to be exclusively feminine; nevertheless, their tales are concerned with political history whereas Ayse's are more typically fairytales concerned with convention and custom. The effect of this essentializing tendency within the text is to feminize the 'alternative'

national identity based on cultural difference that the narrator is striving for, establishing thereby a dualism that pits the feminized Orient against the masculinized West.

The narrator attempts to repudiate an abstract concept of national identity by emphasizing the primacy of individual interaction within a specific community, and, similarly, she refutes a notion of history removed from the sphere of the individual and her or his immediate experience. The role that storytelling plays in both suggesting new historical perspectives and limiting those perspectives by reinforcing a gendered discourse has been discussed. Yet perhaps the narrator's most radical insistence on the importance of remembering the individual in history is made through the theme of death. Death is omnipresent in this book; the second sentence already refers to the smell of dead and not-dead soldiers, establishing the point that being alive is no more than being not yet dead. Shortly afterwards the narrator herself is left in a freshly dug grave as a baby, to let Allah decide if she is to live or die. Fortunately Ayse intervenes. From this point on the narrator is concerned with death and the dead, and her narrative traces a development from initial fear to positive affirmation of death's presence. As a girl she fears the immanence of death, but sees it reflected in the faces of the poor quarry workers of Yenisehir: 'Ich sah in ihren Gesichtern die Gesichter der Soldaten, die ich aus dem Bauch meiner Mutter im schwarzen Zug gesehen hatte' (87). (I saw in their faces the faces of the soldiers I had seen from my mother's stomach in the black train.) The proximity of death triggers a period of sorrow and anxiety in the girl; she wants Ayse to tell her the warning sign of death's approach and learns from her superstitious methods for deceiving death, so that he should pass by. The narrator then attempts to deceive death on behalf of each of the forty quarry workers, listing them individually and weeping inconsolably. Her sorrow is finally alleviated by finding one of the Prophet Mohammed's eyelashes in the Koran with Ayse, evidence of his own weeping. This is a significant episode for two reasons: it shows the ways in which the narrator comes to terms with the fear and sorrow that death engenders, in a cultural context in which the effects of death are not palliated or denied; furthermore, it is the first time that the narrator responds to death by listing individuals, a response that soon gains in ritual importance.

The narrator learns that death is an inseparable part of life, and that the affirmation of life and love enables her concurrently to affirm death and the dead. Thus in the 'Seelenlose Gasse' (129) (soulless alley) in Bursa, where the wealthy women keep themselves to themselves and there is no life on the street, the lifelessness also makes death ominous once again: 'Die Gasse

ist still, so still, daß ich den Tod nicht mehr liebe, nicht mehr mit ihm spiele' (121). (The alley is quiet, so quiet that I no longer love death, no longer play with him.) In contrast, when the dead are accepted as part of the living community of the present, the experience of the present is enhanced. Fatma and Ayse tell each other of the dead while making the winter macaroni supply, and graveyards are places for the living and for life; the communal picnic takes place in the graveyard in Bursa, where 'die Schatten von den Friedhofsbäumen die Lebenden mit den Toten [verbinden]' (316) (the shadows of the graveyard trees bind the living with the dead). Past lives are considered central to the present, and this natural inclusion of the dead in the activities and thoughts of the living brings with it the potential for a history which emphasizes the specificity of the ordinary life. This other face of history is powerfully evoked in the imagery of W. H. Auden's 'Homage to Clio', in which he differentiates between Artemis and Aphrodite, who 'are Major Powers', and Clio, who 'look[s] like any / Girl one has not noticed'. He tells Clio, who is easily overlooked

> I have seen
> Your photo, I think, in the papers, nursing
> A baby, or mourning a corpse: each time
>
> You had nothing to say and did not, one could see,
> Observe where you were, Muse of the unique
> Historical fact [. . .][4]

The poet goes on to admit that 'Making of silence decisive sound: it sounds / Easy, but one must find the time.' Michael Wood comments that '[f]inding the time means abandoning the privileged perch . . . remembering in their unrepeatable individuality the baby and the corpse and the nurse and the mourner'.[5]

Finding the time to remember is precisely what the narrator repeatedly does each night in her prayers. She returns from a long walk with Fatma and Ayse: 'Ich fiel ins Bett . . . und fing von diesem Abend an, bevor ich schlief, für die Seelen der Toten die arabischen Gebete zu sagen und die Namen der Toten, die ich kannte oder deren Namen ich gehört hatte, zu nennen' (140). (I fell into bed . . . and from that evening, before I slept, I started to say the Arabic prayers for the souls of the dead and to say the names of the dead that I knew or whose names I had heard.) Her prayers for the dead bring together the disparate people she has met or heard of, and as she lists them the narrator invites her reader to take the time to remember also. For, as Horrocks point out,[6] the repetition of names forces the reader to remember characters who have only very

briefly appeared and would otherwise be quickly forgotten, and as she grows older, these lists of names become longer. The prayers often produce some surprising and amusing juxtapositions, neatly proving the point that death is a great leveller: 'Ich betete . . . "Für Atatürk, für Isadora Duncan, meine tote Großmutter, die tote armenische Frau, die im Hauseingang in Istanbul gestorben war, alle acht Kinder meiner Großmutter" [etc.]' (146). ('I prayed . . . "For Atatürk, for Isadora Duncan, for my dead grandmother, the dead Armenian woman who had died in the doorway in Istanbul, for all eight children of my grandmother" [etc.].') However, the narrator's repetitions also make a more serious point. Taking the time to remember is not just an amusing game of memory but can be an onerous exercise, as onerous as reading through the pages of the narrator's prayers for the dead soldiers of the First World War. After hearing Mehmet Ali Bey's account of the suffering inflicted by that conflict, the narrator lists the names of the dead of whom she has heard, but 'dann kamen die vier Millionen Soldaten' (199) (then came the four million soldiers). Not knowing their names, she lists them by number over the next three pages: 'Für den ersten toten Soldaten, für den zweiten toten Soldaten . . . für den hundertdreiundzwanzigsten toten Soldaten' (199–202). (For the first dead soldier, for the second dead soldier . . . for the one hundred and twenty-third dead soldier.) Luckily she falls asleep, and it is only the most careful of readers who does not hasten through or skip the list. '[I]t sounds / Easy, but one must find the time'; the narrator reminds the reader of the importance of the ordinary individual in history, of their place in the present, and of the fact that remembering the ordinary can require effort on the part of the audience too. Perhaps that is why, as Auden puts it, 'So few of the Big / Ever listen.'[7]

QUESTIONING AND METAPHOR

Das Leben ist eine Karawanserei is alive with the narrator's recollections and impressions of smells, sounds, people, their customs and episodes from her childhood, linked only chronologically in order to trace her growing-up in Turkey. What is evidently absent from her account is analysis or explanation; description dominates, and the narrator takes no opportunity to offer retrospective comment on what she depicts, to question its nature or to reflect on the implications of events from a position of narratorial authority. This lack of questioning, of seeking explanation, is evident both in what she describes, and the manner in which she describes it. So, in relation to Grandfather Ahmet's murder of Fatma's mother, the narrator remarks: 'Was mich etwas erstaunte, war, daß meine Mutter ihn nie fragte,

warum er es gemacht hatte' (306). (What rather surprised me was that my mother never asked him why he had done it.) Yet, although surprised at this observation, she does no more than report it, neither asking her mother about her reticence, nor herself reflecting upon what the reasons might be. There are numerous examples of such parallel levels of reserve; when Tante Rezzan rents a flat for them in Ankara, no one asks why she has done so, nor does the narrator comment; when the narrator decides to leave for Germany, no one asks her why, nor does she comment; and when the narrator spends five months alone with her father on the Eastern border of Turkey at Mount Ararat, neither of them speaks about the loneliness, and the narrator merely reports it in a matter-of-fact tone: 'Ich wußte nicht, wohin er ging, ich wußte nur, daß er im Offiziershäuserbau arbeitete' (362). (I didn't know where he went, I only knew that he worked building the officers' homes.)

In this last example, the lack of comment or elaboration is a device which evokes the sense of loneliness and silence of the area. Nevertheless, the fact that the narrator so often restricts herself to a bland, almost reporter-like tone is evidence of her reluctance to judge or comment on a situation, or even to contextualize it. So after the coup, when the family are living in Tante Rezzan's house, the narrator wanders between the third and fourth floor, listening to the different political conversations. On the third floor Rezzan is telling Fatma of the benefits of the Democratic Party, on the fourth, Ali, his schizophrenic friend and their teacher are presenting an anti-American and pro-communist argument. Once again, the narrator merely relates what she hears. Her remoteness is perhaps most marked at moments of extreme emotional upheaval and confusion, and is manifested in a lack of psychologizing and in the grammatically simple sentence structures used. When Fatma threatens suicide, the narrator's description is restricted to external observations:

Ich saß vor der Tür des Sofa-und-Sessel-Zimmers und schaute auf meine Füße. Ali und meine Großmutter sagten: 'Sie stirbt.' Ich blieb weiter vor der Tür stehen und konnte nicht reingehen. Meine Mutter saß auf dem Sofa, und Großmutter steckte ihren Finger in ihren Hals. (234)

(I sat in front of the door of the sofa-and-armchair room and looked at my feet. Ali and my grandmother said, 'She's dying.' I stood still again in front of the door and couldn't go in. My mother sat on the sofa and grandmother stuck her fingers down her throat.)

Similarly, when the narrator takes an overdose, she lets the reader assume her state of mind and emotions through the depiction of external events, not the description of those emotions. The first occasion is in response to

her mother's severe depression, and although she describes the hallucinatory experience she has, she does not mention her emotions:

Ich trank vierzehn Aspirin, mein Magen kam in Wellen hoch . . . Als mein Körper im Hurrican von der Steppe in Richtung Schnellstraße verschwand, fiel mein am Fenster sitzender Körper vom Stuhl auf den Boden . . . Großmutter brachte mich zum Kotzen und gab mir Knoblauchyoghurt. (290–1)

(I drank fourteen aspirin, my stomach came up in waves . . . As my body disappeared within the hurricane from the Steppes, travelling in the direction of the fast road, my body sitting at the window fell from the chair to the floor . . . Grandmother made me sick and gave me garlic yoghurt.)

The second occasion is triggered by her father's refusal to let her go and see 'Porky and Bes': 'Er sagte . . . er könnte mich nicht allein zwischen den hungrigen Wölfen sitzen lassen. Ich schluckte anstatt einer halben Tablette zwei Tabletten, machte in der Küche den Gashahn auf, steckte den Schlauch in meinen Mund und schlief ein' (351). (He said . . . he couldn't let me sit alone between the hungry wolves. I swallowed two tablets instead of a half, turned on the gas tap in the kitchen, put the tube in my mouth and went to sleep.)

It could well be argued that this narrative style is a device to emphasize the perspective of the child, who is limited in her understanding both of others' emotions and complex reasons for behaving as they do, and her own; as though the reader is offered only the perceptions and impressions available to the narrator at the time. However, although the style may partly function in this way, and may often be successful in evoking the supposed naive perspective of a child, this explanation is not in itself an adequate one. This is because the perspective is neither systematically that of the child, nor does it develop coherently in relation to the narrator's age. Özdamar's narrator does not attempt the detailed realism of, for example, Esther Freud's narrator in *Hideous Kinky*, whose perspective adheres to that of a five-year-old girl, and whose story is limited to a period of just over a year.[8] In *Karawanserei*, there is no attempt at such realism and the narrator at different times knows more than her age, or reveals little of what she thinks; so whereas she starts her tale by recounting what she sees and thinks from her mother's womb, she conceals the processes of her decision to leave for Germany. Thus, whereas the chronology of Özdamar's book spans about nineteen years, the narrative style never develops to reflect the narrator's age as it does in such marked form in Joyce's *A Portrait of the Artist as a Young Man*;[9] the style of Özdamar's narrator remains the same whether she is seven or seventeen, whether she is playing or menstruating.

I would like to argue that Özdamar's apparent naivety of presentation, her narrator's general reluctance to psychologize, analyze or comment, has little to do with the attempt to emulate a child's perspective, and a great deal to do with the privileging of metaphor as explanation. There are numerous instances in the text that point to the importance of the role of metaphor for answering or responding to questions, be it directly, or in the extended form of a story. So when the narrator asks her grandmother 'warum die Menschen mal so, mal so sind' (69) (why people are sometimes this way and then sometimes that), Ayse responds with an image: ' "Ein Hals, aus dem die Stimme rauskommt, hat vierzig Etagen. Wenn man was sagen will, muß man erst vierzig mal schlucken und dann sprechen, manche Leute sprechen, ohne zu schlucken, dann steht in der Mitte eine Hand voller Scheiße" ' (69). ('A throat out of which the voice comes has forty floors. If you want to say something, you have to swallow forty times first and then speak. Some people speak without swallowing, then you're left with a handful of shit.') When the narrator asks Ayse why she tried to imitate a limping boy, offending him in the process, Ayse remarks, ' "manchmal hat man Affenappetit" ' (136) ('sometimes you feel like behaving like a monkey'), and she encourages Fatma not to think too much about Mustafa's nightclub exploits, saying, ' "hebe nicht so viele Steine auf, sonst triffst du Schlangen oder Skorpione" ' (234) ('don't lift so many stones or you'll meet snakes or scorpions'). Similarly Fatma, when the children ask about why she attempted suicide and why Mustafa goes to the nightclub, responds briefly, ' "Meine Seele hat mich erdrückt' " (236) ('My soul was oppressing me'), then goes on to offer a fuller explanation of Mustafa's behaviour by relating the story of his great grandfather, the moral of which is that ' "die Sippe eures Vaters sind heilige naive Menschen'" (237) ('your father's clan are holy, naive people'). Events or people become understandable through analogy with animals, ancestors and events, often in familiar story form, a framework for comprehending the world that rejects processes of detached analysis or comment from a privileged position.

The inadequacy or even impossibility of distanced analysis is emphatically exposed on the occasion when the narrator suffers a day of extreme existential crisis. Time seems to slow down for her, she no longer recognizes herself, and repeatedly asks her family who she is and what she is called. Such fundamental questions about herself, with which she seeks to objectify the nature of existence, soon sound hollow in her own ears and can receive no adequate reply: 'Irgendwann fragte ich nicht mehr, denn diese Fragen verloren ihr fragende Stimme und klangen in meinen Ohren wie die Antworten der anderen, die für mich keine Antworten waren, weil sie

mir nicht die Augen über mein Leben öffneten' (313). (Then the time came when I didn't ask any more questions, because these questions lost their questioning tone and sounded to me like other people's answers, which for me weren't answers since they didn't open my eyes about my life.) Neither the narrator nor her family ever know what happened to her, for she wakes up the next morning her normal self. But it is important to juxtapose with this experience of futile questions and answers the only other explicit response to the problem of the meaning of life. This is the metaphor offered up by the book as a whole; that life is 'eine Karawanserei hat zwei Türen aus einer kam ich rein aus der anderen ging ich raus' (a caravanserai; it has two doors, I came in through one and went out of the other). Like the progression of events and impressions for which it acts as the title, this metaphor emphasizes sequence and not causality, the participation in tangible and familiar actions, not a self-reflexive response to them.

In its privileging of the role of metaphor the text expresses its scepticism of reflection and questions the value of ratiocination, celebrating instead forms of thinking that are not rational and a culture in which metaphor is depicted as being central to daily communication. The juxtaposition of metaphor to reason is a more complex development of the opposition between the values associated with community and storytelling, and the ceaseless Americanization and corruption of official state politics, discussed earlier. Metaphor, and with it, reason, thus stands in a crucial and defining relationship to the text's understanding of national identity, a relationship heavily inflected by how metaphor is itself understood. For if *Karawanserei* is viewed in relation to the tradition of rhetorical and philosophical debate in which metaphor and reason are evaluated in terms of the epithets 'primitive' or 'progressive', it is difficult to see the narrator escaping the trap of idealizing orientalism. If, however, metaphor is seen in its broadest sense as ontological, the potential for understanding Özdamar's text is broadened. It is these interpretative possibilities that I shall now explore.

The understanding of metaphor has, of course, developed historically, but the undermining of metaphor in relation to more valued forms of expression can already be identified in Aristotle. In *On Rhetoric*, Book III, his references to poetic language are derogatory: 'in speech such things are not only rather unsuitable, but if used immoderately they convict [the writer of artificality (*sic*)] and make it clear that this is "poetry".'[10] As Stephen Halliwell comments:

Even when, as in *Poetics* 21–2, Ar. is attempting to formulate a positive doctrine of poetic style, it is clear that he is concerned primarily with stylistic ornament in the choice of vocabulary, and not with any deeper features of poetic writing. Ar.

assumes, in other words, that the poet, at any rate if he is a good poet, will always be striving for an essential standard of clarity, and this means that the question of style can be reduced to a matter of the degree and kind of verbal embellishment which will secure a distinctive poetic flavour without detracting unduly from lucidity.[11]

For Aristotle, style is secondary to content, to the meaning that must be conveyed, and as George Kennedy argues, given that his approach was then followed by most ancient rhetoricians, 'the result is that invention and style became separate processes: thoughts, already worked out and arranged, are then deliberately cast into words'.[12]

Reacting vehemently and with inspired polemic against the tradition that was so influenced by the 'father of the study of metaphor',[13] Giambattista Vico set out to 'demolish two common errors of the grammarians: that prose is the proper form of speech, and poetic speech improper; and that men spoke first in prose and later in verse'.[14] In his analysis of the origins of language, Vico refutes the 'unclear, frivolous, inept, conceited, and ridiculous, not to mention . . . numerous' opinions of many scholars,[15] arguing instead that language started as an 'innate poetic faculty' among the ancient pagans, and that their poetry 'sprang naturally from their ignorance of causes'.[16] Poetic logic is thus intrinsic to language: 'All figures of speech may be reduced to these four types – metaphor, metonymy, synecdoche, and irony – which were previously thought to be the ingenious inventions of writers.'[17] Central to Vico's argument is the comparison of the historical development of language to children's language acquisition; the first words are onomatopoeic, followed by exclamation, then by pronouns and nouns, until finally the 'authors of languages formed verbs'.[18] Verbs represent a more advanced form of language, since, whereas nouns result in 'clear mental imprints', verbs 'signify motion, which implies past and future moments measured against an indivisible present, a concept which even the philosophers find difficult to grasp'.[19] Thus Vico relates changes in language and consciousness to an individual life: 'In other words, the first peoples were the children of the human race, and founded the world of the arts. Coming much later, the philosophers were the old men of the nations and founded the world of the sciences, by which civilization was completed.'[20] He does not, however, evaluate the development from poetic to philosophical logic as an advance, but views it as a cyclical process 'in the sense that individuals constitutionally rework an inherited pattern of evolution on their own terms. Our lives are repetitions of the same self at different stages of its development.'[21]

If, in distinguishing between poetic and philosophic conscience, Vico refused to privilege one over the other, seeing continuity and not opposition

between the two,[22] in contrast the Romantic tradition was eager to valorize poetic consciousness, and with it primitivity. Characteristics deemed to be typical of primitivity became highly valued, such as, for example, authenticity, naivety, proximity to nature and greater spirituality. In his *Defence of Poetry*, originally written to defend poetry against attacks on its relevance in a rational age, Shelley praises poetry's link with the primitive: 'Poetry is connate with the origin of man.'[23] 'In the youth of the world, men dance and sing and imitate natural objects, observing in these actions, as in all others, a certain rhythm or order' (481). He asserts: 'Their language is vitally metaphorical' (482). It is in relation to the Romantic tradition that Özdamar's text and its privileging of metaphor can be understood. Looked at in terms of both the culture described and how it is depicted, the typical features of the 'primitive poetic consciousness' are present in the text; the primacy of metaphor, onomatopoeia, assumed naivety, the rejection of analysis or comment, orality. In this respect Özdamar is placing herself within the Romantic tradition of privileging the primitive. But although the impact of the positive depiction of a Turkish childhood on the reader may be to enhance sympathy for another culture and encourage a shift in attitude from suspicion of that culture to understanding of it, it probably does little to invite the reader to ponder the tacit assumptions underlying and sustaining the opposition. Certainly, what the blurb of the book tries to sell is an escape into a reassuring oriental fantasy:

Özdamar erzählt in einem magischen Deutsch – ferne Bilder, unbekannte Erfahrungen, wunderbare Rhythmen. So kunstvoll die unendliche Zahl der Geschichten . . . erzählt wird, so natürlich klingt diese Sprache, wie aus einer orientalischen Welt, in der Geschichten noch erzählt und nicht geschrieben wurden.

(Özdamar writes magical German, conjuring up distant pictures, unknown experiences and wonderful rhythms. As creative as the endless stories . . . that are told is the natural sound of this language, as though from an oriental world in which stories are still told and not written.)

The publishers are, of course, keen to profit from their public's oriental fantasies, but is it adequate to conclude that the book, in its celebration of metaphor, merely reinscribes conventional assumptions about Turkey's more primitive culture, even if the 'poetic consciousness' is positively evaluated? There are undoubtedly aspects of the text that do function to reinscribe in this way. However, by looking at definitions of metaphor that refuse the polarity of primitive – civilized, it is possible to point to an alternative movement in the text which counteracts, although it does not dissolve, the

idealization of the primitive through the juxtaposition of metaphor with the colonializing certainties of ratiocination.

As is clear from Vico's work, relating poetic consciousness to primitivity need not result in a hierarchized opposition between the poetic and the philosophical or metaphor and reason. Indeed, to place the terms in opposition simplifies the complexity, even ambiguity, of their interrelationship. The awareness of such ambiguity has lurked behind many of the theories of metaphor, and Aristotle too hints at the difficulty of separating metaphor and meaning: 'Metaphor entails the perception of similarities.'[24] Halliwell clarifies the significance of this formulation, commenting that it 'is an acknowledgement that metaphor is simultaneously a stylistic and a cognitive feature of language, capable of communicating thoughts which may not be readily translatable into "standard" language'.[25] That metaphor is not merely stylistic embellishment but a cognitive feature, a mode of perception, is precisely what the Romantic poets were concerned to emphasize, and Shelley further defines metaphorical language as that which 'marks the before unapprehended relations of things and perpetuates their apprehension'.[26] Ricoeur, referring to his own *Rule of Metaphor*, has much sympathy for this view, arguing that

poetic discourse brings to language aspects, qualities, and values of reality that lack access to language that is directly descriptive and that can be spoken only by means of the complex interplay between the metaphorical utterance and the rule-governed transgression of the usual meanings of our words.[27]

He argues that the frontier between 'metaphorical redescriptions' and the mimetic function of narrative is unstable; 'metaphorical redescription and mimesis are closely bound up with each other, to the point that we can exchange the two vocabularies and speak of the mimetic value of poetic discourse and the redescriptive power of narrative fiction'.[28] But, taking the idea of metaphorical reference and its mimetic function yet further, he suggests that ' "seeing-as", which sums up the power of metaphor, could be the revelatory of a "being-as" on the deepest ontological level'.[29]

The linking of metaphor and ontology is, ironically, the critical final step in undermining the opposition between metaphor (poetic apprehension) and reason. For if metaphor reveals being, being can never be a stable notion, but can itself only ever be represented 'as', even if the 'as' takes on the form of reasoned discourse unaware of its own status of metaphor: 'Every philosophy, then, is basically metaphorical, because it names and opens up with the means of the known what is not yet known.'[30] Nietzsche is, of course, well aware of the status of his writing as metaphorical. He is

quite explicit about the metaphorical status of language in *Über Wahrheit und Lüge im aussermoralischen Sinne*, which therefore makes any postulation of reality, even the proposition of a persisting self, nothing more than an illusion:

Was ist also Wahrheit? Ein bewegliches Heer von Metaphern, Metonymien, Anthropomorphismen kurz eine Summe von menschlichen Relationen, die poetisch und rhetorisch gesteigert, übertragen, geschmückt wurden, und die nach langen Gebrauche einem Volke fest, canonisch und verbindlich dünken: die Wahrheiten sind Illusionen, von denen man vergessen hat, dass sie welche sind, Metaphern, die abgenutzt und sinnlich kraftlos geworden sind . . .[31]

(So what is truth? A mobile herd of metaphors, metonymies, and anthropomorphisms, in short a sum of human relations which are poetically and rhetorically intensified, transferred and elaborated, and which after long use appear to a people as firm, canonical and binding. Truths are illusions about which one has forgotten that they are illusory, metaphors that are worn out and have lost their sensuous force . . .)

Nietzsche is an obvious antecedent to the twentieth-century concern with the relationship of metaphor and being. Andrew Bowie examines the different ways in which thinkers as diverse as Heidegger, Rorty, Derrida and Ricoeur have cast doubt on the meaning and fixity of the signifier '*sein*', and have explored its metaphoric function. Thus, for example, Bowie writes that in 'Rorty's terms . . . the signifier *Sein* is a metaphor: it does not have "meaning" and Derrida suggests the same of *différence*'.[32] In the context of psychoanalysis, the link between metaphor and ontology is taken to its logical conclusion in current Lacanian theory, where subjectivity is seen to be constituted by a series of three metaphors involved in the processes of alienation, separation and desire. Hence 'metaphor's creative spark *is* the subject; metaphor creates the subject . . . There is no such thing as a metaphor without subjective participation, and there is no subjectification without metaphorization.'[33]

It is not my concern here to weigh up the particular strengths of these various thinkers who undermine fixed notions of being by seeing it as in itself metaphorical. What is important is the challenge to a static and definable notion of being that they all make by their use of the concept of metaphor. For it is possible to discern this challenge in *Karawanserei*, which counteracts, although by no means revokes, the tendency towards idealization of the 'primitive'. Such a counterbalance is provided by the narrator's refusal to name herself; throughout the novel she is never referred to by name, and, as was mentioned before, only twice lets her age be known. In a book in which names are otherwise used naturally and with ease, this gap takes

on evident weight. In combination with the impressionistic and episodic mode of representation, the 'I' of the narrating self becomes definable predominantly in relation to the immediate events that she describes. Indeed, the very fact that the novel starts with the fiction of a knowing self at a stage when this is impossible because she is not yet born, and then proceeds to present an 'I' who consistently 'knows' rather little, is an ironic reversal of conventional expectations of subjectivity. Characterization that depends on psychological progression, causality or the narrator's own retrospective understanding or interpretation of herself and her motives is eschewed in favour of an emphasis on the perception of the moment. Unity, coherence, understanding are denaturalized and all explanation and even form itself takes on the status of metaphor. Metaphor and fiction take on central structural importance, both for the narrator as child and the form of the book. For if life consists of entering and leaving with a progression of events in between, then what becomes important, and what must be actively celebrated, are the fictions with which it is lived and enjoyed, since questioning will not alter the door marked 'exit'.

Thus the narrator's optimism, her positive celebration of metaphor, encompasses two positions. First, it without doubt involves a political affirmation of Turkish culture. As such it hovers between the demand on the reader to acknowledge the wealth, breadth and immense variety of what it is to be Turkish, while concurrently reinforcing the association of the Orient with a primitive consciousness. But secondly, and at the same time, her celebration of metaphor is an attempt to affirm the importance and centrality of fiction to subjectivity. Far from heralding a descent into nihilism, this book, like the short stories of *Mutterzunge*, is an optimistic assertion of the value and the meaning of fiction. Because although the challenge made to conventional ontology allows for the theoretical reduction, if not dissolution, of the self into an endless number of impressionistic episodes, it is through metaphor and its extended fictions that form can be imposed or new possibilities of conceiving of the self created. However, Özdamar's optimism is not blind; it does not rest on the denial of mortality or the recognition of the potential futility of existence. Her advocacy of life as metaphor mirrors that of Ayse, for whom fable certainly does convey truth, however fabulous, and is so important precisely because of the woeful failure of human communication. Ayse's defence of stories resides in the very fact that 'die Menschen können mit den Menschen nicht sprechen' (257) (people can't speak with people), and, like one of her grandmother's fairytales, the narrator begins her tale in a mythic period: 'Damals war der Weg einfach, keiner wußte, wie die Berge heißen, und

wie die Flüsse heißen' (9). (In those days the path was easy, no one knew what the mountains and the rivers were called.) She also incorporates moments of fantasy into the text, thereby placing her own life in the tradition of her grandmother's storytelling. Life is a story, the final metaphor with which Özdamar seeks to point beyond the polarity of poetic consciousness (ordinary Turkish culture) and prosaic consciousness (the increasingly corrupting influence of Americanization).

In the last analysis, though, she does not entirely succeed in this quest. Her optimistic emphasis on the creative potential is weakened by the very form that her metaphors assume. The clue to this resides in the proximity of the narrator's storytelling to Ayse's, the continuity of a tradition. Many of the metaphors are proverbial in nature, articulating common truths or maxims. In this manifestation, metaphor can quickly become clichéd or stereotyped, its potential creative spark lessened or lost in the service of common sense. In a text that is sceptical of reflection, the non-reflective mode has a hint of schematization about it, a schematization that limits the creativity of metaphor and which in consequence complements the textual drift towards the idealization of Turkey as exotic Other. The language of *Karawanserei* fails, then, to find the new level of creative expression that it seeks, although, and this is one of its major strengths, it does not fail in inviting the reader to think about such language. The narrator does not succeed in resolving the tension between identifying metaphor with Turkishness and the desire to confirm the emancipatory potential of understanding meaning as metaphor. Yet this tension in Özdamar's text is itself witness to both the possibility and the difficulty of metaphor and its fictions. For although metaphor may generate new apprehension or meaning, its referential field resides in and is specific to the present. This double-sidedness of metaphor is perhaps how Özdamar's writing can best be understood; it is in constant balance between looking forward for new ways of understanding identity, the desire to effect changes in present attitudes, while at the same time affirming that the present is also good and also productive. The pleasure of the text lies in Özdamar's dialectical optimism. For even though her language remains too much in the service of idealizing non-ratiocination, undermining the potential in language that she herself aspires to, it is also a symptom of her refusal to denigrate the present in favour of a utopian future vision. She questions her flawed world, while celebrating what it offers.

Conclusion: *das war es*

[E]s klaffte etwas zwischen Jordan und Franza, und was klaffte, wollte sie schließen. (Bachmann, *'Todesarten'* II, 242)

(Something gaped open between Jordan and Franza and she wanted to close the rift.)

[M]eine Geschichten sind wahr. Sie haben den Vorzug dieser Unvollkommenheit. (Bachmann, *'Todesarten'* I, 365)

(My stories are true. They have the advantage of such imperfection.)

[Jung] beobachtet jeden zuende, man kann aber jemanden nicht zuende beobachten und deswegen nicht zuende beschreiben. (Bachmann, *'Todesarten'* I, 365)

(Jung observes everyone totally, but it is not possible to observe someone totally and therefore not possible to describe them totally.)

Das Judasschaf dreht sich um und führt die Herde *unfehlbar* und *klar* auf eine Plattform . . . um Ecken herum; die Schafe folgen und kommen so schließlich bei einer Tür an. Das Judasschaf tritt jetzt zur Seite, die anderen Schafe gehen durch die Tür und werden sofort betäubt, aufgehängt undsoweiter. (Duden, *Das Judasschaf*, 56. My italics.)

(The Judas sheep turns round and *unerringly* and *clearly* leads the herd to a platform, and around corners. The sheep follow and so finally come to a door. The Judas sheep now steps aside, the other sheep go through the door and are immediately numbed, hung up and so on.)

Ich habe es euch doch gesagt, ich habe soviel Blödsinn wie alle Toten. (Özdamar, 1993: 118)

(I've already told you, I've got as much nonsense as all dead people.)

It is only when the sovereign incalculability of the subject is acknowledged that perceptions of difference will no longer nourish demands for the surrender of difference to processes of 'homogenization', 'purification', or any of the other crimes against otherness with which the rise of racism has begun to acquaint us. (Copjec, *Read My Desire*, 208)

I have had two related aims in this book. The first has been to discuss the different ways in which narrative fiction makes ambiguity and tension central to the critical exploration of identity and to the relationship between female and national identity. Irresolution is explicitly thematized or it forms part of the aesthetic complexity of the author's creative engagement with her themes. Yet irresolution is crucial not only in primary works of literature. The awareness of conflict and ambiguity must also remain central to any (feminist) critical project if it is to resist simplification or schematization in order to enter into constructive dialogue with challenging and often disturbing texts. My second and closely related aim has been to show that feminist literary criticism diminishes itself and its chosen texts if, often as a result of direct identification with the protagonist, narrator and author, it does not acknowledge or attend to women's negativity or failure. This may, as in Bachmann's and Duden's stories, be an integral part of the complex representation of narcissistic identity, or as in *Karawanserei*, relate much more basically to the quality of the text. Either way, however, the avoidance of aspects of a text that might be deemed threatening to the positive, emancipatory trajectory of feminism because they would involve the critic in a 'negative' judgement of a woman (protagonist, narrator, author), denies feminist discourse its insistently radical, unstable, and non-conformist edge.

There has recently been a much greater willingness amongst critics to move away from idealization and take into account problematic aspects of a text, as is particularly evident in Bachmann criticism. This willingness is part of a greater emphasis on understanding texts in relation to broader historical and cultural settings. Literary texts are increasingly interpreted as products of the discourses of the time in which they were and are written, and the flaws, tensions or aporia they evince thus can be comprehended as manifestations of underlying conflicting discourses. This tendency for literary criticism to move more closely towards cultural studies and, indeed, often to become part of a 'cultural studies approach' which treats literary texts as one of many types of 'cultural production', has resulted in many outstanding and enlightening analyses. However, an attendant danger of this approach is a certain levelling: the literary text becomes a piece of evidence for a cultural and historical context; it becomes the symptom of prevailing discourses. It is both of these things, but the specificity of literature's diagnostic rather than solely symptomatic contribution must not be ignored, nor, even more importantly, must its ability to fashion modes of understanding that are unique to it. It is the stylistic, and, above all, narrative polyvalence of prose texts which enables them to thematize and represent the ambivalence and contradictions that structure identity,

and it is precisely this polyvalence that makes the close study of literary texts significant for evaluating theoretical discourse.

As Bachmann's texts demonstrate, it is the inability to live with uncertainty and unresolved questions that leads to destruction and self-destruction in a variety of forms. Thus ambiguity, not knowing, not being able to close the gaps as Franza wishes to do, assumes ethical significance. At a critical level I have shown that it is possible to make an awareness of the unresolved conflicts within feminist discourse part of the process of interpretation. Going yet further, such awareness clearly acts as a safeguard against dogmatism, but it does not need to bring with it a refusal to assess the relative value and contribution of differing theories. The refusal to close the theoretical gap is not the same as suspending judgement. Thus I would point to the importance of ideas that (in different ways) centrally incorporate the notion of the impossibility of knowing, of inevitable ambiguity, into their structure. For not only is the 'sovereign incalculability of the subject' politically crucial through its resistance to the dangers of all-encompassing discourses, as Copjec makes clear; it also guarantees the space for further emancipatory potential. The theoretical emphasis on what cannot be known and articulated is the critical affirmation of Bachmann's insistence that 'im Widerspiel des Unmöglichen mit dem Möglichen erweitern wir unsere Möglichkeiten'[1] (in the interplay of the impossible with the possible, we broaden our possibilities).

Notes

INTRODUCTION

1 See Richard Rutherford's notes in *Euripides. Alcestis and Other Plays*, trans. John Davie (London: Penguin, 1996), p. 43.
2 Christa Wolf, *Medea. Stimmen*. All references will be to the dtv edition (Munich: dtv, 1998) and will be given in parentheses.
3 Helen King, 'That Stupid Pelt', *London Review of Books*, 12 November 1998, p. 20.
4 *Ibid.*, p. 21.
5 Paul Ricoeur, *Time and Narrative*, trans. Kathleen McLaughlin and David Pellauer, 3 vols. (Chicago and London: University of Chicago Press, 1984), III, p. 192.
6 Mary Fulbrook, *German National Identity after the Holocaust* (Cambridge: Polity, 1999), p. 13. Fulbrook offers an accessible discussion of theories of nation and national identity, and an extensive bibliography. Key texts referred to are: Ernest Gellner, *Nations and Nationalism* (Ithaca, N.Y.: Cornell University Press, 1983); Benedict Anderson, *Imagined Communities*, revised edition (London: Verso, 1991); E. J. Hobsbawm, *Nations and Nationalism since 1780* (Cambridge: Cambridge University Press, 1990); Anthony Smith, *National Identity* (Harmondsworth: Penguin, 1991); John Breuilly, *Nationalism and the State*, 2nd edition (Manchester: Manchester University Press, 1993).
7 Timothy Brennan, 'The National Longing for Forms' in Homi Bhabha (ed.), *Nation and Narration* (London and New York: Routledge, 1990), pp. 45–70 (p. 49).
8 I am not alone in wishing to study this relationship more closely. For an interesting collection of essays examining the relationship between gender and national identity, not only in narrative fiction, but in 'a wide range of cultural productions', see Patricia Herminghouse and Magda Mueller (eds.), *Gender and Germanness. Cultural Productions of Nations* (Providence and Oxford: Berghahn, 1997). In their introduction, Herminghouse and Mueller discuss the varying depictions of the figure of Germania, the allegorical figure unequivocally linking Nation and Woman, whereas the essays move away from such a clear icon to discuss poetry, narrative texts, films, etc.

9 To a greater or lesser degree this tendency can be observed in much (feminist) criticism.

1 FRANZA AND THE RIGHTEOUS SERVANT

1 Christa Wolf, *Voraussetzungen einer Erzählung: Kassandra* (Darmstadt und Neuwied: Luchterhand, 1983), p. 151.
2 Stefanie Golisch, *Ingeborg Bachmann. Zur Einführung* (Hamburg: Junius, 1997), p. 115.
3 *Ibid.*, p. 114.
4 Monika Albrecht, 'Poetologische Anthropologie. Zur Strukturgenese von Ingeborg Bachmanns fragmentarischem *Todesarten-Roman*' in Dirk Göttsche and Hubert Ohl (eds.), *Ingeborg Bachmann. Neue Beiträge zu ihrem Werk* (Würzburg: Königshausen & Neumann, 1993), pp. 129–45 (p. 144).
5 Ingeborg Bachmann to Klaus Piper, 14 November 1970. Quoted in Ingeborg Bachmann, '*Todesarten*'-*Projekt*, ed. Monika Albrecht and Dirk Göttsche, 4 vols. (Munich and Zurich: Piper, 1995), II p. 398.
6 Monika Albrecht, ' "Es muß erst geschrieben werden." Kolonisation und magische Weltsicht in Ingeborg Bachmanns Romanfragment *Das Buch Franza*' in Monika Albrecht and Dirk Göttsche (eds.), *Über die Zeit Schreiben. Literatur- und Kulturwissenschaftliche Essays zu Ingeborg Bachmanns 'Todesarten'-Projekt* (Würzburg: Königshausen & Neumann, 1998), pp. 59–91.
7 Sigrid Weigel, ' "Ein Ende mit der Schrift. Ein andrer Anfang." Zur Entwicklung von Ingeborg Bachmanns Schreibweise', in Heinz Ludwig Arnold (ed.), *Ingeborg Bachmann. Text und Kritik Sonderband* (Munich: Text und Kritik, 1984), pp. 58–92. For her discussion of *Das Buch Franza*, see sections V and VI.
8 *Ibid.*, p. 90.
9 Sara Lennox, ' "White Ladies" and "Dark Continents". Ingeborg Bachmanns "*Todesarten*"-Projekt aus postkolonialer Sicht' in Albrecht and Göttsche, *Über die Zeit*, pp. 13–31 (p. 23).
10 *Ibid.*, Lennox, p. 30.
11 'Die Wahrheit ist dem Menschen zumutbar' in Ingeborg Bachmann, *Werke I–IV*, ed. Christine Koschel, Inge von Weidenbaum and Clemens Münster (Munich and Zurich: Piper, 1978), IV, p. 276.
12 Albrecht and Göttsche, *Über die Zeit*, p. 8.
13 Karen McAuley, 'Critical Profiles of *Kind* and *Kindlichkeit* in Ingeborg Bachmann's Prose', PhD thesis, University of Cambridge (2000).
14 For the edited final draft of *Das Buch Franza* see Bachmann, '*Todesarten*', II, pp. 131–347. For the edited drafts of *Requiem für Fanny Goldmann* and the *Goldmann/Rottwitz-Roman* see Bachmann, '*Todesarten*', II, pp. 285–333 and pp. 335–452 respectively.
15 'Das zerstoßene Rohr wird Er nicht brechen, und den glimmenden Docht wird Er nicht auslöschen' (149). (He will not break a bruised reed nor quench a smouldering wick.)

16 I discuss the significance of the Bible quotation on pp. 37–38.
17 Sabine Grimkowski, 'Erzählerfiguren und Erzählperspektive in *Der Fall Franza*' in Göttsche and Ohl, *Ingeborg Bachmann* pp. 95–103 (p. 99).
18 See Bachmann, *Werke*.
19 Albrecht, 'Poetologische Anthropologie', p. 140.
20 Albrecht, ' "Es muß erst geschrieben werden" ', p. 88. Albrecht considers that the immediacy of the narrator–protagonist relationship has to be understood as a product of the fragmentary status of the novel.
21 Robert Knight, 'Education and National Identity in Austria after the Second World War' in Ritchie Robertson and Edward Timms (eds.), *The Hapsburg Legacy. National Identity in Historical Perspective* (Edinburgh: Edinburgh University Press, 1994), pp. 178–95.
22 Knight, 'Education and National Identity', p. 184.
23 For a detailed study of the violence in Austrian politics in the years leading up to the *Anschluß*, see Gerhard Botz, *Gewalt in der Politik. Attentate, Zusammenstöße, Putschversuche, Unruhen in Österreich 1918–1938* (Munich: Wilhelm Fink Verlag, 1983).
24 On 8 July, 1991 the Social Democrat Chancellor, Franz Vranitzky, addressed the National Assembly and offered the first public revision of the 'victim' version: 'Es ist unbestritten, daß Österreich im März 1938 Opfer einer militärischen Aggression mit furchtbaren Konsequenzen war: die unmittelbar einsetzende Verfolgung brachte hunderttausende Menschen unseres Landes in Gefängnisse und Konzentrationslager, lieferte sie der Tötungsmaschinerie des Nazi-Regimes aus, zwang sie zur Flucht und Emigration . . . Dennoch haben auch viele Österreicher den Anschluß begrüßt, haben das nationalsozialistische Regime gestützt, haben es auf vielen Ebenen der Hierarchie mitgetragen. Viele Österreicher waren an den Unterdrückungsmaßnahmen und Verfolgungen des Dritten Reiches beteiligt, zum Teil an prominenter Stelle.
  Über eine moralische Mitverantwortung für Taten unserer Bürger können wir uns auch heute nicht hinwegsetzen . . .
  Wir bekennen uns zu allen Daten unserer Geschichte und zu den Taten aller Teile unseres Volkes, zu den guten wie zu den bösen; und so wie wir die guten für uns in Anspruch nehmen, haben wir uns für die bösen zu entschuldigen – bei den Überlebenden und bei den Nachkommen der Toten.' Quoted by Gerhard Botz, 'Historische Brüche und Kontinuitäten als Herausforderungen – Ingeborg Bachmann und post-katastrophische Geschichtsmentalitäten in Österreich' in Göttsche and Ohl, *Ingeborg Bachmann* pp. 199–214 (pp. 209f.). (It is undisputed that in March 1938 Austria was the victim of military aggression which had terrible consequences: persecution began immediately and led to hundreds of thousands of this country's citizens being put in gaols and concentration camps; being at the mercy of the Nazi regime's death machine; being forced to flee and emigrate . . . Yet many Austrians also welcomed the *Anschluß*, supported the National Socialist regime, and helped bolster the hierarchy at many levels. Many Austrians participated in the oppression and persecution perpetrated by the Third Reich; some were in prominent positions. We can

no longer ignore our moral responsibility for the deeds of our citizens . . . We admit to all the facts of our history and the deeds of all our people, the good as well as the bad; and just as we lay claim to the good people, so too must we apologize to the survivors and their descendants for the bad.)

25 Jean Améry, *Geburt der Gegenwart. Gestalten und Gestaltungen der westlichen Zivilisation seit Kriegsende* in Botz, *Gewalt in der Politik*, pp. 201–2.

26 *Ibid.*, p. 207. See also Hella Pick, *Guilty Victim. Austria from the Holocaust to Haider* (London and New York: I. B. Tauris, 2000).

27 See Botz, *Gewalt in der Politik*, pp. 211–13.

28 Hans-Ulrich Thamer, 'Nationalsozialismus und Nachkriegsgesellschaft. Geschichtliche Erfahrung bei Ingeborg Bachmann und der öffentliche Umgang mit der NS-Zeit in Deutschland' in Göttsche and Ohl, *Ingeborg Bachmann* pp. 215–21 (p. 217).

29 *Ibid.*, p. 216.

30 See Holger Gehle, *NS-Zeit und literarische Gegenwart bei Ingeborg Bachmann* (Wiesbaden: DUV, 1995), p. 23, footnote 2.

31 This powerful passage serves a useful moral purpose when quoted out of the context of the complex narrative strategy of the book. It expresses the narrator's anger as she stands in front of Cornelia Goethe's grave in Sigrid Damm's *Cornelia Goethe* (Berlin and Weimar: Aufbau, 1990), and Christa Wolf quotes it as a chapter epigraph in her *Medea*.

32 After seeing the way in which an Arabic woman is tied up in Cairo, Franza does not wish to return to the city: 'So wird Kairo zum fremdkulturellen Pendant Wiens und die Wüste zum wiedergefundenen Galizien.' (Thus Cairo becomes the foreign cultural counterpart of Vienna and the desert becomes the redis-covered Galicia.) M. Moustapha Diallo, ' "Die Erfahrung der Variabilität." Kritischer Exotismus in Ingeborg Bachmanns "*Todesarten*"-Projekt im Kontext des interkulturellen Dialogs zwischen Afrika und Europa' in Albrecht and Göttsche, *Über die Zeit*, pp. 33–58, (p. 38).

33 Albrecht, ' "Es muß erst geschrieben werden" ', p. 82.

34 Bachmann, *Werke*, IV, p. 335.

35 Ingeborg Bachmann, *Wir müssen wahre Sätze finden. Gespräche und Interviews* (Munich and Zurich: Piper, 1983), p. 144.

36 Thamer, *Nationalsozialismus*, p. 223.

37 In marked contrast to the Greek Luke, who wishes to present Christ more universally as mankind's saviour.

38 The Book of Isaiah, 42.1–4; 49.1–6; 50.4–9; 52.13–53. 12. See H. H. Rowley, *The Servant of the Lord and Other Essays on the Old Testament* (London: Lutterworth Press, 1952), pp. 5–6.

39 This is particularly clear in Isaiah 53. 4–5:

Surely he has borne our griefs / and carried our sorrows: / yet we esteemed him stricken, / smitten by God, and afflicted.
    But he was wounded for our transgressions, / he was bruised for our iniquities / upon him was the chastisement that made us whole, / and with his stripes we are healed.

2 ON SHARKS AND SHAME

1 The narrator in the *Goldmann/Rottwitz-Roman*, as is evident from his inter-changeability with the character Malina, is male. This might indicate that the narrator of the earlier drafts of the Goldmann story (i.e. *Requiem für Fanny Goldmann*), is also male. However, it seems to me that the narrator figure of these earlier drafts is closer to the narrator of *Das Buch Franza* than to the narrator of the later framework narrative. Furthermore, if these two earlier texts were abandoned in favour of Malina and the emergent male narrative voice that is retained in the *Goldmann/Rottwitz-Roman*, it suggests that the earlier narrative voices were female.

2 *Malina* (Frankfurt am Main: Suhrkamp, 1991), p. 288.

3 'Obwohl die komplexe Erzählsituation dieses Fragments die Entscheidung er-schwert, ob Ekas Reaktionen die Darstellung der sexuellen Begegnung bestim-men oder ob ein etwas weniger voreingenommener Erzähler spricht, auf jeden Fall wird der Geschlechtsakt als gewalttätig, brutal und einseitig geschildert.' (Although the complex narrative technique of this fragment makes the decision more difficult as to whether it is Eka's reaction which determines the represen-tation of the sexual encounter, or whether it is the voice of a somewhat less prejudiced narrator, at any rate, the sex act is depicted as violent, brutal and one-sided.) Lennox, " 'White Ladies' ", p. 29.

4 For a largely statistical analysis of the extent to which Austrian identity has been defined with reference to a German nation, language and culture, and how this has developed since the Second World War, see Ernst Bruckmüller, 'The Development of Austrian National Identity' in *Austria 1945–95. Fifty Years of the Second Republic*, ed. Kurt Richard Luther and Peter Pulzer (Aldershot and Brookfield: Ashgate, 1998), pp. 83–108. See also Mark Allinson, *Germany and Austria 1814–2000* (London: Arnold, 2002).

5 Homi Bhabha, 'DissemiNation: Time, Narrative, and the Margins of the Mod-ern Nation' in Bhabha (ed.), *Nation and Narration* (London and New York: Routledge, 1990), pp. 291–322 (p. 294).

3 *MALINA*: EXPERIENCE AND FEMINISM

1 Karen Achberger, 'Beyond Patriarchy: Ingeborg Bachmann and Fairytales', *Modern Austrian Literature* 18 (1985), 211–22.

2 Gudrun Kohn-Waechter, *Das Verschwinden in der Wand. Destruktive Moderne und Widerspruch eines weiblichen Ich in Ingeborg Bachmanns* Malina (Stuttgart: Metzler, 1992).

3 Monika Albrecht and Jutta Kallhof, 'Vorstellungen auf einer Gedankenbühne: Zu Ingeborg Bachmanns "Todesarten" ', *Modern Austrian Literature* 18 (1985), 91–104.

4 Elizabeth Boa, 'Reading Ingeborg Bachmann' in Chris Weedon (ed.), *Post-war Women's Writing in German*, (Providence and Oxford: Berghahn, 1997), pp. 269–89 (p. 284).

5 Elizabeth Boa, 'Unnatural Causes: Modes of Death in Christa Wolf's *Nach-denken über Christa T.* and Ingeborg Bachmann's *Malina*' in Arthur Williams, Stuart Parkes and Roland Smith (eds.), *German Literature at a Time of Change 1989–1990* (Bern: Peter Lang, 1991), pp. 139–54 (p. 145).

6 Sigrid Schmid-Bortenschlager, 'Spiegelszenen bei Bachmann: Ansätze einer psychoanalytischen Interpretation', *Modern Austrian Literature* 18 (1985), 39–52.

7 Angelika Rauch, 'Sprache, Weiblichkeit und Utopie bei Ingeborg Bachmann', *Modern Austrian Literature* 18 (1985), 21–38 (p. 27).

8 Christa Bürger, 'Ich und Wir. Ingeborg Bachmanns Austritt aus der ästhetischen Moderne' in Heinz Ludwig Arnold (ed.), *Ingeborg Bachmann. Text und Kritik Sonderband* (Munich: Text und Kritik, 1984), pp. 7–27.

9 Sara Lennox, 'The Feminist Reception of Ingeborg Bachmann', *Women in German Yearbook* 8 (1993), 73–111 (p. 104).

10 Erika Swales, 'Die Falle binärer Oppositionen' in Robert Pichl and Alexander Stillmark (eds.), *Kritische Wege der Landnahme*, (Vienna: Hora Verlag, 1994), pp. 67–79.

11 All references to *Malina* will be to the Suhrkamp Taschenbuch edition (Frankfurt am Main: Suhrkamp, 1991) and will be given in parentheses.

12 Ingeborg Bachmann, *Wahre Sätze*, pp. 90–1.

13 *Ibid.*, pp. 69–70.

14 Michel Foucault, 'What is an Author?' in D. Bouchard (ed.), *Language, Counter-Memory, Practice. Selected Essays and Interviews* (Ithaca, N.Y.: Cornell University Press, 1977), pp. 113–38. Translated by Donald F. Bouchard and Sherry Simon.

15 Marcia Westcott, quoted in Marnia Lazreg, 'Women's Experience and Feminist Epistemology. A Critical Neo-Rationalist Approach' in Kathleen Lennon and Margaret Whitford (eds.), *Knowing the Difference. Feminist Perspectives in Epistemology* (London and New York: Routledge, 1994), pp. 45–62 (p. 48). This is an interesting article from the point of view of offering a brief overview of the problems of experience in the methodology of the natural and social sciences. It is, however, generally disappointing, in that Lazreg fails to mention parallel discussions in the humanities, and appears to be unaware of the highly developed criticisms of what she sees as essentializing traits. Thus she claims that 'The insistence upon the dichotomy sex/gender has escaped feminist criticism of binary oppositions' (p. 56), which in view of such thinkers as Gayatri Chakravorty Spivak, Judith Butler, Joan W. Scott and Parveen Adams, to name but four, is nothing less than extraordinary.

16 Shulamit Reinharz, quoted in Lazreg, 'Women's Experience and Feminist Epistemology, p. 48.

17 Luce Irigaray, 'The Culture of Difference' in *je, tu, nous: Toward a Culture of Difference*, trans. Alison Martin (London and New York: Routledge, 1993), pp. 45–50 (p. 45).

18 Luce Irigaray, 'The Neglect of Female Genealogies' in *je, tu, nous*, pp. 15–22 (p. 21).

19 Luce Irigaray, 'Your Health: What, or Who, Is It?' in *je, tu, nous*, pp. 101–5 (p. 101).

20 Joan W. Scott, ' "Experience" ' in Judith Butler and Joan W. Scott (eds.), *Feminists Theorize the Political* (New York and London: Routledge, 1992), pp. 22–40 (p. 31).

21 *Ibid.*, p. 37.

22 Gayatri Chakravorty Spivak, 'Feminism and Deconstruction, Again: Negotiating with Unacknowledged Masculinism' in Teresa Brennan (ed.), *Between Feminism and Psychoanalysis* (London and New York: Routledge, 1989), pp. 206–23 (p. 218).

23 Margaret Whitford, *Luce Irigaray. Philosophy in the Feminine* (London and New York: Routledge, 1991), p. 83.

24 Judith Butler, 'Contingent Foundations: Feminism and the Question of "Postmodernism" ' in Butler and Scott, *Feminists Theorize*, pp. 3–21 (p. 15).

25 See Schmid-Bortenschlager, *Spiegelszenen*.

26 The narrator's address is Ungargasse 6, Wien III. I discuss the significance of the address to the theme of national identity on p. 88.

27 Sabine Hotho-Jackson, 'Subversiveness in Ingeborg Bachmann's Later Prose', *New German Studies* 18 (1994), 55–71.

28 *Ibid.*, p. 67. Hotho-Jackson's reference to *Malina* is to Ingeborg Bachmann, *Werke*.

29 Boa, 'Unnatural Causes', p. 145.

30 Hotho-Jackson, 'Subversiveness', p. 59.

31 *Ibid.*, pp. 70–1.

32 *Ibid.*, p. 71.

33 Butler, 'Contingent Foundations', p. 16.

34 *Ibid.*, pp. 22–5.

35 H. C. Artmann, *Glückliches Österreich. Literarische Besichtigung eines Vaterlands*, ed. Jochen Jung (Salzburg and Vienna: Residenz Verlag, 1978), p. 24.

36 Sigrid Weigel, ' "Ein Ende mit der Schrift" ' in Arnold, *Ingeborg Bachmann* pp. 58–92.

37 Even outside the fictional context of a novel, in which dream sequences are conceptualized as an integral part of the whole, dreams belong to the range of narratives that can be taken as historical evidence. As Reinhart Kosellek argues, 'Gewiß stehen Träume am äußersten Ende einer denkbaren Skala historischer Rationalisierbarkeit. Aber streng genommen zeugen die Träume von einer unentrinnbaren Faktizität des Fiktiven, auf die sich einzulassen ein Historiker nicht verzichten sollte.' (Certainly dreams stand at the far end of a conceivable scale of what can be historically rationalized. But actually dreams testify to the inescapable factuality of the fictional, which the historian should not abstain from exploring.) Reinhart Kosellek, 'Terror und Traum. Methodologische Anmerkungen zu Zeiterfahrungen im Dritten Reich' in *Vergangene Zukunft. Zur Semantik geschichtlicher Zeiten* (Frankfurt am Main: Suhrkamp, 1979), pp. 283–4.

38 Kosellek, *Vergangene Zukunft*, p. 24.

39 A certain form of resolution is found by the narrator of Özdamar's *Mutterzunge*, who, rather than setting up her emotional attachment to Arabic and Islamic tradition in opposition to her secular and emancipated present, experiences

identity as a type of palimpsest. See my analysis of Özdamar's *Mutterzunge* in Chapter 5.

In a more flippant moment one could develop Gudrun Kohn-Waechter's excellent interpretation of the life and death struggle in *Malina* between modernist and pre-modernist forms of writing, and see in *Mutterzunge* the post-modern, more superficial, but liveable solution to the fight.

4 THE SHORT STORIES. THOUGHTS ON THE BODY AND ETHICS

1 I am using the term 'economy' here in its metaphorical sense to describe not only the modes of production and exchange of goods in society, but also, more broadly, modes of relating and perceiving. Thus a masculine economy might be understood as one based on the application of reason and calculation to maximize utility, power, etc., which has its equivalent in relationships in which the pursuit of pleasure and individual satisfaction are paramount. A feminine economy is contrasted to this and related to a gift economy with no anticipation of profit, but with emotional reward. As with so many terms used in debates over gender, 'economy' is used in different ways. Feminist thinkers tend to privilege any notion of a feminine economy, but clearly its characteristics will depend upon what is understood to be 'masculine' or 'feminine'. In my discussion of Duden's work I do not automatically identify the individual woman with a feminine economy, for this would assume the biologically necessary relationship of the two. Instead, I distinguish between a feminine economy as constructed in the text and an individual subject position, which refers to the subject's masculine or feminine identification. See Elizabeth Wright (ed.), *Feminism and Psychoanalysis. A Critical Dictionary* (Oxford: Blackwell, 1992), pp. 90–2.

2 Leslie Adelson, *Making Bodies, Making History* (Lincoln and London: University of Nebraska Press, 1993), p. 54.

3 *Ibid*.

4 Hereafter page references to the volume *Übergang* will be given as 'Ü', and references to the volume *Wimpertier* will be given as 'W'.

5 Erich Fried, 'Mein Gedächtnis ist mein Körper. Anne Dudens Erzählungen', *Die Zeit*, 13 May 1983, p. 45.

6 *Ibid*.

7 Anne Duden, 'Der wunde Punkt im Alphabet' in *Der wunde Punkt im Alphabet* (Hamburg: Rotbuch, 1995), pp. 77–84.

8 *Ibid*., p. 81.

9 *Ibid*., p. 83.

10 *Ibid*., p. 81.

11 *Ibid*.

12 Judith Butler, *Gender Trouble: Feminism and the Subversion of Identity* (New York and London: Routledge, 1990), p. 132.

13 Julia Kristeva, 'La Femme', quoted in Toril Moi, *Sexual/Textual Politics* (London and New York: Methuen, 1985), p. 163.

14 Kristeva, 'About Chinese Women' in Toril Moi (ed.), *The Kristeva Reader* (Oxford: Blackwell, 1986), p. 154.
15 *Ibid.*, p. 155.
16 *Ibid.*, p. 156.
17 Kristeva, 'La femme, ce n'est jamais ça' in Elaine Marks and Isabelle de Courtivron (eds.), *New French Feminisms* (Brighton: Harvester Press, 1985), p. 137.
18 Kristeva, 'Chinese Women', p. 156.
19 Jacques Lacan, *Écrits. A Selection* (London: Routledge, 1977), p. 264.
20 Bruce Fink, *The Lacanian Subject. Between Language and Jouissance* (Princeton: Princeton University Press, 1995), p. 55.
21 *Ibid.*, p. 59.
22 *Ibid.*, p. 60.
23 *Ibid.*, p. 60.
24 Joan Copjec, '*m/f*, or Not Reconciled' in Parveen Adams and Elizabeth Cowie (eds.), *The Woman in Question*: m/f (Cambridge, Massachusetts: MIT Press, 1990), p. 17.

5 DESIRE AND COMPLICITY IN *DAS JUDASSCHAF*

1 Anne Duden, *Das Judasschaf* (Berlin: Rotbuch, 1985). All references will be to the 1994 edition and will be given in parentheses.
2 Anne Duden, *Übergang* (Berlin: Rotbuch, 1982).
3 Suzanne Greuner, *Musik in der Schreibweise von Ingeborg Bachmann und Anne Duden* (Hamburg: Argument Verlag, 1990), p. 123.
4 See the discussion of Sigrid Weigel's interpretation of the text on p. 134.
5 Greuner, *Musik*, p. 118.
6 Margaret Littler, 'Diverging Trends in Feminine Aesthetic: Anne Duden and Brigitte Kronauer' in Arthur Williams, Stuart Parkes, Julian Preece (eds.), *Contemporary German Writers, Their Aesthetics and Their Language*, (Bern: Peter Lang, 1996), pp. 161–80 (p. 167).
7 *Ibid.*, p. 168.
8 *Ibid.*, p. 171.
9 Greuner, *Musik*, pp. 135–6.
10 Sigrid Weigel, 'Korrespondenzen zwischen Bild- und Körpergedächtnis', *Neue Zürcher Zeitung*, 23 April 1993, p. 38.
11 *Ibid.*
12 Johanna Bossinade, 'Original Differentiation. The Poetics of Anne Duden' in Chris Weedon (ed.), *Postwar Women's Writing in German* (Oxford: Berghahn, 1997), pp. 131–51 (p. 150, note 15).
13 Fulbrook, *German National Identity*.
14 *Ibid.*, p. 114.
15 *Ibid.*, p. 121.
16 For a detailed account of the *Historikerstreit* see Charles S. Maier, *The Unmasterable Past: History, Holocaust and German National Identity* (Cambridge,

Mass.: Harvard University Press, 1997). For the central texts of the dispute see '*Historikerstreit*' (Munich: Piper Verlag, 1987). The English translation is *Forever in the Shadow of Hitler?* (Atlantic Highlands, N.J.: Humanities Press, 1993) trans. J. Knowlton and T. Cates.

17 Fulbrook, *German National Identity*, p. 127.

18 As Karsch remarks in Uwe Johnson's *Das dritte Buch über Achim*, 'Irgend wie . . . Irgend wie . . . war sehr genau. Irgend wie war Irgend wie vielleicht auch zu beschreiben.' (Somehow . . . Somehow . . . was very precise. Somehow it might also be possible to describe somehow.) (Frankfurt am Main: Suhrkamp, 1992), p. 209.

19 See Dan Bar-On, 'Children as Unintentional Transmitters of Undiscussable Traumatic Life-Events' in H. Adam, P. Riedessier, H. Riquelene, A. Verderber and J. Walter, *Children – War and Persecution* (Osnabrück: Secolo Verlag, 1995), pp. 67–74.

20 Jacques Lacan, *The Ethics of Psychoanalysis, 1959–1960* (London: Routledge, 1992), p. 108.

21 *Ibid.*, p. 109.

22 Franz Kafka, letter to Oskar Baum, June 1922. In *Franz Kafka. Letters to Friends, Family, and Editors*, trans. Richard and Clara Winston (New York: Schocken Books, 1977), p. 327.

23 Slavoj Zizek, *For They Know Not What They Do* (London and New York: Verso, 1991), p. 239.

24 Weigel, *Korrespondenzen*, p. 38.

25 Jacqueline Rose, *Sexuality in the Field of Vision* (London and New York: Verso, 1986), p. 177.

26 *Ibid.*, p. 190.

27 Jacques Lacan, *The Four Fundamental Concepts of Psycho-Analysis* (London: Penguin, 1979), p. 101.

28 Georg Wilhelm Friedrich Hegel, *Phänomenologie des Geistes*. Hegel's use of the *schöne Seele* is not to be confused with the feminine ideal as represented in certain German classical texts. He refers to the *schöne Seele* in section VI.c.c. of *Phänomenologie*, in the context of his discussion of the unhappy consciousness. He writes:

Insofern nun der seiner selbst gewisse Geist, als schöne Seele, nicht die Kraft der Entäußerung des an sich haltenden Wissens ihrer selbst besitzt, kann sie nicht zur Gleichheit mit dem zurückgestoßnen Bewußtsein und also nicht zur angeschauten Einheit ihrer selbst im Andern, nicht zum Dasein gelangen; die Gleichheit kommt daher nur negativ, als ein geistloses Sein, zustande. Die wirklichkeitslose schöne Seele, in dem Widerspruche ihres reinen Selbsts und der Notwendigkeit desselben, sich zum Sein zu entäußern und in Wirklichkeit umzuschlagen, in der *Unmittelbarkeit* dieses festgehaltnen Gegensatzes – einer Unmittelbarkeit, die allein die Mitte und Versöhnung des auf seine reine Abstraktion gesteigerten Gegensatzes, und die reines Sein oder das leere Nichts ist – ist also als Bewußtsein dieses Widerspruches in seiner unversöhnten Unmittelbarkeit zur Verrücktheit zerrüttet, und zerfließt in sehnsüchtiger Schwindsucht. Es gibt damit in der Tat das harte Festhalten seines *Für-sich-seins* auf, bringt aber nur die geistlose Einheit des Seins hervor' (Stuttgart: Reclam, 1987), pp. 470–1.

(Now, in so far as the self-certain Spirit, as a 'beautiful soul', does not possess the power to renounce the knowledge of itself which it keeps to itself, it cannot attain to an identity with the consciousness it has repulsed, nor therefore to a vision of the unity of itself in the other, cannot attain to an objective existence. Consequently, the identity comes about only negatively, as a being devoid of Spirit. The 'beautiful soul', lacking an actual existence, entangled in the contradiction between its pure self and the necessity of that self to externalize itself and change itself into an actual existence, and dwelling in the *immediacy* of this firmly held antithesis – an immediacy which alone is the middle term reconciling the antitheses, which has been intensified to its pure abstraction, and is pure being or empty nothingness – this 'beautiful soul', then, being conscious of this contradiction in its unreconciled immediacy, is disordered to the point of madness, wastes itself in yearning and pines away in consumption. Thereby it does in fact surrender the *being-for-itself* to which it so stubbornly clings, but what it brings forth is only the non-spiritual unity of [mere] being.) Translated as *Phenomenology of Spirit* by A. V. Miller (Oxford: Oxford University Press, 1977), pp. 406–7.

29 Michael Inwood, *A Hegel Dictionary* (Oxford: Blackwell, 1992), p. 190.
30 Lacan, *Écrits*, p. 70.
31 Slavoj Zizek, *The Sublime Object of Ideology* (London and New York: Verso, 1989), p. 216.
32 Jacques Lacan, 'God and the *Jouissance* of Woman. A Love Letter' in Juliet Mitchell and Jacqueline Rose (eds.), *Feminine Sexuality. Jacques Lacan and the* École Freudienne (London: Macmillan, 1982), p. 147.
33 Lacan, *Ethics*, p. 187.
34 Rose, *Sexuality*, p. 12.
35 *Ibid.*, p. 16.
36 *Ibid.*, p. 14.
37 In *Das Judasschaf* and 'Übergang' there is a clear link established between victimhood and Germanness. One might wish to comment retrospectively on the pervasive theme of victimhood in Duden's other short stories, and speculate about the relationship of victimhood and Germanness in general terms. I myself, however, have not found examples of interpretation based on the undifferentiated linking of any story involving themes of victimhood/authority, etc. to National Socialism very illuminating. Rather, I would suggest that the absence of clear cause for the narrators' suffering in those stories raises interesting ethical issues which I start to consider in my article 'Considering Ethics in the Short Prose of Anne Duden' in Heike Bartel and Elizabeth Boa (eds.), *Anne Duden. A Revolution of Words. Approaches to her Fiction, Poetry and Essays* German Monitor, 2003), pp. 62–71.

6 TRADITION OUT OF CONTEXT

1 Margaret Littler, 'Diasporic Identity in Emine Sevgi Özdamar's *Mutterzunge*' in Frank Finley and Stuart Taberner (eds.), *Recasting German Identity* (Cambden House, forthcoming). See too Elizabeth Boa's article 'Sprachenverkehr. Hybrides Schreiben in Werken von Özdamar, Özakin und Demirkan' in Mary

Howard (ed.), *Interkulturelle Kommunikationen. Zur deutschsprachigen Prosaliteratur von Autoren nichtdeutscher Herkunft* (Munich: iudicium, 1997), pp. 115–37. Boa is convinced that the application of Lacanian thought to *Mutterzunge* would be a form of violence to the text. I would argue that that depends on how it is done.

2 Leslie A. Adelson, 'Response to Ülker Gökberk, *"Culture Studies* und die Türken"', *The German Quarterly* (Summer 1997), pp. 277–82 (p. 277). See too the article by Ülker Gökberk, '*Culture Studies* und die Türken: Sten Nadolnys *Selim oder Die Gabe der Rede* im Lichte einer Methodendiskussion', *The German Quarterly* (Spring 1997), pp. 97–122.

3 Hans-Georg Gadamer, *Wahrheit und Methode. Grundzüge einer philosophischen Hermeneutik* (Tübingen: J.C.B. Mohr, 1990), p. 274. Translation by Joel Weinsheimer and Donald G. Marshall, *Truth and Method* (London: Sheed and Ward, 1989), p. 269.

4 For as Gadamer argues: 'Ein hermeneutisch geschultes Bewußtsein [muß] für die Andersheit des Textes von vornherein empfänglich sein. Solche Empfänglichkeit setzt aber weder sachliche "Neutralität" noch gar Selbstauslöschung voraus, sondern schließt die abhebende Aneignung der eigenen Vormeinungen und Vorurteile ein' (Gadamer, *Wahrheit*, pp. 273–4). (That is why a hermeneutically trained consciousness must be, from the start, sensitive to the text's alterity. But this kind of sensitivity involves neither 'neutrality' with respect to content nor the extinction of one's self, but the foregrounding and appropriation of one's own fore-meanings and prejudices) (Weinsheimer and Marshall, *Truth*, p. 269).

5 Annette Wierschke, *Schreiben als Selbstbehauptung: Kulturkonflikte und Identität in den Werken von Aysel Özakin, Alev Tekinay und Emine Sevgi Özdamar* (Frankfurt am Main: Verlag für Interkulturelle Kommunikation, 1996).

6 Annette Wierschke, 'Auf den Schnittstellen kultureller Grenzen tanzend: Aysel Özakin und Emine Sevgi Özdamar' in Sabine Fischer and Moray McGowan (eds.), *Denn du tanzt auf einem Seil. Positionen deutschsprachiger MigrantInnen-literatur* (Tübingen: Stauffenburg, 1997), pp. 179–94 (p. 189).

7 'Living and Writing in Germany. Emine Sevgi Özdamar in Conversation with David Horrocks and Eva Kolinsky' in David Horrocks and Eva Kolinsky (eds.), *Turkish Culture in German Society Today* (Oxford: Berghahn, 1996), p. 47.

8 *Turkish Culture*, p. xiii.

9 Wierschke, 'Auf den Schnittstellen', p. 188.

10 Ngugi Wa Thiong'o, 'The Language of African Literature' in Bill Ashcroft, Gareth Griffiths and Helen Tiffin (eds.), *The Post-Colonial Studies Reader* (London and New York: Routledge, 1995), pp. 285–90 (p. 287).

11 Chantal Zabus, 'Relexification' in Ashcroft, Griffiths and Tiffin, *Post-Colonial Studies*, pp. 314–18 (p. 315).

12 *Ibid.*, p. 317.

13 Littler too uses the concept of palimpsest in her article to point to the overlapping traditions of pre-Islamic, Ottoman and Kemalist notions of 'Turkishness' evoked in 'Großvaterzunge'. (Littler, 'Diasporic Identity'.)

14 Stuart Hall, 'New Ethnicities' in Ashcroft, Griffiths and Tiffin, *Post-Colonial Studies*, pp. 223–7 (p. 224–5).
15 *Ibid.*, p. 226.
16 *Ibid.*, p. 227.
17 See also Thomas H. Eriksen, 'Ethnicity, Race, Class and Nation' in John Hutchinson and Anthony D. Smith (eds.), *Ethnicity* (Oxford and New York: Oxford University Press, 1996). As he points out, although the term 'race' is now discredited, for as modern genetics shows 'there is often greater variation within a "racial" group than there is systematic variation between two groups . . . concepts of race can nevertheless be important to the extent that they inform people's actions: at this level, race exists as a cultural construct, whether it has a "biological" reality or not' (p. 29).
18 Sabine Fischer and Moray McGowan, 'From Pappkoffer to Pluralism: On the Development of Migrant Writing in the German Federal Republic' in Horrocks and Kolinsky (ed.), *Turkish Culture*, pp. 1–22 (p. 17). Also quoted in A. Burkhard, 'Vom Verlust der Zunge. Annäherung an das Fremde: Emine Sevgi Özdamar im Literaturhaus', *Frankfurter Rundschau*, 23 February 1991.
19 Following this scheme of things, writers like Gayatri Chakravorty Spivak and Sara Suleri become honorary representatives of the West through, for example, their refusal to accept personal narratives as a critical category.
20 Jacques Derrida, 'Signature Event Context' in *Limited Inc* (Evanston: Northwestern University Press, 1988), pp. 1–23 (p. 9).
21 *Ibid.*, p. 12.
22 Heiner Müller and Alexander Kluge, *'Ich schulde der Welt einen Toten.' Alexander Kluge im Gespräch mit Heiner Müller* (Hamburg: Rotbuch, 1995), p. 49.
23 Ferdinand Freiligrath, *Werke in einem Band* (Berlin and Weimar: Aufbau, 1980), pp. 74–6.
24 Johann Wolfgang Goethe, *Wilhelm Meisters Lehrjahre* (Basel: Verlag Birkhäuser, 1944), book 5, end of chapter 6.
25 For a detailed discussion on Wilhelm Meister and the theatre, see T. J. Reed's discussion of Goethe's *Theatralische Sendung* in his chapter 'Theatre and Nation' in *The Classical Centre. Goethe and Weimar 1775–1832* (Oxford: Oxford University Press, 1986).
26 Müller and Kluge, *Ich schulde der Welt*, p. 42.
One might also like to see proof of the German enthusiasm for Hamlet in the fact that the so-famous soliloquy has even been translated into Bavarian dialect:

Lewenddig odá gschdoámá, ja, dees frágd si:
Wiá hásd ás gmiáddlichá, wannsd schee geduidig ságst:
Nuá heár auf mi, odá wannsd oáfach zuádrásd,
Schluß, aus Ebbfi amen. Dees wanssd dá iwálegsd, dá kimsd
bfeigrád ins Schleidán. Várregg Kaffäähaus! Gäh, hau di hi
und schlaf á Gsátzl.

And so on.

27 Elaine Showalter, 'Representing Ophelia: Women, Madness, and the Responsibilities of 'Feminist Criticism' in Patricia Parker and Geoffrey Hartman (eds.), *Shakespeare and the Question of Theory* (New York and London: Methuen, 1985), pp. 77–94 (p. 78).

28 Showalter, 'Representing Ophelia', p. 79.

29 *Ibid.*, p. 80.

30 *Ibid.*, pp. 91–2.

31 *Ibid.*, p. 89.

32 Wierschke, *Schreiben als Selbstbehauptung*, p. 195

33 *Ibid.*, pp. 195–6.

34 *Ibid.*, p. 196.

35 Heiner Müller, *Die Hamletmaschine* in Joachim Fiebach (ed.), *Stücke* (Berlin: Henschelverlag, 1988), p. 419.

36 Judith Butler, *Excitable Speech. A Politics of the Performative* (New York and London: Routledge, 1997), p. 16.

37 Judith Butler, *Bodies That Matter. On the Discursive Limits of 'Sex'* (New York and London: Routledge, 1993), p. 12.

38 Judith Butler, *Gender Trouble*, p. 145.

39 Saliha Scheinhardt, *Frauen, die sterben, ohne daß sie gelebt hätten* (Freiburg: Herder, 1991). In this story a young woman murders her husband, who repeatedly and violently abused her. In *Drei Zypressen* (Freiburg: Herder, 1990), three stories tell of women, who, in the words of the blurb, live 'unter der traditionellen Herrschaft ihrer Väter und Brüder. Sie sind zerrieben zwischen nackter Angst und Gewalt, Isolation und der kraftvollen Sehnsucht nach Eigenständigkeit.' (under the traditional domination of their husbands and brothers. They are crushed between naked fear and violence, isolation and the powerful yearning for independence.)

40 Betty Mahmoody and William Hoffer, *Nicht ohne meine Tochter* (Lübbe: Berg.-Gladb, 1995).

7 METAPHOR'S CREATIVE SPARK

1 Özdamar's readership is broad in scope, including German and Turkish–German readers. Clearly, the latter form a more competent readership, sooner able to fill in the gaps of Turkish history, to work out the events referred to and whose response to the use of Turkish and Arabic will be different from those for whom these are unknown languages.

2 See p. 167.

3 See p. 159.

4 W. H. Auden, 'Homage to Clio' in *Collected Shorter Poems 1927–1957* (London: Faber, 1966), pp. 307–10.

5 Michael Wood, 'What Kind of Guy?', *London Review of Books*, 10 June 1999, p. 3.

6 See Horrocks and Kolinsky, *Turkish Culture*, p. 38.

7 Auden, 'Homage to Clio'.

8 Esther Freud, *Hideous Kinky* (London: Penguin, 1993).
9 James Joyce, *A Portrait of the Artist as a Young Man* (London: Penguin, 1992).
10 Aristotle, *On Rhetoric. A Theory of Civic Discourse*, trans. George A. Kennedy (New York and Oxford: OUP, 1991), p. 227.
11 Aristotle, *Poetics*, translation and commentary by Stephen Halliwell (London: Duckworth, 1987), p. 161.
12 Aristotle, *On Rhetoric*, p. 311.
13 *Ibid.*, p. 311.
14 Giambattista Vico, *New Science. Principles of the New Science Concerning the Common Nature of Nations*, trans. David Marsh with an introduction by Anthony Grafton (London: Penguin, 1999), p. 162.
15 *Ibid.*, p. 171.
16 *Ibid.*, p. 144.
17 *Ibid.*, p. 162.
18 *Ibid.*, p. 187.
19 *Ibid*. Vico goes on to clinch his argument thus: 'This scientific observation is confirmed by the following case. There is living in Naples a gentleman who has suffered a severe stroke, and can only utter nouns, having completely forgotten the verbs.'
20 *Ibid.*, p. 203–4.
21 Paul Hamilton, *Historicism* (London: Routledge, 1996), p. 35.
22 See Hayden White, *Metahistory. The Historical Imagination in Nineteenth-Century Europe* (Baltimore and London: The Johns Hopkins University Press, 1973), p. 32.
23 Percy Bysshe Shelley, 'In Defence of Poetry' in Donald H. Reiman and Sharon B. Powers (eds.), *Shelley's Poetry and Prose* (New York and London: Norton Critical Edition, 1977), pp. 480–508 (p. 480).
24 Aristotle, *Poetics*, p. 57.
25 Ibid., p. 162.
26 Shelley, *In Defence*, p. 482.
27 Paul Ricoeur, *Time and Narrative* I, p. xi.
28 *Ibid.*, vol I, p. xi.
29 *Ibid*.
30 H. H. Holz, cited in Andrew Bowie, *Schelling and Modern European Philosophy* (London and New York: Routledge, 1993), p. 8.
31 Friedrich Nietzsche, *Unzeitgemäße Betrachtungen I–IV*, ed. Giorgio Colli and Mazzino Montinari (Munich: dtv, 1988), pp. 880–1.
32 Bowie, *Schelling*, p. 70. See also pp. 5–12 and 115–26.
33 Bruce Fink, *The Lacanian Subject*, p. 70.

CONCLUSION

1 'Die Wahrheit ist dem Menschen zumutbar' in Bachmann, *Werke* IV, p. 276.

Bibliography

Achberger, Karen, 'Beyond Patriarchy: Ingeborg Bachmann and Fairytales', *Modern Austrian Literature* 18 (1985), 211–22.

Adams, Parveen and Elizabeth Cowie (eds), *The Woman in Question: m/f* (Cambridge, Mass.: MIT Press, 1990).

Adelson, Leslie A., *Making Bodies, Making History* (Lincoln and London: University of Nebraska Press, 1993).

 'Response to Ülker Gökberk, "*Culture Studies* und die Türken"', *The German Quarterly* (Summer 1997), pp. 277–82.

Albrecht, Monika, 'Poetologische Anthropologie. Zur Strukturgenese von Ingeborg Bachmanns fragmentarischem *Todesarten*-Roman' in Göttsche and Ohl (eds.), *Ingeborg Bachmann*, pp. 129–45.

Albrecht, Monika and Dirk Göttsche, (eds.), *Über die Zeit Schreiben. Literatur- und Kulturwissenschaftliche Essays zu Ingeborg Bachmanns 'Todesarten'-Projekt* (Würzburg: Königshausen & Neumann, 1998).

 ' "Es muß erst geschrieben werden." Kolonisation und magische Weltsicht in Ingeborg Bachmanns Romanfragment *Das Buch Franza*' in Albrecht and Göttsche (eds.), *Über die Zeit*, pp. 59–91.

Albrecht, Monika and Jutta Kallhof, 'Vorstellungen auf einer Gedankenbühne: Zu Ingeborg Bachmanns "Todesarten"', *Modern Austrian Literature* 18 (1985), 91–104.

Allinson, Mark, *Germany and Austria 1814–2000* (London: Arnold, 2002).

Améry, Jean, *Geburt der Gegenwart. Gestalten und Gestaltungen der westlichen Zivilisation seit Kriegsende* in Botz, *Gewalt in der Politik*, pp. 201–2.

Anderson, Benedict, *Imagined Communities*, revised edition (London: Verso, 1991).

Aristotle, *Poetics*, translation and commentary by Stephen Halliwell (London: Duckworth, 1987).

Aristotle, *On Rhetoric. A Theory of Civic Discourse*, trans. George A. Kennedy (New York and Oxford: Oxford University Press, 1991).

Arnold, Heinz Ludwig (ed.), *Ingeborg Bachmann. Text und Kritik Sonderband* (Munich: Text und Kritik, 1984).

Artmann, H. C., *Glückliches Österreich. Literarische Besichtigung eines Vaterlands* ed. Jochen Jung (Salzburg and Vienna: Residenz Verlag, 1978).

Ashcroft, Bill, Gareth Griffiths and Helen Tiffin (eds.), *The Post-Colonial Studies Reader* (London and New York: Routledge, 1995).

Auden, W. H., 'Homage to Clio' in *Collected Shorter Poems 1927–1957* (London: Faber, 1966), pp. 307–10.

Bachmann, Ingeborg, *Werke*, I–IV, ed. Christine Koschel, Inge von Weidenbaum and Clemens Münster (Munich and Zurich: Piper, 1978).

Wir müssen wahre Sätze finden. Gespräche und Interviews (Munich and Zurich: Piper, 1983).

Malina (Frankfurt am Main: Suhrkamp, 1991).

'Todesarten'-Projekt, 4 vols., ed. Monika Albrecht and Dirk Göttsche (Piper: Munich and Zurich, 1995).

Bar-On, Dan, 'Children as Unintentional Transmitters of Undiscussable Traumatic Life-Events' in H. Adam, P. Riedessier, H. Riquelene, A. Verderber and J. Walter, *Children – War and Persecution* (Osnabrück: Secolo Verlag, 1995) pp. 62–74.

Bartel, Heike, and Elizabeth Boa (eds.), *Anne Duden. A Revolution of Words. Approaches to her Fiction, Poetry and Essays* (German Monitor, 2003).

Bhabha, Homi (ed.), *Nation and Narration* (London and New York: Routledge, 1990).

'DissemiNation: Time, Narrative, and the Margins of the Modern Nation' in Bhabha (ed.), *Nation and Narration*, pp. 291–322.

Bird, Stephanie, 'Considering Ethics in the Short Prose of Anne Duden' in Bartel and Boa (eds.), *Anne Duden*, pp. 62–71.

Boa, Elizabeth, 'Unnatural Causes: Modes of Death in Christa Wolf's *Nachdenken über Christa T.* and Ingeborg Bachmann's *Malina*' in Williams, Parkes and Smith (eds.), *German Literature*, pp. 139–54.

'Sprachenverkehr. Hybrides Schreiben in Werken von Özdamar, Özakin und Demirkan' in Howard (ed.), *Interkulturelle Kommunikationen*, pp. 115–37.

'Reading Ingeborg Bachmann' in Weedon (ed.), *Postwar Women's Writing*, pp. 269–89.

Bossinade, Johanna, 'Original Differentiation. The Poetics of Anne Duden' in Weedon (ed.), *Postwar Women's Writing*, pp. 131–51.

Botz, Gerhard, *Gewalt in der Politik. Attentate, Zusammenstöße, Putschversuche, Unruhen in Österreich 1918–1938* (Munich: Wilhelm Fink Verlag, 1983).

'Historische Brüche und Kontinuitäten als Herausforderungen – Ingeborg Bachmann und post-katastrophische Geschichtsmentalitäten in Österreich' in Göttsche and Ohl (eds.), *Ingeborg Bachmann*, pp. 199–214.

Bowie, Andrew, *Schelling and Modern European Philosophy* (London and New York: Routledge, 1993).

Brennan, Teresa (ed.), *Between Feminism and Psychoanalysis* (London and New York: Routledge, 1989).

Brennan, Timothy, 'The National Longing for Forms' in Bhabha (ed.), *Nation and Narration*, pp. 45–70.

Breuilly, John, *Nationalism and the State*, 2nd edition (Manchester: Manchester University Press, 1993).

Bruckmüller, Ernst, 'The Development of Austrian National Identity' in Luther and Pulzer (eds.), *Austria 1945–95*, pp. 83–108.

Bürger, Christa, 'Ich und Wir. Ingeborg Bachmanns Austritt aus der ästhetischen Moderne' in Arnold (ed.), *Ingeborg Bachmann*, pp. 7–27.

Burkhard, A., 'Vom Verlust der Zunge. Annäherung an das Fremde: Emine Sevgi Özdamar im Literaturhaus', *Frankfurter Rundschau*, 23 February 1991.

Butler, Judith, *Gender Trouble: Feminism and the Subversion of Identity* (New York and London: Routledge, 1990).

    Bodies That Matter. On the Discursive Limits of 'Sex' (New York and London: Routledge, 1993).

    Excitable Speech. A Politics of the Performative (New York and London: Routledge, 1997).

    'Contingent Foundations: Feminism and the Question of "Postmodernism"' in Butler and Scott (eds.), *Feminists Theorize*, pp. 3–21.

Butler, Judith and Joan W. Scott (eds.), *Feminists Theorize the Political* (New York and London: Routledge, 1992).

Copjec, Joan, *Read My Desire. Lacan Against the Historicists* (Cambridge, Mass. and London: MIT Press, 1994).

    '*m/f*, or Not Reconciled' in Adams and Cowie (eds.), *Woman in Question* pp. 10–18.

Damm, Sigrid, *Cornelia Goethe* (Berlin and Weimar: Aufbau, 1990).

Derrida, Jacques, 'Signature Event Context' in *Limited Inc* (Evanston: Northwestern University Press, 1988) pp. 1–23.

Diallo, M. Moustapha, ' "Die Erfahrung der Variabilität." Kritischer Exotismus in Ingeborg Bachmanns "*Todesarten*"-Projekt im Kontext des interkulturellen Dialogs zwischen Afrika und Europa' in Albrecht and Göttsche (eds.), *Über die Zeit*, pp. 33–58.

Duden, Anne, *Übergang* (Berlin: Rotbuch, 1982).

    Das Judasschaf (Berlin: Rotbuch, 1985).

    Der wunde Punkt im Alphabet (Hamburg: Rotbuch, 1995).

    Wimpertier (Cologne: Kiepenheuer & Witsch, 1995).

Eriksen, Thomas H., 'Ethnicity, Race, Class and Nation' in Hutchinson and Smith (eds.), *Ethnicity*, pp. 28–31.

Fink, Bruce, *The Lacanian Subject. Between Language and Jouissance* (Princeton: Princeton University Press, 1995).

Finley, Frank and Stuart Taberner (eds.), *Recasting German Identity*, (Cambden House, forthcoming).

Fischer, Sabine and Moray McGowan, 'From Pappkoffer to Pluralism: On the Development of Migrant Writing in the German Federal Republic' in Horrocks and Kolinsky (eds.), *Turkish Culture*, pp. 1–22.

Fischer, Sabine and Moray McGowan (eds.), *Denn du tanzt auf einem Seil. Positionen deutschsprachiger MigrantInnenliteratur* (Tübingen: Stauffenburg, 1997).

Foucault, Michel, 'What is an Author?' in D. Bouchard (ed.), *Language, Counter-Memory, Practice: Selected Essays and Interviews* (Ithaca, N.Y.: Cornell

University Press, 1977), pp. 113–38. Translated by Donald F. Bouchard and Sherry Simon.

Freiligrath, Ferdinand, *Werke in einem Band* (Berlin and Weimar: Aufbau, 1980).

Freud, Esther, *Hideous Kinky* (London: Penguin, 1993).

Fried, Erich, 'Mein Gedächtnis ist mein Körper. Anne Dudens Erzählungen', *Die Zeit*, 13 May 1983, p. 45.

Fulbrook, Mary, *German National Identity after the Holocaust* (Cambridge: Polity, 1999).

Gadamer, Hans-Georg, *Wahrheit und Methode. Grundzüge einer Philosophischen Hermeneutik* (Tübingen: J. C. B. Mohr, 1990); trans. Joel Weinsheimer and Donald G. Marshall as *Truth and Method* (London: Sheed and Ward, 1989).

Gehle, Holger, *NS-Zeit und literarische Gegenwart bei Ingeborg Bachmann* (Wiesbaden: DUV, 1995).

Gellner, Ernest, *Nations and Nationalism* (Ithaca, N.Y.: Cornell University Press, 1983).

Goethe, Johann Wolfgang, *Wilhelm Meisters Lehrjahre* (Basel: Verlag Birkhäuser, 1944).

Gökberk, Ülker, '*Culture Studies* und die Türken: Sten Nadolnys *Selim oder Die Gabe der Rede* im Lichte einer Methodendiskussion', *The German Quarterly* (Spring 1997), pp. 97–122.

Golisch, Stefanie, *Ingeborg Bachmann. Zur Einführung* (Junius: Hamburg, 1997).

Göttsche, Dirk and Hubert Ohl (eds.), *Ingeborg Bachmann. Neue Beiträge zu ihrem Werk* (Königshausen & Neumann: Würzburg, 1993).

Greuner, Suzanne, *Musik in der Schreibweise von Ingeborg Bachmann und Anne Duden* (Hamburg: Argument Verlag, 1990).

Grimkowski, Sabine, 'Erzählerfiguren und Erzählperspektive in *Der Fall Franza*' in Göttsche and Ohl (eds.), *Ingeborg Bachmann*, pp. 95–103.

Hall, Stuart, 'New Ethnicities' in Ashcroft, Griffiths and Tiffin (eds.), *Post-Colonial Studies*, pp. 223–7.

Hamilton, Paul, *Historicism* (London: Routledge, 1996).

Hegel, Georg Wilhelm Friedrich, *Phänomenologie des Geistes* (Stuttgart: Reclam, 1987).

Herminghouse, Patricia and Magda Mueller (eds.), *Gender and Germanness. Cultural Productions of Nations* (Providence and Oxford: Berghahn, 1997).

Hobsbawm, E. J., *Nations and Nationalism since 1780* (Cambridge: Cambridge University Press, 1990).

Horrocks, David and Eva Kolinsky (eds.), *Turkish Culture in German Society Today* (Oxford: Berghahn, 1996).

Hotho-Jackson, Sabine, 'Subversiveness in Ingeborg Bachmann's Later Prose', *New German Studies* 18 (1994), 55–71.

Howard, Mary (ed.), *Interkulturelle Kommunikationen. Zur deutschsprachigen Prosaliteratur von Autoren nichtdeutscher Herkunft* (Munich: iudicium, 1997).

Hutchinson, John and Anthony D. Smith (eds.), *Ethnicity* (Oxford and New York: Oxford University Press, 1996).

Inwood, Michael, *A Hegel Dictionary* (Oxford: Blackwell, 1992).

Irigaray, Luce, *je, tu, nous: Toward a Culture of Difference*, trans. Alison Martin (London and New York: Routledge, 1993).

Johnson, Uwe, *Das dritte Buch über Achim* (Frankfurt am Main: Suhrkamp, 1992).

Joyce, James, *A Portrait of the Artist as a Young Man* (London: Penguin, 1992).

Kafka, Franz, *Franz Kafka. Letters to Friends, Family, and Editors*, trans. Richard and Clara Winston (New York: Schocken Books, 1977).

King, Helen, 'That Stupid Pelt', *London Review of Books*, 12 November 1998.

Knight, Robert, 'Education and National Identity in Austria after the Second World War' in Robertson and Timms (eds.), *The Hapsburg Legacy*, pp. 178–95.

Knowlton, J. and T. Cates (trans.), *Forever in the Shadow of Hitler?* (Atlantic Highlands, N.J.: Humanities Press, 1993).

Kohn-Waechter, Gudrun, *Das Verschwinden in der Wand. Destruktive Moderne und Widerspruch eines weiblichen Ich in Ingeborg Bachmanns* Malina (Stuttgart: Metzler, 1992).

Kosellek, Reinhart, *Vergangene Zukunft. Zur Semantik geschichtlicher Zeiten* (Frankfurt am Main: Suhrkamp, 1979).

Lacan, Jacques, *Écrits. A Selection* (London: Routledge, 1977).
   The Four Fundamental Concepts of Psycho-Analysis (London: Penguin, 1979).
   The Ethics of Psychoanalysis, 1959–1960 (London: Routledge, 1992).
   'God and the *Jouissance* of Woman. A Love Letter' in Mitchell and Rose (eds.), *Feminine Sexuality*, pp. 137–48.

Lazreg, Marnia, 'Women's Experience and Feminist Epistemology. A Critical Neo-Rationalist Approach' in Lennon and Whitford (eds.), *Knowing the Difference*, pp. 45–62.

Lennon, Kathleen and Margaret Whitford (eds.), *Knowing the Difference. Feminist Perspectives in Epistemology* (London and New York: Routledge, 1994).

Lennox, Sara, 'The Feminist Reception of Ingeborg Bachmann', *Women in German Yearbook* 8 (1993), 73–111.
   ' "White Ladies" and "Dark Continents". Ingeborg Bachmanns *"Todesarten"*-Projekt aus postkolonialer Sicht' in Albrecht and Göttsche (eds.), *Über die Zeit* (1998), pp. 13–31.

Littler, Margaret, 'Diverging Trends in Feminine Aesthetic: Anne Duden and Brigitte Kronauer' in Williams, Parkes and Preece (eds.), *Contemporary German Writers*, pp. 161–80.
   'Diasporic Identity in Emine Sevgi Özdamar's *Mutterzunge*' in Finley and Taberner (eds.), *German Identity*.

Luther, Kurt Richard and Peter Pulzer (eds.), *Austria 1945–95. Fifty Years of the Second Republic* (Aldershot and Brookfield: Ashgate, 1998).

Mahmoody, Betty and William Hoffer, *Nicht ohne meine Tochter* (Lübbe: Berg.-Gladb, 1995).

Maier, Charles S., *The Unmasterable Past: History, Holocaust and German National Identity* (Cambridge, Mass.: Harvard University Press, 1997).

Marks, Elaine and Isabelle de Courtivron (eds.), *New French Feminisms* (Brighton: Harvester Press, 1985).

McAuley, Karen, 'Critical Profiles of *Kind* and *Kindlichkeit* in Ingeborg Bachmann's Prose', PhD thesis, University of Cambridge (2000).

Miller, A. V. (trans.), *Hegel. Phenomenology of Spirit* (Oxford: Oxford University Press, 1977).

Mitchell, Juliet and Jacqueline Rose (eds.), *Feminine Sexuality. Jacques Lacan and the* École Freudienne (London: Macmillan, 1982).

Moi, Toril, *Sexual/Textual Politics* (London and New York: Methuen, 1985).

(ed.), *The Kristeva Reader* (Oxford: Blackwell, 1986).

Müller, Heiner, *Die Hamletmaschine*, in Joachim Fiebach (ed.), *Stücke* (Berlin: Henschelverlag, 1988), pp. 411–19.

Müller, Heiner and Alexander Kluge, *'Ich schulde der Welt einen Toten.' Alexander Kluge im Gespräch mit Heiner Müller* (Hamburg: Rotbuch, 1995).

Ngugi Wa Thiong'o, 'The Language of African Literature' in Ashcroft, Griffiths and Tiffin, (eds.), *Post-Colonial Studies*, pp. 285–90.

Nietzsche, Friedrich, *Unzeitgemäße Betrachtungen I–IV*, ed. Giorgio Colli and Mazzino Montinari (Munich: dtv, 1988).

Özdamar, Emine, *Das Leben ist eine Karawanserei* (Cologne: Kiepenheuer & Witsch, 1992).

Mutterzunge (Berlin: Rotbuch Verlag, 1993).

Die Brücke vom Goldenen Horn (Cologne: Kiepenheuer & Witsch, 1998).

Der Hof in Spiegel (Cologne, Kiepenheuer & Witsch, 2001).

Parker, Patricia and Geoffrey Hartman (eds.), *Shakespeare and the Question of Theory* (New York and London: Methuen, 1985).

Pichl, Robert and Alexander Stillmark (eds.), *Kritische Wege der Landnahme* (Vienna: Hora Verlag, 1994).

Pick, Hella, *Guilty Victim. Austria from the Holocaust to Haider* (London and New York: I. B. Tauris, 2000).

Rauch, Angelika, 'Sprache, Weiblichkeit und Utopie bei Ingeborg Bachmann', *Modern Austrian Literature* 18 (1985), 21–38.

Reed, T. J., *The Classical Centre. Goethe and Weimar 1775–1832* (Oxford: Oxford University Press, 1986).

Ricoeur, Paul, *Time and Narrative*, trans. Kathleen McLaughlin and David Pellauer, 3 vols. (Chicago and London: University of Chicago Press, 1984).

Robertson, Ritchie and Edward Timms (eds.), *The Hapsburg Legacy. National Identity in Historical Perspective* (Edinburgh: Edinburgh University Press, 1994).

Rose, Jacqueline, *Sexuality in the Field of Vision* (London and New York: Verso, 1986).

Rowley, H. H., *The Servant of the Lord and Other Essays on the Old Testament* (London: Lutterworth Press, 1952).

Rutherford, Richard, *Euripides. Alcestis and Other Plays*, trans. John Davie (London: Penguin, 1996).

Scheinhardt, Saliha, *Drei Zypressen* (Freiburg: Herder, 1990).

Frauen, die sterben, ohne daß sie gelebt hätten (Freiburg: Herder, 1991).

Schmid-Bortenschlager, Sigrid, 'Spiegelszenen bei Bachmann: Ansätze einer psychoanalytischen Interpretation', *Modern Austrian Literature* 18 (1985), 39–52.

Scott, Joan W., ' "Experience" ' in Butler and Scott (eds.), *Feminists Theorize*, pp. 22–40.

Shelley, Percy Bysshe, 'In Defence of Poetry' in *Shelley's Poetry and Prose*, ed. Donald H. Reiman and Sharon B. Powers (New York and London: Norton Critical Edition, 1977).

Showalter, Elaine, 'Representing Ophelia: Women, Madness, and the Responsibilities of 'Feminist Criticism' in Parker and Hartman (eds.), *Shakespeare*, pp. 77–94.

Smith, Anthony, *National Identity* (Harmondsworth: Penguin, 1991).

Spivak, Gayatri Chakravorty, 'Feminism and Deconstruction, Again: Negotiating with Unacknowledged Masculinism' in Brennan (ed.), *Feminism and Psychoanalysis*, pp. 206–23.

Swales, Erika, 'Die Falle binärer Oppositionen' in Pichl and Stillmark (eds.), *Kritische Wege*, pp. 67–79.

Thamer, Hans-Ulrich, 'Nationalsozialismus und Nachkriegsgesellschaft. Geschichtliche Erfahrung bei Ingeborg Bachmann und der öffentliche Umgang mit der NS-Zeit in Deutschland' in Göttsche and Ohl (eds.), *Ingeborg Bachmann*, pp. 215–21.

Vico, Giambattista, *New Science. Principles of the New Science Concerning the Common Nature of Nations*, trans. David Marsh with an introduction by Anthony Grafton (London: Penguin, 1999).

Weedon, Chris (ed.), *Postwar Women's Writing in German* (Providence and Oxford: Berghahn, 1997).

Weigel, Sigrid, ' "Ein Ende mit der Schrift. Ein andrer Anfang." Zur Entwicklung von Ingeborg Bachmanns Schreibweise' in Arnold (ed.), *Ingeborg Bachmann*. 'Korrespondenzen zwischen Bild- und Körpergedächtnis', *Neue Zürcher Zeitung*, 23 April 1993, p. 38.

White, Hayden, *Metahistory. The Historical Imagination in Nineteenth-Century Europe* (Baltimore and London: The Johns Hopkins University Press, 1973).

Whitford, Margaret, *Luce Irigaray. Philosophy in the Feminine* (London and New York: Routledge, 1991).

Wierschke, Annette, *Schreiben als Selbstbehauptung: Kulturkonflikte und Identität in den Werken von Aysel Özakin, Alev Tekinay und Emine Sevgi Özdamar* (Frankfurt am Main: Verlag für Interkulturelle Kommunikation, 1996).

'Auf den Schnittstellen kultureller Grenzen tanzend: Aysel Özakin und Emine Sevgi Özdamar' in Fischer and McGowan (eds.), *Denn du tanzt*, pp. 179–94.

Williams, Arthur, Stuart Parkes and Roland Smith (eds.), *German Literature at a Time of Change 1989–1990* (Bern: Peter Lang, 1991).

Williams, Arthur, Stuart Parkes and Julian Preece (eds.), *Contemporary German Writers, Their Aesthetics and Their Language* (Bern: Peter Lang, 1996).

Winston, Richard and Clara (trans.), *Franz Kafka. Letters to Friends, Family and Editors* (New York: Schocken Books, 1977).

Wolf, Christa, *Voraussetzungen einer Erzählung: Kassandra* (Luchterhand: Darmstadt und Neuwied, 1983).

Medea. Stimmen. (Munich: dtv, 1998).

Wood, Michael, 'What Kind of Guy?', *London Review of Books*, 10 June 1999.

Wright, Elizabeth (ed.), *Feminism and Psychoanalysis. A Critical Dictionary* (Oxford: Blackwell, 1992).

Zabus, Chantal, 'Relexification' in Ashcroft, Griffiths and Tiffin (eds.), *Post-Colonial Studies*, pp. 314–18.

Zizek, Slavoj, *The Sublime Object of Ideology* (London and New York: Verso, 1989).

For They Know Not What They Do (London and New York: Verso, 1991).

Index

9 780521 824064